NEW DIRECTIONS IN RHETORIC AND MATERIALITY

Barbara A. Biesecker, Wendy S. Hesford, and Christa Teston, Series Editors

VISUALIZING POSTHUMAN CONSERVATION IN THE AGE OF THE ANTHROPOCENE

AMY D. PROPEN

THE OHIO STATE UNIVERSITY PRESS

COLUMBUS

CONTENTS

ACKNOWLEDGMENTS

THIS IS the book I've imagined writing for some time. But it hardly would have been possible without the support, insight, and feedback of so many others for whom I am truly grateful. From casual conversation to more specific feedback, this book has been made possible through and is part of the many broader intra-actions of material discursive practice, and I hope it can continue to participate in the ongoing dialogues about productive environmental discourse in the Anthropocene.

While I did not realize it at the time, the writing of this book actually began when I finished my earlier project, *Locating Visual-Material Rhetorics*, in 2012. At that time, something was nagging at me about the next set of stories I wanted to tell, even though I wasn't yet sure what specifically they would be about. I knew I wanted to pick up where I had somewhat unintentionally left off—with the idea that we need a visual-material rhetoric that looks even farther beyond the realm of the human in accounting for our relationships with nonhuman species. Such a visual-material rhetoric would need to diffract the light a bit differently. Those ideas also informed early discussions with Dennis Weiss and Colbey Emmerson Reid as we later edited *Design, Mediation, and the Posthuman* (Weiss, Propen, and Reid), and they continue to underpin my thinking on posthumanism, agency, and human/nonhuman animal relationships in this book. I am grateful to Colbey and Dennis for the inspiration that their intellectual camaraderie has provided.

My thinking on the affective intra-actions of vulnerable species and visuality in Anthropocene technoscience would also not have been possible without many productive and fascinating discussions with and feedback from friends and colleagues. I would specifically like to thank Bridie McGreavy, Justine Wells, Guy McHendry, and Samantha Senda-Cook for sharing their insights on the work of the visual and the haptic image, related to the early ideas that eventually developed into chapter 2. I am so excited to know that our work can be in dialogue together. I would also like to thank my geographer colleagues Kevin McHugh and Jennifer Kitson for an interesting discussion of animals, sense, and microplastics, and Kevin for reminding me of Barthes's work in *Camera Lucida*. And I would especially like to thank Sasha Engelmann for prompting me to consider more broadly ideas about the elemental in this book.

Thanks also to the faculty and graduate students at the UCSB Center for Information Technology and Society for their sharp questions and ideas about the intersections of posthumanism, bodies, and materiality. At UCSB, I've also been fortunate to work with Melody Jue, my colleague in all things ocean, whose quick and keen insights always improve my own thinking. I'm especially grateful for her insights into the corporeal frequencies of sonic testing as they pertain to chapter 3.

So many of my friends and colleagues at UCSB have provided support throughout the writing of this book. I would especially like to thank John Majewski, Linda Adler-Kassner, Madeleine Sorapure, and Jim Donelan for giving me the time and space to write, which I do not take for granted and which I truly appreciate. Other friends and colleagues in the Writing Program have provided perspective, support, and great conversation, which has helped keep the writing process from getting too insular. Thanks especially to Katie Baillargeon, Kara Mae Brown, Chris Dean, Trish Fancher, Deb Harris, Jennifer Johnson, and Karen Lunsford—my colleague in campus birding. Caren Converse and Nicole Warwick, I'm ever-appreciative of our regular dinners. Really, though, I have all of my Writing Program colleagues to thank in making this such a wonderful place to work.

Portions of this book have appeared in previous form and are reprinted with permission. Chapter 3 is reprinted in modified form with permission from the Rhetoric Society of America (RSA), from "Technologies of Mediation and the Borders and Boundaries of Human-Nonhuman Animal Relationships in Marine Species Advocacy." *Rhetoric Across Borders*. Ed. Anne Teresa Demo. Anderson: Parlor Press, 2015. 213–24. I gratefully acknowledge permission from the Rhetoric Society of America to reproduce a modified version of this work here.

I would also like to thank Harvard University Press for permission to reprint the Emily Dickinson poem, "Forever—is composed of Nows" in chapter 2: Franklin, Cambridge, Mass.: The Belknap Press of Harvard University Press, Copyright © 1998, 1999 by the President and Fellows of Harvard College. Copyright © 1951, 1955 by the President and Fellows of Harvard College. Copyright © renewed 1979, 1983 by the President and Fellows of Harvard College. Copyright © 1914, 1918, 1919, 1924, 1929, 1930, 1932, 1935, 1937, 1942 by Martha Dickinson Bianchi. Copyright © 1952, 1957, 1958, 1963, 1965 by Mary L. Hampson. And I thank New Directions Publishing Corp. for their permission to reprint the following poem as an epigraph in chapter 3: "Seascape with Sun and Eagle" by Lawrence Ferlinghetti, from WILD DREAMS OF A NEW BEGINNING, copyright © 1979 by Lawrence Ferlinghetti. Reprinted by permission of New Directions Publishing Corp. Chapter 4 includes an excerpt from "Please Call Me By My True Names" in *Being Peace* (1987, 2005) by Thich Nhat Hanh, and is gratefully reprinted with permission of Parallax Press, Berkeley, California, www.parallax.org. Chapter 4 is republished with permission of Taylor & Francis Group, LLC from "Reading the *Atlas of the Patagonian Sea*: Toward a Visual-Material Rhetorics of Environmental Advocacy." *Environmental Rhetoric: Ecologies of Place.* Ed. Peter Goggin. New York: Routledge, 2013. 127–42; permission conveyed through Copyright Clearance Center, Inc. I gratefully acknowledge permission from Taylor & Francis Group, LLC to reproduce a modified version of this work here.

I would also like to thank the editors of the *Atlas of the Patagonian Sea*: Valeria Falabella and Claudio Campagna at the Wildlife Conservation Society, and John Croxall at Birdlife International, for their permission to reprint the maps included in chapter 4. Thanks also to Victoria Zavattieri for permission to reprint the photograph in figure 3. Additionally, I would like to thank Valeria Falabella for her helpful clarifications and feedback throughout the writing of this chapter, as well as Peter Goggin for his earlier comments and suggestions in this regard.

Very special thanks to Chris Jordan for permission to reprint the photograph in Figure 1: CF010257, Unaltered stomach contents of a Laysan albatross fledgling, Midway Island, 2012. Credit: Photo by Chris Jordan. May your brilliant work continue to inspire us all to build more productive, loving worlds.

Several mentors and colleagues also provided insight and guidance in the direction of this project. I owe great thanks to Mary Schuster and Alan Gross, without whom the original proposal for this project might not even have made its way to my laptop. In his no-nonsense style that is not easily ignored, Alan instructed me not to delay in the writing of the proposal. Both Alan and Mary provided invaluable early feedback that helped me to refine and eventually submit the initial proposal for the book.

Sharing my book proposal with Tara Cyphers and series editors Barbara Biesecker, Wendy Hesford, and Christa Teston then marked the start of what has perhaps been the most wonderfully supportive and collegial relationship I've ever had with anyone involved in scholarly publishing. Tara and the series editors have been more attentive, patient, and hugely helpful than I could have ever imagined. Their guidance and suggestions have provided perspective when I needed it, and ultimately helped shape this project into the book that I've been wanting to write for so long. Tara in particular responded promptly and with clarity and helpful guidance to my countless, sometimes neurotic emails and questions, and I am truly grateful for her support throughout this process. Thank you to Angela Moody for her gorgeous cover design, and to Michelle Hoffmann for her assistance during the editorial process. I would also like to thank the two external manuscript reviewers, Marguerite Helmers and Steve Katz, for their intriguing and invaluable questions and suggestions, all of which helped me improve and fine-tune the book.

Special thanks to my great friend and sharp-witted colleague Clancy Ratliff for providing some early feedback about the story of my scrub jay friends. These feathered kin have been inspirational and ever-present throughout the writing of this book in the most joyful and audible ways, and I'm glad to be able to convey at least one version of their potential story here. Speaking of nonhuman kin, I cannot imagine having written this book without the furry companionship of Milo, my best and most mischievous feline friend. I'm also infinitely appreciative for the friendship and support of some other wonderful humans, including Marc Weinstein, my companion in wildlife observation and appreciation, whose friendship long predates this project but who has, most recently, listened patiently to all of my writing angst. Thanks to Elizabeth Shea, protector of squirrels, even when it means sacrificing order. Thanks also to my many other friends and colleagues who have been supportive over the years and during the writing of this book, including Cristina Hanganu-Bresch, Beth Britt, Dominic DelliCarpini, Karen Dias, Kenny Fountain, Laura Gurak, Sarah Johnson, Krista Kennedy, Brian Larson, Salma Monani, Jessica Reyman, Brian Salerno, and Mike Zerbe, as well as my friends at the Santa Barbara Wildlife Care Network, who practice compassionate conservation every day.

Finally, I would like to thank my family, especially my parents, Beverly and Michael Propen, who have provided feedback on many ideas related to this project, and who have always supported my love of writing; my siblings and fellow wildlife advocates, David Propen and Mindy Howley Propen; and my uncle, Allen Schoen, with whom I've shared many conversations about the nature of our relationships with our nonhuman kin. This book truly would not be possible without the support of my family, and I dedicate this work to them.

The Scrub Jay and the Peanut

BLUE JAY species reside throughout North America. A native of the northeastern United States myself, I grew up with eastern blue jays—loud, raucous, assertive, and curious songbirds that kind of resemble large blue budgies with head crests. In central California, my home of several years now, I have come to know the California scrub jay, or the "Blue Jay of the Pacific seaboard," as it is sometimes known (Cornell Lab of Ornithology, "California Scrub-Jay"). The California scrub jay is similarly assertive, resourceful, curious, and cheeky. They bear a similar appearance to their eastern counterpart but lack the familiar head crest, and rather than the light bluish, grayish, and whitish color combination, they sport a consistently deep-to-bright turquoise plumage throughout, with grayish backs, blue cheeks, and long, bright blue tails.

Here on the West Coast, I happily coexist, mostly peacefully, with a lovable pair of scrub jays who live in the hills outside my home in Santa Barbara. Every morning and afternoon, in what seems remarkably well-timed to my teaching and work schedule, this pair of jays descend from the hills and into the large carrotwood tree that overlooks the balcony off my living room.

Whilst in the tree and during their descent to my balcony, they announce their arrival with a raucous and cheeky squawk that sounds a bit how I would imagine the call of a small pterodactyl. Their call, at least in my interpretation, is not neutral. It is a communication, a greeting (I like to think), and a request.

There, they wait—mostly patiently, for what has now become my daily offering to them of roasted, unsalted peanuts.[1]

From atop the carrotwood tree, the jays have a clear line of sight not only into my living room but also into my bedroom upstairs. From there, they watch and wait. I realize that in another context this may sound a bit like cause for voyeuristic concern, but here instead I offer this perhaps predictable note about Derrida and his cat.[2] Unlike Derrida, however, my concern is rooted not in shame about the jays' potentially being privy to my various states of morning routine, but rather in a curiosity about what they may be thinking—about what they may be experiencing—as they gaze expectantly into my home.

I step outside—we make direct eye contact, and I arrange a handful of peanuts along the ledge of the balcony. Then I step barely back inside, at which point the jays take turns swooping down, landing on the ledge, selecting peanuts, and carrying them back to the hills, where I imagine they must have a rather large stash accumulated.

In February 2017, however, the strongest storm in nearly a decade moved through southern, central, and northern California. This was the same storm system that made national news when it threatened the main and auxiliary spillways of the Oroville Dam (Chappell). The storm had followed (though did not resolve) a drought of historic proportions, and much like the rest of California, Santa Barbara's landscape was wholly unprepared to absorb such vast quantities of rainfall at such a fast pace; as a result, significant mudslides and flooding plagued the region. More specifically, before this storm, Lake Cachuma, which provides much of Santa Barbara's drinking water, "had dwindled to a weedy channel at just 7% of capacity and was perilously close to being written off as a regional water supply" (Sahagun, "Yes"). The February storm "swamp[ed] historical records and caus[ed] the lake to rise a whopping 31 feet in depth in just a few days" (Sahagun, "Yes").

During the several days of torrential rains and mudslides, the jays did not appear. This is unsurprising, as birds seek shelter where they can find it during storms—on the lee sides of trees, in the brush, in shrubs, and so on. But this storm was exceptional, and the hills they call their home had succumbed to mudslides and had even formed small rivers in places. Plus, this was California—storms this severe were rare here. How prepared could these jays possibly be?

In mild anxiety, I found myself Googling questions like "Where do scrub jays go during storms?" "Can birds in California survive monsoons?" I entertained perhaps conflicting thoughts, given the critical analysis I am about to embark upon in this book, like, "If only my jays wore geolocators, I could know whether they're safe."

When the rain finally let up, I wondered if the jays might return or if the storm had somehow reset their routine. Then one morning, as I surveyed the newly modified landscape of the hillside, I heard the familiar pterodactyl-like call announcing the jays' presence. It is hard to describe the relief I felt to anyone unfamiliar with this sort of relationship. To some it may sound silly (although I hope it does not), but I was deeply relieved to know that they were safe. I teared up as I quickly set out peanuts along the ledge of the balcony, and I watched with joy as the pair of scrub jays took turns swooping down to collect them. After the first couple of trips, though, I realized that their exigency was different—this was no ordinary trip. Rather, they returned repeatedly; they sat in the tree, peered into the living room, and squawked, clearly requesting more peanuts. They required the extra peanuts, I then realized, because their stash had likely been washed away during the storms. So, in a slight anthropomorphism, I will put it this way: they needed to restock. I went through a good many peanuts that morning, continuing to distribute them until the jays were satisfied. I felt flattered and honored that they chose to return—that they came back to the place where they trusted they could replenish this portion of their food source. That said (and as note 1 further discusses), the jays are not wholly dependent on me for their sustenance, nor would I ever want them to be; rather, I generally understand these exchanges to take place in moderation.

While I will not ever truly know what the jays were thinking, or how they perceive of our relationship, I nonetheless feel confident in calling it that—a *relationship*. More skeptical readers may quite understandably question whether the jays were simply food motivated, and I would perhaps be remiss not to acknowledge that this may be the case. I would also suggest, though, that to understand our relationship as embodied communication is to consider the possibility that even food motivation does not necessarily override an intuition of safe space and trust—that even if the jays needed to replenish their food supply, they would not approach my balcony until they felt it was safe to do so. In this sense, we know each other—we share and communicate energy. We have a place in common. A shared, safe food source. A shared connection: we make eye contact—we recognize each other. We watch and observe each other. We are consistent in our actions and routines. We share communication—communication about relationship. It is interesting, too, that a large part of the development of our relationship has been made possible through the provisioning of that little material artifact, that thing, the peanut.

The peanut is sure enough an aesthetically pleasing, symbolic token of our connection, but it is more than that; it is a material artifact that moves between us, that has become part of our communication—our connection.[3] That is, in many ways, the peanut itself has become part of the relationship—one that provides nourishment and a consistent thread, as long as we both choose to continue to participate in the communication. I would not go so far as to say that the peanut constitutes the whole of the relationship, because there are other, ineffable variables at play, like knowing, seeing, curiosity, consistency, and trust, for starters. But the peanut provides both a literal and figurative part of our connection. It is an ideal thing for both of us—a protein source for humans and jays alike.[4] Easily stored in the pantry and in the hills, easily enough replenished by me, easily enough transported by them. Peanuts continue to move between us—they are a physical and affectual thing necessary to the ongoing cultivation of our relationship.

Developing this relationship with the scrub jays, or their developing a relationship with me, is an ongoing process that has taken time and will continue to take time. I like to believe that we see from each other's perspectives. I am not sure what the scrub jays would call it, or how they feel about our connection, but they seem interested in maintaining it, albeit likely in different ways and for different reasons. But we pay attention to each other—we know each other, and we have established and continue to develop a relationship built on trust, consistency, and a mutual, ongoing attentiveness to each other's individual daily lives and routines. We are, then, fellow beings in relationship.

I begin with this narrative because it illustrates in a hopefully accessible way some of the larger themes and questions addressed in this book,[5] such as: How do we understand the lives of nonhuman animals and our relationships with and perceived responsibilities to them? What are the artifacts or things that help configure or perform such perceived responsibility or an interest in communication with or about nonhuman animals, and what are the implications of those artifacts for productive knowledge-making? And, how, then, might we go about engaging in productive, compassionate practices of communication and knowledge-building about or with nonhuman species in an age of technoscience? Or, what does it mean to act with compassion and practice conservation in an age of technoscience, and in the age of the Anthropocene?

In the chapters that follow, I describe the theoretical concepts and the broader contexts that allow for an exploration of such questions. These concepts draw largely upon the work of material feminist scholars including Stacy Alaimo (*Bodily, Exposed*), Karen Barad (*Meeting*), Jane Bennett (*Vibrant*), Rosi Braidotti, and Donna Haraway (*ModestWitness, Simians, Staying, When*). I apply and extend these theoretical concepts in stories of Anthropocene technoscience set in and around areas of the Pacific Ocean, from the Midway Atoll of the Hawaiian archipelago, to the Central Coast of California, to the Patagonian Sea. This book is an Anthropocene love letter to these vulnerable ecosystems and the many species, our kin, that reside within them.

CHAPTER 1

Agential Entanglements and the Paradoxes of Anthropocene Technoscience

Visualizing Posthuman Conservation in the Age of the Anthropocene aims to bring visual-material rhetorics into conversation with material feminisms and environmental humanities in ways that consider the implications and worldly consequences of the rhetorical artifacts and genres of Anthropocene technoscience—artifacts and genres, configured as environmental accounts, that emerge through the intra-actions of world-making. World-making, as I understand and use the term, speaks to the ways that we may participate in the becoming of the world through the practices of embodied knowledge-making in which we are always already entangled and in which we are not the only participants; in this way, world-making is knowledge-making, and knowledge-making is world-making.[1]

To the hypothetical reader whom I may encounter in the proverbial elevator, I would perhaps more briefly describe this book as about how technologies, environments, bodies, and matter work together in ways that often shape, reshape, and raise questions about how we connect with and perceive our responsibilities to the worlds in which we coexist with our nonhuman kin. To the reader currently physically engaged with this book, I would suggest with more nuance that this book asks us to rethink our relationship with conservation as not necessarily about managing or controlling bodies in the natural world but as emanating from a place of curiosity and an interest in *becoming with* (Haraway, *When*)—and as informed even more so by an ethic of compassion (Bekoff, *Animal*; Bekoff, *Rewilding*).

Such an ethic would more explicitly decenter the human vantage point, eschew anthropocentrism, and subsequently embrace a version of posthumanism (Wolfe, "From") that decenters the human enough to consider more closely ideas about the environment and conservation from the vantage point of the nonhuman animal, while also not trading humanism for antihumanism (Mara and Hawk), or "flipping the privilege," as Diane Davis puts it when making a not dissimilar point in her critique of gynocentrism (137).[2] That is, posthuman theory, I would argue, especially when considered in the context of environmental rhetoric, can not only serve as "a generative tool to help us re-think the basic unit of reference for the human" in the age of the Anthropocene, but in a more measured way "can also help us re-think the basic tenets of our interaction with both human and non-human agents on a planetary scale" (Braidotti 5–6). It likewise eschews human exceptionalism and acknowledges multispecies entanglements in the age of the Anthropocene, or, as Rosi Braidotti has described, "the historical moment when the Human has become a geological force capable of affecting all life on this planet" (5). And yet, as Braidotti's posthumanism also suggests, the force and capability of human intervention hardly make us the only characters in this story; that is, as Jeremy Davies adds: "Humanity is not at the center of the picture of the Anthropocene, opposing, by its powers of mind, the passive matter that encircles it. Instead, human societies are themselves constructed from a web of relationships between human beings, nonhuman animals, plants, metals, and so on" (7).

Additionally, based on Jane Bennett's conceptualizations of agency and vital new materialisms (*Vibrant*), this book also, not incompatibly, asks us to work from an ethics of ecological relationality that manifests not through an adversarial or moralistic vantage point but rather through potential enactments of ethical responsibility. Broadly speaking, this book takes a vantage point that, somewhat similar to what Nathan Stormer and Bridie McGreavy describe, "presumes connectedness and attachment between all manner of things and that sees beauty and value in rhetoric's unruly variability" (3).[3] Likewise, in the sense that this book calls into question and asks us to think on our perceived responsibilities to the nonhuman species with whom we coexist, this book also engages animal studies.

As rhetoric scholars engaged with animal studies have recently argued, we would do well to consider the various ways that rhetoric might participate in questions of how to "balanc[e] the 'control of our environment' with the dialogic responsibility we all have to our wilder kin" (Gordon, Lind, and Kutnicki 223). And as Debra Hawhee has noted, to incorporate "rhetoric in cross-disciplinary conversations about animals" can help do the necessary work of engaging rhetoric in interdisciplinary conversations, as it can help demonstrate how animals often traverse rhetorical theory as they "travel into other disciplinary traditions" (3). Moreover, the decentering of the human vantage point required of animal studies implicitly aligns with the posthumanist conservation ethic that this book seeks to conceptualize. With such ideas in mind, then, each chapter in this book demonstrates, through different illustrative cases, what emerges as our sometimes implicit, sometimes explicit interest in furthering connections with or engaging curiosities about the lives of nonhuman animals, often through the configuration of rhetorical artifacts and technologies of visualization that attempt to enact an ethics of ecological relationality, or what I argue marks the beginnings of a posthuman conservation.

As I seek to demonstrate, the cases in this book implicitly signal, to varying extents, an interest in ethical responsibility that aligns with the posthuman agency and environmentalism inherent in Stacy Alaimo's notion of trans-corporeality (*Bodily*; *Exposed*), Rosi Braidotti's notion of "co-presence," Jane Bennett's distributive agency (*Vibrant*), and Karen Barad's agential realism and posthumanist, performative approach to understanding technoscience (*Meeting*). They also draw upon Donna Haraway's (*ModestWitness*; *Simians*; *Staying*; *When*) material feminist approach to grappling with the cultural assumptions that both codify and destabilize understandings of human/nonhuman animal relationships in an age of technoscience. This book is thus about the paradoxical enactments and intra-actments of ethical responsibility, and how they matter in an age of technoscience and in the Anthropocene—where responsibility is not just ours alone, but where the agential intra-actments and entanglements of bodies, environments, and matter also do not preclude consideration of our own relationships and responsibilities to productive, sustainable, compassionate world-making.

Stacy Alaimo's trans-corporeality, for instance, understands posthumanism as "always already part of intra-active networks and systems that are simultaneously material, discursive, ecological, and biopolitical" (*Exposed* 133). Importantly, Alaimo aligns her notion of trans-corporeality, which is very much rooted in an ethics of ecological relationality, with Barad's theory of intra-action and agential realism; in doing so, she also notes that "while Barad does not (and could not) offer specific guidance as to how to determine what particular ethical practices would entail, she emphasizes ontological entanglements rather than encounters with discrete objects" (*Exposed* 133). This book endeavors to contribute to and extend that conversation by demonstrating how visual-material rhetorical artifacts and emergent texts can participate in the posthuman intra-actments of ethical practice that agential realism may entail. For, as Alaimo writes, environmental accounts "often reconceptualize material agencies—the often unpredictable and always interconnected actions of environmental systems, toxic substances, and biological bodies" (*Bodily* 3). While Alaimo refers more so, here, to artifacts of literature such as memoirs, I would add that emergent texts related to visual-material rhetoric and professional writing, such as position statements, opposition letters, media articles, maps, and even memos, may help illuminate questions about our trans-corporeal entanglements in ways that implicitly reveal an interest in compassionate conservation.[4]

While it is possible to suggest that such emergent texts or accounts perpetuate a human-centered vantage point, I argue, drawing again primarily on ideas from Alaimo, Barad, and Bennett in this area, that visual-material rhetorical artifacts may constitute specific configurations of knowledge-making that enact a kind of ethical obligation and explorations of power and accountability that agential realism does not preclude, but that also does not happen solely via the efforts of the individual. This does not necessarily mean that visual-material artifacts are impervious to critiques of representationalism or human attribution, but rather that the rhetorical configurations of ethical enactment are nuanced and paradoxical—and that as such, rhetorical artifacts may also bear recuperative power and participate in the larger agential workings of material discursive practice and world-making. In other words, this book operates not from the vantage point of "either/or," but rather from an openness to "both/and." This is a book about paradox, and paradox requires acceptance and inclusivity. Such understandings, as I imagine them here, can ultimately help us conceptualize a visual-material, posthuman environmental rhetoric informed by an ethic of compassionate conservation. This book endeavors to get us *there* by remaining attentive to entanglements of the *here* and *now*. Or, as Donna Haraway has recently put it, to grapple with questions of human exceptionalism and multispecies entanglements in the Anthropocene requires not that we throw in the towel but rather that we "stay with the trouble" (*Staying* 4).

The stories I wish to tell with this book thus cannot be told solely or even predominantly from the perspective of the human. And neither can they be told solely from the perspective of the inanimate artifact or the nonhuman animal body. They must be told in a way that acknowledges and respects the ongoing relationships of all beings, matter, and bodies, and that likewise brings to the fore questions of what accountability and ethical responsibility might then look like when we acknowledge the entangled, embodied relationships of the Anthropocene—an age in which humans can no longer maintain the façade of privileged exceptionalism. When we let go of exceptionalism, our worlds open up in potentially productive ways. Our vantage points become partial, and multiple, and entangled. Blinders will not do anymore, if they ever did.

With these ideas in mind, this book explores how life in what we have come to call the "Anthropocene" has reconfigured naturecultures and their attendant human/nonhuman animal relationships in ways that catalyze a range of rhetorical configurations that incorporate and perform critical awareness, ethical obligation, affirmation, catharsis, grief, and new modes of unwitting collaboration. As my colleague Melody Jue helps describe: "The Anthropocene attempts to name a historical shift in Earth history that is not only marked by layers and inscriptions, but also by the forces of erasure and unmaking that are largely related to anthropogenic rise of petroculture and resource extraction" (84). Moreover, Jue argues, how we tell the story of the Anthropocene matters greatly to our own perceptions of ethical obligation and how we perceive our relationships to and with our nonhuman kin and the environments in which we coexist; for example, to focus on

> megafaunal extinction implie[s] something inherently destructive about human nature, a violent tendency to eradicate (by hunting or habitat destruction) other species. The advent of agriculture implie[s] a more distributed responsibility, where plants were also agents in climate warming. The industrial revolution and great acceleration implied a greater share of responsibility with the West, affinity with ecological Marxism, and critiques of our global reliance on oil. (86–87)

In each of these potential frames, humans, nonhuman species, environments, and technologies intermingle in acts of world-making. However, how we imagine the nature of this intermingling and our own responsibilities therein has great implications for the worlds that we help build and in which all reside.

Similarly focused on questions of accountability and the implications of human exceptionalism in knowledge production, Bruno Latour reflects on the challenges of the Anthropocene when he says, in the context of describing a sobering journalistic account in *Le Monde* about the state of global warming:

> I think that it is easy for us to agree that, in modernism, people are not equipped with the mental and emotional repertoire to deal with such a vast scale of events; that they have difficulty submitting to such a rapid acceleration for which, in addition, they are supposed to feel responsible while, in the meantime, this call for action has none of the traits of their older revolutionary dreams. How can we simultaneously be part of such a long history, have such an important influence, and yet be so late in realizing what has happened and so utterly impotent in our attempts to fix it? ("Agency" 1–2)

Being attentive to the present while also learning from the past and considering with care our possible futures—this is a difficult lesson to (try to) learn on many fronts, and a difficult balance to achieve. It requires that we remain present—that we *be here now* in a productive and relational manner that does not fall prey to the pitfalls of human exceptionalism, the Great Divides, or the pendulum swinging too far in the direction of, as Haraway has put it, either "hope" or "despair" (Haraway, *Staying* 4). That is, to grapple with the seemingly conflicting crises of consciousness that Latour describes above requires not only a capacity for critical self-awareness but also a related understanding that humans do not work alone in the mattering of the world—that it is actually to our detriment to think that we do. As Haraway writes: "Alone, in our separate kinds of expertise and experience, we know both too much and too little, and so we succumb to despair or to hope, and neither is a sensible attitude. Neither despair nor hope is tuned to the senses, to mindful matter, to material semiotics, to mortal earthlings in thick copresence" (*Staying* 4). Thus to engage with the world from a point of curiosity and what Braidotti calls "co-presence," or "the simultaneity of being in the world together" (169), and to start from a point of acknowledging a more ecological vantage point that also decenters human exceptionalism, places us at the heart of this book's thinking on agency, human/nonhuman animal relationships, and posthumanism, and allows us to engage more productively in more nuanced questions about what ethical obligation might look like in an age of Anthropocene technoscience, and the place of rhetoric therein.

To begin exploring these ideas, this chapter addresses the following main themes and discussions: (1) how we understand agency in an age of Anthropocene technoscience; (2) trajectories in rhetoric and materiality; (3) compassionate conservation, embodied communication, and visuality; and (4) conceptualizing a posthuman conservation ethic. In the discussion that follows, then, a fuller accounting of agency and its connections to ethical obligation helps paint a clearer picture of how and where ideas about visual-material rhetorics and compassionate conservation fit into environmental, agential realist accounts of mattering.

WHAT'S SO IMPORTANT ABOUT HOW WE THINK ABOUT AGENCY?

In this section, I will describe some of the dominant positions that inform rhetoric's understanding of the agency of matter, specifically as they pertain to the analytical chapters in this book. I understand Bennett's notions of thing-power and the agential assemblage (*Vibrant*), combined with Barad's thinking on agential realism and intra-action (*Meeting*), as each offering subtly different but productive means of thinking through the place of ethical responsibility and rhetoric within the agential intra-actments of world-making.

Informed by Barad's notion of agential realism, for example, I understand visual-material rhetorical artifacts as emergent configurations of, and as participating in, the larger intra-actments of material discursive practice. That is, as Barad describes, "in contrast to the usual 'interaction,' which assumes that there are separate individual agencies that precede their interaction, the notion of intra-action recognizes that distinct agencies do not precede, but rather emerge through, their intra-action" (*Meeting* 33). With this, I consider the always ongoing intra-actions of spaces, bodies, matter, technologies, and environments as helping to enact specific and ongoing rhetorical configurations that characterize material discursive practice. Or, as Christa Teston says of material discursive practice in a helpful and perhaps clearer paraphrase, "things and the words used to describe them are mutually constitutive" (*Bodies* 19). Moreover, I see Barad's agential realism as bearing recuperative power through its ecological understanding of the entanglements of all bodies and matter and in its consideration of the place of ethical accountability within material discursive practice.

For Barad, the idea of entanglements comes from quantum theory, and "refers not to the intertwining of separate states but, rather, to their inseparability. To put it another way, spatially separated particles in an *entangled state* do not have separate identities; they are instead part of the same phenomena" ("Invertebrate Visions" 241, emphasis in original). For Barad, the very nature of "matter itself entails *entanglements*," and the term pertains to her "agential realist ontology" and its own reconfiguring of materiality and agency (*Meeting* 160, emphasis in original). By extension, or in acknowledging the inseparability of humans and nonhuman animals, to maintain a focus on the ethical accountabilities of our trans-corporeal entanglements means always considering our responsibilities to our worlds and the vulnerable, nonhuman kin with which we share them, and the different enactments that are constituted through material discursive practice.

Jane Bennett similarly considers whether nonhuman artifacts might bear agential properties. In her essay "The Force of Things," she subsequently questions what the agential power of things might mean from the perspective of policy-making. Bennett views life not as specific to the human realm but also as pertaining to nonhuman matter. In this view, then, we might take the example of plastic ocean debris, the subject of chapter 2, as bearing the capacity for life, or liveliness, or as having agency. As such, ocean plastic, which she might then term "vibrant matter," is not a neutral entity and would ultimately take on a power, a "thing-power," all its own. Writing later, in *Vibrant Mat-*

ter, Bennett continues to contend that things themselves may bear a lively capacity for agency: "Our trash is not 'away' in landfills but generating lively streams of chemicals and volatile winds of methane as we speak" (vii). Here, she notes that, on the one hand, thing-power is a good point of entry to moving beyond the "life-matter binary," but on the other hand, she wants to clarify that the drawback to the term is its tendency to "overstate the thinginess or fixed stability of materiality"; rather, her goal, via thing-power, is to "theorize a materiality that is as much force as entity, as much energy as matter, as much intensity as extension" (20).

Moreover, Bennett feels that another drawback to thing-power is "its latent individualism," or how "the figure of 'thing' lends itself to an atomistic rather than a congregational understanding of agency" (*Vibrant* 20). That is, in Bennett's thing-power, things never act on their own and are not merely social constructs but function more as actors; likewise, humans are not mere "autonoms" but rather "vital materialities" (21). As Scot Barnett and Casey Boyle likewise note, "we do not simply point *at* things but act *alongside* and *with* them" (1, emphasis in original). Bennett thus posits a "theory of *distributive* agency," which she contextualizes using the case of the blackout that impacted much of North America in the summer of 2003 (21, emphasis in original). Bennett seeks to demonstrate how theorizing the electrical power grid as an agentic assemblage can help illuminate, first, "an understanding of agency as a confederation of human and nonhuman elements," and ultimately, the implications of such an understanding for "established notions of moral responsibility and political accountability" related to agency (21). Bennett's vital materialism also draws on Spinoza's notion of the body as affective, relational, and always in flux, which allows her to argue that "bodies enhance their power *in* or *as a heterogeneous assemblage*" (Bennett 23, emphasis in original). For Bennett, agency is then "distributed across an ontologically heterogeneous field, rather than being a capacity localized in a human body or in a collective produced (only) by human efforts" (23).

In terms of the 2003 blackout, for instance, the elements of Bennett's assemblage collaborate, and include "some very active and powerful nonhumans: electrons, trees, wind, fire, electromagnetic fields," all of which play a role in the blackout but, interestingly, none of which are at fault or to blame in its unfolding (24). Bennett's agential assemblage is thus not grounded in what she understands as less productive questions of moralism and blame per se, for she acknowledges that "this federation of actants is a creature that the concept of moral responsibility fits only loosely and to which the charge of blame will not quite stick" (28). Here, Bennett also distinguishes moralism from ethical responsibility.

That is, Bennett's ethics, informed by Spinoza, likewise eschews the transcendent, oppositional values that would judge "Good" versus "Evil" and instead entails relational enactments of ethical responsibility. These enactments come about in relation to the possibility of "a being of which we could be a function," and involve the ways that we then "incorporate into that being" (Deleuze 22). In other words, how we relate to the worlds around us determines our ethical relationships to those worlds.

These relationships are composed in certain ways that can function either more productively: compositionally, or less productively: decompositionally. As Deleuze helps us to understand, "there are always relations that enter into composition in their particular order, according to the eternal laws of nature. There is no Good or Evil, but there is good and bad" (22). The notion of good and bad has two levels of meaning: a more objective, relative meaning, and a more subjective, modal meaning. Of the objective meaning, Deleuze writes: "The good is when a body directly compounds its relation with ours, and with all or part of its power, increases ours. A food, for example. For us, the bad is when a body decomposes our body's relation, although it still combines with our parts, but in ways that do not correspond to our essence, as when a poison breaks down the blood" (22). Thus, "good and bad have a primary, objective meaning, but one that is relative and partial: that which agrees with our nature or does not agree with it" (22). Good and bad also have a secondary, more subjective meaning. An individual is considered to be good "who strives, insofar as he is capable, to organize his encounters, to join with whatever agrees with his nature, to combine his relation with relations that are compatible with his, and thereby to increase his power" (23). Goodness is then dynamic and compositional, or productive in its power. On the other hand, Deleuze says: "That individual will be called *bad,* or servile, or weak, or foolish, who lives haphazardly, who is content to undergo the effects of his encounters, but wails and accuses every time the effect undergone does not agree with him and reveals his own impotence" (23, emphasis in original).

Spinoza's ethics thus functions as "a typology of immanent modes of existence" that "replaces Morality, which always refers existence to transcendent values. Morality is the judgment of God, the *system of Judgment.* But Ethics overthrows the system of judgment. The opposition of values (Good-Evil) is supplanted by the qualitative difference of modes of existence (good-bad)" (Deleuze 23, emphasis in original). Moreover, for Spinoza, an individual is "a singular essence, which is to say, a degree of power. A characteristic relation corresponds to this essence, and a certain capacity for being affected corresponds to this degree of power" (Deleuze 27). It is here that we see in this notion of ethics the ecological orientation to which Bennett subscribes and with which I also align, and which helps account for our affective relationships with the material world. Our ethical enactments thus shape and are shaped by our relationships with and responses to the worlds and beings with whom we coexist. Whether we engage positively or negatively in these affectual relations is then a marker of our ethics.

While Bennett's federation of actants does not look to place blame for the potentially anthropogenic crises of the assemblage, questions of ethical responsibility and human intentionality, while not disregarded, are also not readily foregrounded. This, again, is a reflection of Bennett's ecological orientation, which would suggest that to situate agency more squarely within the realm of the human is not necessarily the answer to questions of ethical responsibility, either. She acknowledges that even though humans can form intentions and have the capacity for self-reflection, nonhuman forces nonetheless have much influence in the equation:

> The vital materialist must admit that different materialities, composed of different sets of protobodies, will express different powers. Humans, for example, can experience themselves as forming intentions and as standing apart from their actions to reflect on the latter. But even here it may be relevant to note the extent to which intentional reflexivity is also a product of the interplay of human and nonhuman forces. (*Vibrant* 31)

It bears noting that while Bennett does not explicitly say so, it appears that her focus on nonhuman elements has more to do with earthly matter and technological things than with nonhuman animal bodies, per se. That said, we may see no reason why Bennett's vital materialism or the agential assemblage would necessarily oppose the inclusion of nonhuman animals. Nonetheless, vital materialism begins to emerge as subtly distinct from Barad's agential realism and intra-activity, and Alaimo's more trans-corporeal, material feminism, in which thing-power is not discounted but in which human accountability is less deemphasized, and in which the lives of nonhuman animals are more readily accounted for.

Nonhuman animals are integral to our trans-corporeal, agential entanglements, perhaps not as explicitly in the context of the 2003 blackout, but certainly in one of many other possible tales from the Anthropocene. And as Barad more explicitly states: "*All bodies, not merely 'human' bodies, come to matter through the world's iterative intra-activity—its performativity*" (*Meeting* 152, emphasis in original). Moreover, while in Barad's account of agential realism, agency is likewise "not aligned with human intentionality or subjectivity" (177), her notion of agency as intra-action does leave more room for consideration of our ethical responsibilities to the worlds in which we coexist with nonhuman animals: "Particular possibilities for (intra-)acting exist at every moment, and these changing possibilities entail an ethical obligation to intra-act responsibly in the world's becoming, to contest and rework what matters and what is excluded from mattering" (178). Again, as noted earlier, while Barad does not specifically describe what exactly such ethical responsibility entails, I argue that it entails the sort of entanglements in which rhetoric plays a role—in which visual-material rhetorical artifacts intra-act with and within the material world and help produce specific versions of world-making. That is, these "different agential cuts" that Barad describes can be said to function in a visual-material rhetorical sense, in that they "materialize different phenomena," and in leaving "different marks on bodies," these "intra-actions do not merely effect what we know and therefore demand an ethics of knowing; rather, our intra-actions contribute to the differential mattering of the world" (178). A posthuman, compassionate conservation that draws on trans-corporeality and an intra-active notion of agency would then consider visual-material rhetoric from a vantage point that is also attuned to our ethical obligations for the species with which our lives and worlds are entangled.

Moreover, Barad's posthumanism "challenges the positioning of materiality as either a given or a mere effect of human agency" (183). Here, nonetheless, we are, rightly, still responsible for the "agential cuts that we help enact," even though we are not the only knowledge-makers in the picture: "We are responsible for the cuts that we help enact not because we do the choosing (neither do we escape responsibility because 'we' are 'chosen' by them), but because we are an agential part of the material becoming of the universe. Cuts are agentially enacted not by willful individuals but by the larger material arrangement of which 'we' are a 'part'" (178–79). Thus we are "co-constituted" by the material discursivities that we help to create and perform.

In *Pandora's Hope*, Latour similarly notes that the energy of coordination is co-constituted with nonhuman artifacts: "Through technoscience, [which he defines] as a fusion of science, organization, and industry—the forms of coordination learned through 'networks of power' are extended to inarticulate entities" (203). Again taking plastic debris circulating in the ocean as a potential example of such "inarticulate entities," Latour might understand ocean plastics as enacting a shared sense of agency, suggesting a variation on the theme of his idea that "nonhumans are endowed with speech, however primitive, with intelligence, foresight, self-control, and discipline, in a fashion both large-scale and intimate. Socialness is shared with nonhumans in an almost promiscuous way" (203–4).

This "socialness" is necessary for agency, as Carolyn Miller has somewhat similarly suggested: "The energy of agency (whether direct or mediated) is rhetorically functional only through interaction. . . . Interaction is necessary for agency because it is what creates the kinetic energy of performance and puts it to rhetorical use" (149–50). Thus, Miller says, agency is "not only the property of an event" but also it is about the relationships and interactions between or among "subjects within a rhetorical situation" (150). In this view, we might co-construct agency with nonhuman artifacts, while nonetheless acknowledging that at the end of the day, there is no easy way around the anthropocentric underpinnings of understanding the matter of circulating ocean plastics as bound up in human knowledge-making and consumer practice. That is, we must also understand agency as an anthropocentric reflection of human patterns of desire, consumption, and so on. In this way, as Miller suggests, "attributions of agency may rely on prefabricated conventions, ideologically imposed or culturally given" (151). Moreover, we "position" agency within the orbit of our "habitual or imposed patterns of attribution" (151). As Thomas Rickert then notes, for Miller, things exist primarily "within human-defined limits" (202). Barad and Bennett, on the other hand, are less embracing of a conceptual model in which agency is situated farther along the "human-defined" end of the continuum.

Rickert aptly makes salient the tensions between these varied ways of understanding agency. He says: "Miller rightly wants to underscore the performative nature of agency, but as soon as she moves to agency as an attribution, she harbors agency within human practice" (203). Bennett, on the other hand, suggests that distributive agency "does not posit a subject as the root cause of an effect. There is instead always a swarm of vitalities at play. . . . This understanding of agency does not deny the existence of that thrust called intentionality, but it does see it as less definitive of outcomes" (*Vibrant* 31–32).

In parsing out the agency continuum, Rickert also acknowledges the perspective of Graham Harman, who makes a related point about what he calls "blowback," or the "unintended consequences" that objects may have; that is, positing fairly little human intervention, he says that "whatever we think about the object, whatever we design or deploy it to do, it always exceeds such assignments" (204). Plastic ocean debris again serves as a decent example of technoscience operating in ways that exceed our assignments. As Rickert fairly suggests, in seeming accord with Bennett, "objects wend their way in the world through their own capacities, too, not just through those we intend for them or attribute to them; blowback provides us some sense of this because it can significantly affect us, doing so outside the orbit of our attribution" (204).

This potential consequence of plastic debris has until recently been outside the orbit of our attribution; once situated on our trans-corporeal radar, it invites new questions of control and ethical obligation.

While I would generally agree that to understand the agential capacities of matter is to necessarily eschew anthropocentrism, I would also suggest that an understanding of agency that to some extent acknowledges human attribution is not a *wholly* negative thing, but *only if* that view at least prompts us to critically question the ideologies that inform our habits and those "patterns of attribution" (Miller 151), with the hopeful goal of decentering our human-centeredness and considering our ethical responsibilities within the assemblage; such a view then requires that we "stay with" rather than delegate, or even relegate the trouble. Moreover, in an agential realist view, the "trouble" is not an "us or them" proposition. Rather, "ethics cannot be about responding to the other as if the other is the radical outside to the self. Ethics is not a geometrical calculation; 'others' are never very far from 'us'; 'they' and 'we' are co-constituted and entangled through the very cuts 'we' help to enact" (Barad, *Meeting* 178–79). Similarly, from the perspective of compassionate conservation, we must understand nonhuman animals not as outside of ourselves and the material discursive practices that we help to enact, but as producing marks on all bodies, not just human bodies.

Such understandings may prove challenging; we may recall that Latour views humans as ill-equipped to deal with blowback as it pertains to the "vast scale of events" and consequences of the Anthropocene, or to reconcile our responsibilities to and relationships with the worlds in which we reside, and to that, I would add, with the nonhuman animals with whom we coexist ("Agency," 1). This crisis of comprehension becomes very clearly significant when we imagine humans embracing the immediate, perceived ease of consumerism without planning or accounting for its consequences—consequences that manifest in ways that invite these questions of agency and ethical responsibility, when the products of human knowledge-making get bound up in intra-active cycles detrimental to the bodies and worlds in which they circulate. Interestingly, Miller makes an analogous point in the conclusion of her article about automation and agency, albeit in a somewhat different context. She contends:

> If agency is an attribution, our ideological concerns have been misplaced. We should be concerned less about empowering subaltern subjects and more about enabling and encouraging attributions of agency *to* them by those with whom they interact—and accepting such attributions *from* them. We should examine the attributions we ourselves are willing to make and work

to improve the attributions that (other) empowered groups are willing to make. (153, emphasis in original)

Miller's points here are well taken, and this "to/from" conceptualization of agency seems just a short trip from the workings of agential realism, or at least not incompatible with the agential concerns of feminist materiality. The challenge or conceptual trickiness arises when we expand the boundaries of the rhetorical situation beyond the more traditional rhetor/audience formulation, or even beyond the human/machine (software) formulation, to consider also the concerns, muddy terrain, and entanglements of trans-corporeality, or the ways that human and nonhuman animal bodies, organisms, environments, and things connect, enmesh, and intra-act. Here, agential realism more closely fits the bill. Nonetheless, such considerations of power and accountability remain key: What are the perceived risks or consequences of more readily attributing agency *to* vulnerable nonhuman bodies? Why might stakeholders or dominant groups be hesitant to attribute agency to vulnerable groups or species? Bekoff acknowledges such concerns in his thinking about compassionate conservation, and Haraway makes compatible points when she thinks on the "semiotic agency" of marine species in the "hermeneutic labor" of knowledge projects like *Crittercam,* a National Geographic documentary that followed the lives of marine creatures by affixing cameras to their bodies (*When* 261).

In her "Crittercams" chapter, Haraway more specifically questions the agency of nonhuman animals. She notes that "there is no way even to think about the issue outside the relentlessly fleshly entanglements of this particular techno-organic world" (*When* 262). According to Don Ihde, Haraway says, "in the human-technology hermeneutic relation, the technology adapts to the humans and vice versa," and subsequently contends that "surely the same insight applies to the animal-human-technology hermeneutic relation" (262). To conceptualize an animal-human-technology hermeneutic relation in such a way then shifts the locus of control; humans, nonhuman animals, and technology participate in the co-construction of knowledge-making. Subsequently, we "are all enmeshed in hermeneutic labor (and play) by the material-semiotic requirements of getting on together in specific lifeworlds" (262–63). Such onto-epistemological shifts raise the argument that "situated human beings have epistemological-ethical obligations to the animals. Specifically, we have to learn who they are in all their nonunitary otherness in order to have a conversation on the basis of carefully constructed, multisensory, compounded languages" (263). Haraway's call for such "carefully constructed" conversations helps to further acknowledge the consequences of how we make and present knowledge about nonhuman animals, and how we understand and conceptualize, implicitly and explicitly, our relationships with them.

Alaimo, in advocating for a "material ecocriticism," notes that "while particular strands of thing theory, object-oriented ontology, speculative realisms, new vitalisms, and material feminisms may or may not be particularly posthumanist or environmentally oriented, material ecocriticism, by definition, focuses on material agencies as part of a wider environmentalist ethos that values ecosystems, biodiversity, and nonhuman life" (*Exposed* 130–31). I would add here that material ecocriticism is then compatible with agential realism; that is, as Angela Willey describes, Barad's notion of agential realism

> asks us to think of science as 'material-discursive' practices. . . . In this formulation, objectivity and agency are bound up with responsibility and accountability—we, producers of knowledge, are thus bound to consider the possibilities, both enabling and violent—of interacting with the world by studying it. In this sense, we become responsible not only for the knowledge we seek but for what exists. (1008)

In conceptualizing agency, then, questions of accountability emerge as key. Do we imagine technology's blowback as perpetuating and sustaining its own momentum, or do we think critically about attribution and the role of humans in what is a crisis largely of our own making? Of course, this is hardly an either/or proposition; rather, as we have seen, the question of agency is nuanced, and one that requires some acceptance of paradox. I appreciate Barad's agential realism especially for its friendliness toward material ecocriticism and its explicit acknowledgement of the need to keep the concerns of ethical responsibility close at hand while also acknowledging that accountability does not fall solely or neatly within the purview of the human. In this way, conceptualizing ethical responsibility means acknowledging the ongoing intra-activity of bodies, materials, discourses, and ecosystems. I contend that we can conceptualize agency in such a way that avoids understanding ethical responsibility as an "us or them" proposition and acknowledges our entanglement with the material world and all its kin, while also acknowledging the consequences of human knowledge-making in these ecological dilemmas. For, as Willey notes, "we have to acknowledge our agency and our role as knowledge producers in shaping the course of knowledge" (1008).

How we see agency, and how we understand our relationships and responsibilities to vulnerable, nonhuman animals, is very important in the stories we tell. As Haraway says, "It matters which stories tell stories" (*Staying* 35). This is why I like the notion of a visual-material, posthuman rhetoric, imbued with the themes of compassionate conservation, trans-corporeality, material feminisms, and agential realism: it is attuned to coexistence with nonhuman animals and engages productively with questions of agency and accountability without moving into anger or blame, and without necessarily relying on technofixes but without forgoing them. In other words, as Haraway describes, "sometimes it is hard to remember that it remains important to embrace situated technical projects and their people. They are not the enemy; they can do many important things for staying with the trouble and for making generative oddkin" (*Staying* 3). To embrace technoscience in a way that "stays with the trouble," to borrow Haraway's phrase, then situates us in the entangled web of material discursive practice for which we likewise bear some responsibility, precisely because, as Barad reminds us, "we are an agential part of the material becoming of the universe" (*Meeting* 178). In the configurations of material discursive practice, "*objectivity means being accountable for marks on bodies*," and ethical responsibility ought not to be an "us or them" proposition; rather, we are entangled in the material discursivities that we help enact (Barad, *Meeting* 178–79, emphasis in original). Likewise, I consider artifacts of visual-material rhetoric as participating in the larger intra-actments of material discursive practice through their potential enactments of ethical responsibility. Moreover, in considering the intra-active workings of agency, we must think of nonhuman animals, for instance, as not outside of ourselves, not outside the orbit of our attribution, but rather as part of our worldly practice—as co-constituted through those material discursive practices in which we intra-act. *This is a conceptualization of agency that I can get on board with.*

TRAJECTORIES IN RHETORIC AND MATERIALITY: OR, VISUAL-MATERIAL RHETORICS AND / INFORMED BY NEW MATERIALISMS

Visual-material rhetorical artifacts then participate in the larger, agential intra-actments of material discursive practice. That is, they may emerge and intra-act with, within, and across spaces and bodies in ways that help create and co-construct new knowledge, perform perceived responsibility for threatened or vulnerable species and ecosystems, and illuminate new ways of thinking about our relationships with nonhuman animals that foreground questions of power and accountability. Visual-material rhetoric is thus compatible with and intersects with some of the overarching themes of new material feminisms. More specifically, it is important to note that I understand visual-material rhetorical artifacts as performing configurations that emerge out of ongoing agential intra-actions; in this way, they are part of the new materialist account but are technically distinct from the notion of new materialisms. The next section describes these distinctions in more depth.

Early Conceptions of Material Rhetoric

It is worth noting that new materialisms, while sharing the "material" terminology, has some commonality with but is distinct from the subdiscipline of material rhetoric, at least in its earlier conceptions. It may be helpful to note, for the sake of clarity, that new materialisms, as an interdisciplinary theory, is not specific to rhetorical studies; however, new materialisms is compatible with rhetorical studies and its subdisciplines such as material and visual rhetorics, as Laurie Gries has recently shown. I likewise see new materialisms as aligned with some of the larger goals of a visual-material rhetorical lens, especially in its attention to the *consequences* of visual and material artifacts, or as Gries puts it, visual things, in the world; however, new materialisms differs primarily in its locating agency beyond solely the realm of human attribution, or even beyond human/machine attribution, to consider even more broadly the ongoing, agential and entangled intra-actions of matter, things, human and nonhuman bodies, spaces, and systems. Importantly, for instance, whereas studies in material rhetoric may analyze the impact of artifacts and spaces on human bodies and attribute *agency* primarily to *humans,* new materialisms would understand matter, bodies, ecosystems, and discourses as participating in broader, always ongoing, agential intra-actions in ways that, as Alaimo reminds us, "often reconceptualize material agencies" (3).

Material rhetoric is a subdiscipline of rhetorical studies and thus has its theoretical and analytical roots in rhetorical theory. Material rhetoric initially established a niche within rhetorical studies through its ability to extend rhetoric's analytical purview from its more traditional focus on printed text to the visual, material, and spatial representations of bodies, incorporating such sites as memorials, museum displays, or other visual-material representations that in some way influence, advocate for, or perform critiques related to vulnerable or marginalized bodies (see Biesecker; Blair; Brouwer; Collins; Fausch; Haas; Mountford; Nicoletti; Propen, *Locating*; and Schuster).[5]

Viewed through a more traditional material rhetoric lens, sculptures or memorials may count as material texts; architectural spaces and walking paths within national parks would count as material texts, through features such as their tactileness, durability, physicality, their focus on space or spatiality, and also primarily through their impact on the body (Blair).

Material texts, like marked walking paths within a park (Propen, *Locating*), influence the body through their potential to prescribe the movements of park visitors and thus influence visitors' interpretations of a space and thus the broader histories described by that space; such marked pathways may then have broader consequences for knowledge-making than their immediate presence on the landscape would indicate. Informational placards are also changeable in the sense that they are subject to the elements and their immediate environment (snow may hide a placard; the noise of local traffic may distract a tourist's decision-making), but those paths and their placards may also be understood as materially fixed artifacts, and their knowledge work, while not to be undervalued in its ability to describe histories and shape understandings of how spaces participate in knowledge-making, is viewed as most relevant for *human* bodies and action.

Similarly, the multimodal experiences ushered forth by a GPS device, for instance, as I have argued elsewhere (*Locating*), would count as materially rhetorical because its audiovisual cues, mobility, tactility, and adaptability constitute more than just a printed text or page. The GPS produces a multimodal text, and in doing so, it also guides us, prompts us, influences bodily action, response, physical direction, and decision-making, and in doing so, co-constructs agency with its user. In such instantiations, however, knowledge-making is still primarily related to human interests. Implicitly supporting this point while also providing a nice definition of material rhetoric, Barbara Dickson, in her analysis of the iconic *Vanity Fair* cover photo of actor Demi Moore when she was seven months pregnant, defined material rhetoric as

> a mode of interpretation that takes as its object of study the significations of material things and corporal entities—objects that signify not through language but through their spatial organization, mobility, mass, utility, orality, and tactility. Of primary interest to material rhetoric are objects that represent the *human* body, because of the way that these representations are then taken up by and inscribed on corporal bodies. (298, my emphasis)

Thus, studies in material rhetoric tend to emphasize how material objects can signify through their spatiality or use of space, or, for instance, how spaces can signify not primarily through language but through their ability to physically guide an audience. And as Blair has described, material rhetoric was initially and does remain concerned with the broader consequences of material artifacts in the world. But again, importantly, earlier studies in material rhetoric tended to focus on how such objects or spaces can engage, mark, enable, or constrain *primarily human action and bodies*. Moreover, material rhetoric would seek to understand how artifacts "can be read as providing for or constraining agency, the ability of persons singly and collectively to produce change" (Dickson 298). Thus, studies in material rhetoric also often addressed notions of agency, but tended to attribute agency to human thought and action, and focused more on the impact of artifacts and spaces on *human* action and bodies.

Importantly, then, while earlier conceptions of material rhetoric understood agency as operating within the human purview, new materialisms understands agency as involving to an even greater extent the entanglements of humans, nonhuman animals, technologies, and the material world. Thus, as Angela Willey notes: "It is matter's agentive properties that distinguish new materialist inquiry from old materialist claims about the presumptively static nature of things" (998). On this point I would agree; however, I might add that the notion of the "static nature of things" may be perceived by some as a bit tricky. That is, on the one hand, it may be said that earlier studies in material rhetoric tended to focus on arguably static or fixed things, such as memorial sculptures, museum exhibits, or marked walking paths; on the other hand, such analyses often focused on these things' physical or multimodal mobility or malleability. Even so, a thing's malleability, for instance, is subtly different from its entanglements in the ongoing intra-activities of matter—that is, it is the nature of intra-activity that is key here, and Willey's concern is likewise with the *agentive* properties of matter in the sense of its ongoing, intra-active entanglements across humans, nonhumans, and environments, and the implications of those entanglements for power and accountability in knowledge-making.

Likewise, this book understands visual-material rhetorics as pertaining to the knowledge-making that can happen in the agential realist, environmental account. It understands visual-material rhetorical artifacts as entangled with, emerging, and participating in the intra-actions of spaces, human *and* nonhuman bodies, technologies, and ecosystems. More concisely, this book understands visual-material rhetorics in the context of new material feminisms, and as bound up in these broader agential intra-actions of world-making.

New Materialisms and Its Intersections with Visual-Material Rhetorics

While material rhetoric and new materialisms emerge as two technically distinct entities, we may also easily consider their interplay when we understand visual-material rhetorical artifacts as participating in posthuman, agential intra-actions in ways that, as Alaimo reminds us, "often reconceptualize material agencies" (*Bodily* 3). That is, when we talk about new materialism, the interdisciplinary theory, and (or versus) theories of material rhetoric, with its roots in rhetorical studies, we are talking about two compatible but technically different areas of focus. More specifically, as Gries describes, new materialism, while "difficult to pin down," can be thought of as "an emergent interdisciplinary theory informed by contemporary scholarship emanating from the intersections of science studies, feminist studies, and political theory" (4). It is a more decentralized mode of inquiry that, while recently taken up in rhetorical studies, is readily associated with the nonhuman turn, in that new materialist scholars "challenge the modernist paradigm" responsible for the dualist thinking that would place "humans/subject/culture on one side and things/object/nature on the other" (5). As Gries further describes, "new materialism, in part, is an ontological project in that it challenges scholars to rethink our underlying beliefs about existence and particularly our attitudes toward and our relationship with matter," and thus invites questions of the agency of things (5; see also Bennett, "Systems"; Barnett and Boyle; Jack; Sheldon; and Teston, *Bodies* and "Rhetoric"). Following Bennett (*Vibrant*), Gries notes that we often do not acknowledge the agency of things because we attribute tool use more so to human agents (12). However, things gain agential and rhetorical power as they work with, sometimes within, sometimes against, human and nonhuman animals, in social, cultural, and political contexts that bear consequences in the world. Finally, a new materialist rhetorical approach, much like the aims of earlier material rhetorical analysis, is thus broadly concerned with consequence, or as Gries says, futurity—"the strands of time beyond the initial moment of production and delivery when rhetorical consequences unfold, often unpredictably, as things circulate and transform across space, form, genre, and function" (14).

This book thus considers visual-material rhetorical artifacts in the context of new material feminist, agential realist, environmental accounts, in which rhetorical artifacts are not necessarily products of human agency, but rather are co- or, really, *multiply*-constituted with bodies, things, matter, and ecosystems. Moreover, while perhaps topically concerned with the impacts of bodies and spaces, such rhetorical artifacts also function intra-actively in the ongoing, emergent configurations of the worlds in which they matter—and they matter, here, both topically and agentially. In other words, visual-material rhetorical artifacts, as agential, environmental accounts, emerge through the ongoing intra-actions of the very bodies, technologies, and worlds in which they continuously participate, and in ways that potentially enact configurations of ethical responsibility.

A visual-material, posthuman environmental rhetoric informed by an ethic of compassionate conservation, then, with its interest in the consequences and agential capacities and intra-actions of visual and material artifacts and things in the world, and with its related considerations of power and accountability, is thus allied with many of the thematic and theoretical leanings of new material feminisms. This book engages those leanings even *more so,* or even more explicitly, from the perspective of their implications for *nonhuman animals.* That is, this book focuses more specifically on the implications of visual and material artifacts and things in the world for vulnerable, nonhuman species. Thus, the material world is not divorced from the rhetorical accounts produced in response to the environmental crises taking place within it. Moreover, such rhetorical accounts are produced not through the agencies of humans alone but through the entanglements of bodies, environments, and technoscientific practices of visualization that sometimes paradoxically make vulnerable as they also seek to *advocate on behalf of.*

A new visual-material, posthuman environmental rhetoric informed by an ethic of compassionate conservation would thus retain its concern for the rhetorical components of visual-material artifacts and how they represent and affect spaces and bodies in ways that create new knowledge and advocate for threatened or vulnerable species. It would, as mentioned above, understand such emergent environmental rhetorical accounts as an extension of the material world and ultimately the very substance of self. It would also, likewise, go even farther in its focus on questions of nonhuman agency—not only in terms of the agentive properties of things and matter, but also in terms of how things and matter, or *things that matter,* are entangled with the lives and well-being of nonhuman animals in ways that can no longer be set aside or viewed as separate, and in ways that have implications for embodied knowledge-making. Such questions then comprise the stuff of not only visual-material rhetorical analysis, but one that is also imbued with some of the themes and concerns of new material feminisms.

Moreover, as the subject matter of our analyses become more complex and less immediately tangible or seeable—as they become more entangled—we need to delve deeper into questions of power and accountability about how exactly we need and want to explore and understand our worlds. And, we ought to consider how the apparatuses of technoscience might leverage power and accountability in ways that are productive of world-making and compassionate in their workings. These types of questions, while anchored in fields like animal studies, new material feminisms, and the environmental humanities, may easily engage visual-material rhetorics in ways that align with what Willey has referred to as "postcolonial feminist science studies."

Willey describes new materialist research as involving a "return/turn to such objects as 'the body,' 'nature' and 'life' in social and critical theory by bringing 'matter' into the purview of our research" (992). She then points to what she perceives as a limitation of new materialist research. Here, she critiques, matter "takes the form of scientific data on bodies and climates," and then gives way to new material feminist theories; however, she argues that new theories based on new data are not enough (992–93). She calls for a postcolonial feminist science studies and argues that "thinking creatively, capaciously, pluralistically, and thus irreverently with respect to the rules of science—about the boundaries and meanings of matter, 'life,' and 'humanness'" could be central to such a project (992). Moreover, a postcolonial feminist science studies would "endeavor to hold feminist materialism" to a "shared vision" that "foregrounds power and accountability" (993). I understand a postcolonial feminist science studies as very much aligned with a visual-material rhetoric of posthuman conservation. Further, this "shared vision" not only aligns with Alaimo's ideas about trans-corporeality and the ways that environments, bodies, and matter intersect to illuminate the ethical and political challenges of technoscience, but also aligns with the main tenets of compassionate conservation in its accounting for the best interests of the lives of nonhuman species. Indeed, as Alaimo notes, ideas about *posthumanist* new materialism and transcorporeality "insist that nonhuman life is a matter of concern," and "even the smallest, most personal ethical practices in the domestic sphere are inextricably tied to any number of massive political and economic predicaments" (*Exposed* 10). Such ideas are also consistent with Bekoff's call for compassionate conservation, and the more creative and pluralistic thinking and attentiveness to the lives of nonhuman animals that it requires.

COMPASSIONATE CONSERVATION, EMBODIED COMMUNICATION, AND VISUALITY

Compassionate conservation is an interdisciplinary movement that has steadily gained international attention and momentum in recent years. A compassionate conservation approach, as the University of Technology Sydney's Centre for Compassionate Conservation (UTS: CfCC) describes it, would advocate for the protection of "wild and captive animals" and "seeks to build the welfare of individual animals into conservation practice" (UTS, "About Us: Who We Are"). Compassionate conservation understands every individual animal life as uniquely important and seeks to promote peaceful coexistence between humans and nonhuman animals. Compassionate conservation is also grounded "in the guiding principle of 'first do no harm'" (UTS, "About Us: What Is").[6] Given these ideas, a compassionate conservation approach would not endorse, for example, the U.S. Army Corps of Engineers' recent plan to kill 11,000 double-breasted cormorants in Oregon's Columbia River Estuary to protect local salmon populations (Anderson). Such an approach not only places value on one species over another but also enacts a "utilitarian" perspective that deems it acceptable to kill species viewed as "pests" due to their high populations within a given area (Tobias). Such vantage points run counter to the tenets of compassionate conservation.

Part of the goal of compassionate conservation is to prompt and foster a critical awareness of how we understand our relationships with nonhuman animals, and to foster an ethic of peaceful coexistence in which decision-making about conservation practice and policy is grounded in a consideration of the most compassionate choice for all beings. Of course, this is easier said than done, and we may easily complicate the notion that conservation is still, at the end of the day, about humans making decisions on behalf of nonhuman animals—a dilemma that chapters 3 and 4 also consider. I argue, however, following Bekoff, that when we begin to ask the right questions, or questions that are more critically engaged and that come from a place of compassion and kinship, and less from the position of attempting to regulate or control our environment or place value on certain kinds of bodies, we might begin to acknowledge the rich, multispecies entanglements that can inform a compassionate, posthuman conservation.

Marc Bekoff, scholar of ecology, evolutionary biology, and animal behavior who initially conceptualized compassionate conservation, likewise advocates such an approach to understanding our lives with other species. He reiterates that the initial step in such processes is to do no harm, but he also emphasizes a necessary shift in perspective that recognizes animals as sentient, individual beings:

> It's critical to avow that sentience matters. Science tells us animals have feelings, emotions, and preferences and individuals care about and worry about what happens to them and to their families and friends. We need to consider what we know about animal sentience when we intrude into their lives, even if it is on their behalf. . . . A humane framework that considers individual animals is long overdue. (Tobias)

The "humane framework that considers individual animals" that Bekoff describes ought not to be mistaken as an interest in trading humanism for antihumanism, or to be misread as an "animal" version of the traditional humanist notion of the "'autonomous, self-willed individual agent'" (Roelvink and Zolkos 1). Rather, compassionate conservation, similar to what Donna Haraway and Judith Butler describe in varied but compatible contexts, is a philosophy of accountability that calls into question the hegemonic power structures underpinning human exceptionalism and modes of disregard, witting or unwitting, for vulnerable bodies.

Visibility, Vulnerability, and Advocacy

Haraway, Butler, and Bekoff raise strikingly similar points about what is at stake in the practices of visualizing vulnerable beings. Writing in 2016, Haraway asks: "Who lives and who dies, and how, in this kinship rather than that one? What shape is this kinship, where and whom do its lines connect and disconnect, and so what? What must be cut and what must be tied if multispecies flourishing on earth, including human and other-than-human beings in kinship, are to have a chance?" (*Staying* 2). And Butler, writing in 2003, in the context of her critique of the U.S. response to 9/11, states:

> The public sphere is constituted in part by what can appear, and the regulation of the sphere of appearance is one way to establish what will count as reality, and what will not. It is also a way of establishing whose lives can be marked as lives, and whose deaths will count as deaths. Our capacity to feel and to apprehend hangs in the balance. But so, too, does the fate of the reality of certain lives and deaths as well as the ability to think critically and publicly about the effects of war. (xx–xxi)

Both Haraway and Butler point to the need for solidarity and kinship, and the need to embrace rather than turn our backs on vulnerable bodies. Both point to the value of and need for self-reflection in considering the most compassionate path forward in the face of what may be understood as the violence that affects vulnerable beings.

In the context of this book, more specifically as it pertains to the analyses in chapters 2 and 3, I understand such violence largely in terms of what Rob Nixon refers to as the "slow violence" incurred by vulnerable bodies in an age of anthropogenic change. Moreover, Butler implicitly speaks to the role of practices of visualization in establishing "what will count as reality," and Haraway, too, implicitly invokes visuality and spatiality in questioning the "shape" of our kinship with vulnerable beings, and the location of these points of connection and disconnection. Such practices of visuality are not merely philosophical exercises but also precarious endeavors; that is, following Christa Teston, who draws upon Butler's work, these practices are grounded in political, economic, and social power structures "that maintain conditions required for securing life" ("Rhetoric" 253). Such practices of visuality then prompt us to question, as Haraway notes, "what must be cut and what must be tied" in order for multispecies entanglements to survive, thrive, and function in the positive (*Staying* 2).

Like Haraway, Bekoff also notes that the differences in how we understand the rights and lives of animals are enormous, and can lead "to very different priorities about who lives, who dies, and why," given the range of approaches to and motivations for conservation endeavors (Tobias). As Bekoff argues,

> Whenever humans seek to "manage" nature, creating parks and artificial boundaries, it is always only for the benefit of humans. Perhaps, to the degree to which animals are left alone within these parks, it might be said that animals benefit, that they have been protected from humans. Otherwise, most of what passes for "wildlife management" looks like nothing so much as a direct attack on wildlife itself. (*Animal* 40)

Instead, as chapter 4 describes in more detail, Bekoff advocates for what he calls "rewilding projects" (*Rewilding*), or approaches to conservation that, not incompatible with a posthumanist approach, soften rather than reinforce the perceived and actual borders between humans, animals, and the natural world.

Haraway similarly alludes to the hegemonic, binary structures often at play in conservation projects when she writes, somewhat sardonically, "I do long for an idiom that considers multispecies flourishing outside the idiom and apparatus of 'Save the Endangered [fill in the blank]'" (*When* 256). Here, the critique is not so much in the fact of our well-intended propensities to want to save the endangered "blank," but rather in the lack of nuance perpetuated in such models of conservation. That is, the "save the endangered" idiom, while well-meaning, nonetheless relies on and perpetuates a more binary, "us/them" mode of understanding our relationships *to* nonhuman species, whereas a more entangled mode of discursive practice might engage a more relational becoming *with* our nonhuman kin. That said, lack of nuance is not necessarily grounds for abandoning knowledge projects; rather, it just means we need to dig a little deeper to find the points of connection, or even the reasons for disconnection, which can then help prompt more nuanced relationalities that posthumanism can accommodate and foster.

Bekoff begins to help us understand some of this nuance when describing the varied range of priorities for valuing species; in doing so, he describes broadly the positions of animal welfarists, animal rightists, utilitarians, and conservation biologists. Bekoff notes that "welfarists and conservation biologists argue over whether, for example, a specific project needs to be put on hold until animal suffering is eliminated, or that a project needs to be terminated if this is not possible" (Tobias). The welfarist position would have that "while humans should not wantonly exploit animals, as long as we make animals' lives comfortable, physically and psychologically, we're respecting their welfare. . . . In the end, welfarists agree that the pain and death animals suffer is sometimes justified because of the benefits that humans derive." Animal rightists, on the other hand, "*stress* that animals' lives are valuable in and of themselves, not valuable just because of what they can do for humans or because they look or behave like us." Animals, Bekoff describes, "are not property or 'things,' but rather living organisms, subjects of a life, who are worthy of our compassion, respect, *friendship,* and support." A utilitarian position, as mentioned earlier, would view it as acceptable to kill species deemed "'pests' such as brown rats, coyotes, and other animals because they are numerous." Finally, Bekoff notes that many conservation biology and environmentalist camps are typically or often composed of "welfarists who are willing to trade-off individuals' lives for the perceived good of higher levels of organization such as ecosystems, populations, or species." Here he cites the example of reintroducing the Canadian lynx into Colorado, where there was not enough food for them in the habitat, causing many lynx to starve; in such a case, "some conservationists and environmentalists, in contrast to rightists, argued that the death of some individuals . . . was permissible for the perceived good of the species" (Tobias). Thus, how we perceive the lives of animals and our relationships to them and the environment can indeed give way to vastly different ideas and priorities about "who lives, who dies, and why" (Tobias).

In addition to these ideas about how we understand the lives of animals, Bekoff raises another important, overarching question about the larger motivations for and consequences of conservation biology—that built into its mission is the assumption that conservation biology, on some level, involves human intervention into the environment, and often accounts for or attempts to course-correct prior human intervention in the first place. That is, conservation biology implicitly places humans at the forefront of efforts to *protect* species through means that, nonetheless, involve modes of human intervention and control, no matter how well-meaning those efforts might be.[7] Here, Bekoff again calls into question human exceptionalism: "Can we really recreate or restore ecosystems? Should other animals pay for our destructive and selfish ways? What are we really doing? Can we or should we try to 'do it all'?" Nonetheless, Bekoff is willing to acknowledge and even engage the paradox that necessarily underpins ideas about compassionate conservation. Occupying the mossy terrain that exists someplace between hope and despair, Bekoff argues that "since we decide who lives and who dies, compassionate conservation can easily be integrated into decisions about the fate of individual animals" (Tobias). Here, Bekoff is acutely aware of the role that humans play in managing vulnerable animal bodies, but wants to trouble hegemonic binaries in ways that look for the potentially nuanced relationalities within them; doing so then requires that we engage more empathetically with the lives of vulnerable nonhuman animals. That is, when Bekoff notes, in a recent interview in *Forbes,* that he is trying to "understand why the trading off of lives 'for the good of their own species' is permissible," and subsequently remarks, "I wonder what the animals would think about it all," he is asking that we set aside our human-centered perspective to engage with curiosity, and relationally, from a vantage point more attentive to the vulnerable other (Tobias). When it comes to countering hegemony, then, curiosity and relationality are both game changers and deal breakers.

The Precarious Paradox of Visualization

If the tracking and visualization of cryptic species, for instance, is a hallmark of legitimate conservation and environmental advocacy in the age of Anthropocene technoscience, then how might we engage with practices of tracking or visualizing vulnerable species in the most compassionate ways possible? I argue in this book that the ability to visualize the heretofore unvisualizable through the practices and products of technoscience is a complicated and somewhat paradoxical form of visual-material rhetoric and embodied communication in which vulnerable bodies are simultaneously made more vulnerable through practices of revealing, and yet perceived as more easily protected through those very practices—a precarious double bind brought on by an interest in understanding and communicating about our relationships with other species through the practices of seeing and tracking that often mark our witting or unwitting attempts to control the natural world. Such visualization practices are paradoxical in their normalization and mechanisms of control, on the one hand, and in their potential for engaging in or performing a sort of "embodied communication," or "becoming with," on the other hand.

Embodied communication entails "communication about relationship, the relationship itself, and the means of reshaping relationship and so its enacters" (Haraway, *When* 26). Embodied communication is not a top-down enterprise—it understands humans and nonhuman animals as "multiple beings in relationship" (26). How, then, might such relationships take shape and manifest in productive ways through material discursive practice? Such attempts to reconcile these issues of embodiment, and what counts as advocacy, and what counts as normalization and control of bodies, continue to fuel scholarship in environmental rhetoric, animal studies, and related fields.

Cary Wolfe, for instance, explores the implications of artists' various representational strategies for portraying nonhuman animals in contemporary works of art ("From" 129). He is interested in what a "particular artistic strategy" might say about the "larger philosophical and ethical challenge of speaking for nonhuman animals, speaking to our relations with them, and how taking those relations seriously unavoidably raises the question of who 'we' are" (130). Not dissimilarly, Spencer Schaffner's study of birding field guides as a form of rhetorical action describes the genre of the field guide as one that "attempt[s] to control environmental encounters" (95). I might argue that birding guides impart such mechanisms of control by normalizing standards of feathered bodies rather than enacting a more embodied communication. More specifically, as Leigh A. Bernacchi describes, via Schaffner, "birders and ornithologists gain knowledge of birds' capacities for coexistence through careful, patient observation as most field guides do not address the ways in which a bird affects or is affected by humans and our artifices" (143–44).

Steve Baker, too, questions the role of visual representation in reflecting ideas about how humans understand their relationship to nonhuman animals. In *Ecosee,* Baker calls for a more nuanced way of seeing the environment and nonhuman animals—one that goes beyond mere "looking" or "watching" and invites a greater level of "attentiveness to animals and their habitats," more akin to an entangled, becoming *with* (155). He argues that artistic representation has the potential to provide this "creative interruption of the ways in which humans habitually look at animals" (166). And in calling for new ways to conceptualize the "presence of animals," Marcus Bullock notes that "the world of animals themselves and our encounters with it have already fallen into a characteristic form of distance" (105).

In *Communicating Nature,* Julia Corbett similarly explores the role of nonhuman animal imagery in communicating about the environment. She finds that nonhuman animals often serve as "symbolic shorthand for environmental issues" (180). More specifically, she notes:

> Over the decades, environmental groups have used grizzly bears, wolves, spotted owls, and other critters to represent pristine places in need of protec-

tion, and to raise funds to use in that protection. Symbols of marine protection have included whales ("Save the Whale"), harp seal pups, dolphins, and manatees. . . . For many people, animals are the most tangible element of the larger environment and environmental issues. (180)

For Corbett, nonhuman animals represent a way for people to express feelings or beliefs "about the nonhuman world. As the most sentient and evident characteristic of the natural world, animals often function as a symbolic barometer of people's fundamental beliefs and valuations of nature" (181). In considering anthropomorphism, or the projection of human characteristics onto nonhuman animals, and its relevance for conceptualizing human/nonhuman animal relationships, Corbett says that "we can only understand [animals] in terms of our own experiences, language, and emotions, and interpreted within our social, historical, and cultural contexts" (178). Noting, however, that not all types of anthropomorphism need be understood in pejorative terms, she also describes the idea of "applied anthropomorphism," or "the use of our own personal perspective about what it's like to be a living being to suggest ideas about what it is like to be some other being of either our own or another species" (Lockwood, qtd. in Corbett 198–99). As Bennett and Stormer and McGreavy have similarly described, Corbett argues that applied anthropomorphism can paradoxically help us "view animals as autonomous creatures with lives separate from our own" (199). To analyze the affordances and limitations of visualizing vulnerable nonhuman bodies, while also recognizing that we are multiple beings in relationship, may prompt us to consider how such practices reshape our relationships with nonhuman animals and how they are enacted, thus allowing us to better conceptualize a visual-material, posthumanist conservation. A visual-material rhetoric of posthuman conservation thus necessarily critiques the complex entanglements that can occur when representation normalizes through its attempts at advocacy. Here there is no easy solution, and while we ought not to put all of our faith in the products of technoscience on the one hand, we must also remember, as Haraway notes, "that it remains important to embrace situated technical projects and their people. They are not the enemy; they can do many important things for staying with the trouble and for making generative oddkin" (*Staying* 3).

With the perceived need to track and visualize, then, we also get the normalization and reification that is tied up in these modes of advocacy through representation. A rhetoric of posthuman conservation, which I argue paradoxically reifies and normalizes through the very practices of representation that attempt to advocate, necessarily needs to embrace the multispecies entanglements that Haraway and Alaimo complicate. These entanglements are not without their own paradoxes. The paradox is part of the mix. So, then, if there is no easy solution, perhaps we must instead accept the paradox as a starting point. Such ideas and questions about how we understand human intervention in nature, and how we conceptualize and perceive the lives of nonhuman animals, also serve as an appropriate point of entry for merging ideas about posthumanism with conservation, or to begin to conceptualize an ethic of posthuman conservation.

TOWARD A POSTHUMAN CONSERVATION ETHIC

As Gerda Roelvink and Magdalena Zolkos describe, "posthumanism stands for diverse theoretical positions which together call into question an anthropocentric belief in the human as a distinctive, unique and dominant form of life" (1). Casey Boyle not dissimilarly posits that "the key for a posthumanist rhetoric . . . is an acknowledgment of a kind of *betweenness* among what was previously considered the human and nonhuman," which can then open the door to a more ecological vantage point ("Writing" 540, emphasis in original). Such vantage points then easily invite the posthuman co-presence, or perhaps even multi-presences, that constitute the "simultaneity of being in the world together" (Braidotti 169). This book is aligned with an understanding of the posthuman that, as Katherine Hayles, Collin Brooke, and Cary Wolfe have all described, is necessarily mindful of the practices of embodiment, and sensitive to the idea that modes of being are inextricably linked to the material world. For Brooke, similar to what Roelvink and Zolkos describe, a "posthuman rhetoric, as a return to embodied information, involves a revaluing of partiality. A posthuman rhetoric would allow us to turn our backs on omniscience and the humanist values of mastery and control that derive from the will to knowledge" (791). Moreover, a posthumanist version of conservation would necessarily work against the humanist version of posthumanism, which as Wolfe has noted, "reinstalls a very familiar figure of the human at the very center of the universe of experience . . . or representation" ("From" 148). Instead, Wolfe posits a more posthumanist version of posthumanism— one that, especially important for conservation and environmental advocacy, "take[s] seriously the ethical and even political challenges of the existence of nonhuman animals" (148). Such a view is also compatible with Bekoff's call for compassionate conservation, which likewise asks us to take seriously the challenges of the lives of nonhuman animals—to consider human and nonhuman lives as enmeshed—to recognize the "ecological vulnerability and resilience that is shared across species, where the human is seen as an 'instantiation of a network of connections, exchanges, linkages and crossings with all forms of life'" (Roelvink and Zolkos 1–2). Such a view of posthumanism not only allows for a more focused exploration of the intersections of technoscience, the environment, and human/nonhuman animal relationships, but also, through Wolfe's "critical interrogation of 'human' as a social norm," Roelvink and Zolkos note that he "illuminate[s] the relevance of posthumanism for theorizing affect" (2).

Affect becomes important for a posthumanist approach that values the lives of nonhuman animals in part because it invites "the creation of a new social nexus and new forms of social connection" with the posthuman subject (Braidotti 103). To understand posthuman affect in such a way is not incompatible with an ecological orientation, which, as described earlier, helps account for our affective relationships with the material world; thus, our ethical enactments inform and are informed by our always already ongoing, relational connections to the worlds and beings with whom we coexist. While interconnectedness and coexistence are not necessarily hallmarks of posthuman thought, to understand affect as compatible with posthumanism in this way begins to merge these two ideas in arguably productive ways.

As Rosi Braidotti argues, "Both kinship and ethical accountability need to be redefined in such a way as to rethink links of affectivity and responsibility not only for non-anthropomorphic organic others, but also for those technologically mediated,[8] newly patented creatures we are sharing our planet with" (103). Like Haraway's notion of "staying with the trouble," Braidotti's version of affect bears recuperative power; that is, as Roelvink and Zolkos note, for Braidotti, "affect is not reducible to the widespread melancholic sentiments that accompany the recognition of shared human and non-human vulnerability in the face of climate change and species extinction, such as feelings of hopelessness and depression that the problem is just too big and all-encompassing for any effective action alone or in concert" (3). While melancholic sentiment may inform notions of affect, it alone will not necessarily move us in the most productive direction; instead, we need to move toward more affirmative conceptualizations that may potentially link affect with the haptic (Marks), and with the elemental (Cohen), in ways that help facilitate becoming *with* places and beings. Again, such ideas are not only compatible with Haraway's notion of "staying with the trouble" and Bekoff's ideas about compassionate conservation but also speak to the ways in which humans and nonhuman animals are implicated and enmeshed in the products and projects of technoscience in the Anthropocene.

Informed by these ideas, this book thinks on the most compassionate path forward in the face of the considerable threats facing vulnerable nonhuman beings or species. In doing so, it merges a visual-material rhetorical framework imbued with the themes of new material feminisms, trans-corporeality, and agential realism with ideas about compassionate conservation and the posthuman, applying these ideas to three cases that involve (1) the impact of ocean plastics on vulnerable seabirds, (2) the debate about seismic testing and its potential impacts on marine species, and (3) the rhetorical implications of conservation maps created by tracking the movements of marine species over time and space. In these cases, technologies of visualization, from photography to GPS tracking, play a prominent role in arguments to protect threatened marine species. Together, the cases in this book then help conceptualize a new visual-material, posthuman environmental rhetoric, informed by an ethic of compassionate conservation that thrives and depends on multispecies entanglements and kinships. Put differently, this book is grounded in a rhetorical approach that not only affirms the role of rhetoric in conservation and technoscience but also extends and transcends these ideas to consider how visual-material rhetorical artifacts, as agential, environmental accounts, emerge through the ongoing intra-actions of the bodies, technologies, and worlds in which they continuously participate, in ways that can enact ethical responsibility and inform an ideal of compassionate conservation. I argue that a visual-material rhetorical approach informed by an ethic of compassionate conservation can help us better understand the ways that rhetoric informs ideas about environmental advocacy and compassion for living, vulnerable nonhuman creatures in an age of technoscience and the posthuman. The chapters in this book each explore and illuminate these ideas in different but intersecting ways.

CHAPTER SUMMARIES

Chapter 2, "Material Rhetoric in the Midway," merges ideas about visual-material, environmental rhetorics with questions of agency, affect, and accountability in human/nonhuman animal relationships, to consider the impact of the "Pacific Garbage Patch" and ocean plastics in the Midway Atoll on resident albatross populations. The Midway Islands, located at the northern end of the Hawaiian archipelago, provide a habitat for threatened albatross species. Here, ocean plastics pose a specific threat to albatross populations, as parents mistakenly feed pieces of plastic to their chicks. Photographer Chris Jordan has been documenting this issue since around 2009; these photographs, while harrowing, are quite powerful and have since circulated in museums and in the media. Thus, in case of the Midway, ocean plastics, bodies, and the products and processes of technoscience function as agential artifacts that situate albatross bodies as materially rhetorical in ways that we perhaps wish they weren't. This chapter argues that bodies, plastics, environments, and visual-material artifacts such as photos help configure and reconfigure worlds via their participation in the intra-activities of matter; as such, they are entangled in the broader material discursive phenomenon that is the ecological crisis of the Midway Atoll. Moreover, I argue that a visual-material, posthuman environmental rhetoric informed by the principles of compassionate conservation can help make salient these rhetorical entanglements, and ultimately, prompt the kind of enactments that can help shape productive intra-action and policy-making.

More specifically, chapter 2 argues that photographs constitute a performative, visual-material rhetorical response to the issue of the inadvertent impacts of technoscience on environment and species—a response that then enacts the ethical obligations that agential realism can entail. In enacting a posthuman performative response, photography also functions as a productive means of sharing the elemental, toxic space of the Midway and the bodies that have borne the consequences of its toxicity. Photographs then constitute affective, haptic, rhetorical inscriptions that make salient, in this case, the vulnerable albatross and the at-once paradoxically beautiful and toxic world in which it resides, and of which we are all inseparably implicated. I argue that the haptic image and the haptic eye enable a "grieving with," to borrow from Haraway (*Staying*), that paradoxically opens the door to more productive knowledge-making and world-making.

Chapter 3, "Seismic Risks and Vulnerable Bodies," analyzes the recent seismic testing debate in central California and the ways that its emergent texts and contexts illuminate rationales for how and why we value species and want to protect, advocate for, or feel a sense of kinship with them. More specifically, in 2009, the California power company, Pacific Gas and Electric Company (PG&E), requested a twenty-year license renewal for the Diablo Canyon nuclear power plant, which is located about halfway between Los Angeles and San Francisco. In 2011, after Japan's nuclear disaster, PG&E delayed the renewal until seismic tests could be conducted to assess nearby earthquake faults. The proposed testing then sparked public debate about potential risk to marine species in the region; moreover, PG&E proposed to monitor the effects of the tests by tracking otters and porpoises to gauge whether the testing would impact their well-being. This measure was itself viewed by some as contentious, as stakeholders perceived tracking as yet another potential risk and disturbance to species.

In step with the book's larger themes, chapter 3 understands the maps and emergent texts associated with the seismic testing debate as artifacts of visual-material rhetoric that participate in and perform the larger intra-actments of material discursive practice. In doing so, it considers how such rhetorical artifacts help enact configurations of ethical obligation related to marine species and ecosystem advocacy. Moreover, this chapter considers the function of public debate in the agential assemblage, or, as Bennett suggests, "the kind of striving that may be exercised by a human within the assemblage" (*Vibrant* 38). That is, I demonstrate that humans engage in material discursive practice in ways that paradoxically call into question the very role of the human, in essence signaling an implicit interest in what Diane Davis has referred to as a "posthumanist ethics" (19). Subsequently, I argue that the rhetorical artifacts associated with this debate paradoxically signal a move away from human exceptionalism and toward an interest in a more posthuman conservation ethic. The seismic testing debate thus emerges as a phenomenon that participates in the configuring and reconfiguring of enactments of ethical obligation that have important consequences for world-making. Rhetorical artifacts emerge and reemerge in the context of shifting perceptions of risk. In doing so, they participate in and perform the larger intra-actments of material discursive practice, and they help enact configurations of ethical obligation in a risk society.

Chapter 4, "Tracking to Sea (in the Anthropo-scene)," analyzes a digital mapping project in order to advocate for a visual-material, posthuman environmental rhetoric informed by the principles of compassionate conservation, and made salient through the practices of conservation mapping and ideas about critical cartography. More specifically, in 2009, the conservation organizations Birdlife International and Wildlife Conservation Society (WCS) partnered to produce a digital text called the *Atlas of the Patagonian Sea: Species and Spaces.* The *Atlas* was created to aid in policy decisions related to fisheries management and the designation of transportation routes within the Patagonian Sea, which ranges from southern Brazil to southern Chile, and is increasingly threatened by development and overfishing. Significantly, the *Atlas* is also the first-ever such work created largely by tracking the movements of seabirds, marine mammals, and sea turtles in the area. These marine species were outfitted with remote tracking devices for a ten-year period, and the resulting satellite data were then used to compile the *Atlas.*

Chapter 4 continues to understand the *Atlas* from the related perspectives of material rhetoric and new materialisms, as an artifact of visual-material rhetoric that participates in and performs the larger intra-actments of material discursive practice. In doing so, it also considers how cartographic practice, when understood as a rhetorical knowledge-making endeavor that is part of larger material discursive practices, can help enact configurations of ethical obligation and marine species and ecosystem protection by advocating for nonhuman animal bodies residing in the spaces represented through the map. Ultimately, I argue in this chapter that the *Atlas* helps move us incrementally closer to visualizing a posthuman conservation. In arriving at these broader conclusions, I explore an approach to environmental rhetoric that is located at the intersections of animal studies, critical cartography, and visual-material rhetorics. Further, to consider the intra-actions of spaces, bodies, technologies, and environments that constitute the *Atlas,* or this specific configuration or instantiation of material discursive practice, then raises questions of agency, or how and to what extent these various agential components, including the bodies of marine species, participate and intra-act in the material discursive practices of world-making. In doing so, I look to Haraway's understanding of agency in human/nonhuman animal relationships, and to Bekoff's notion of compassionate conservation, to consider whether and how these rhetorical, technoscientific artifacts illuminate and instantiate a compassionate, mindful conservation ethic.

Additionally, it is worth noting that in each case chapter, Foucault's concept of heterotopic space emerges to varying extents as a frame for understanding the contested and paradoxical nature of the places in question: the Midway Islands, the region of central California affected by the seismic testing debate, and the area of the Patagonian Sea mapped in the online *Atlas of the Patagonian Sea.* Understanding these areas as heterotopic helps further contextualize the challenges faced by the bodies residing in those spaces, and the material rhetorical, agential intra-actments that characterize them, in ways that paradoxically reify as they also attempt to advocate for vulnerable bodies.

Finally, chapter 5, the conclusion, revisits and expands upon some of the connections among the three cases in the book and considers the implications of a visual-material, posthuman environmental rhetoric informed by an ideal of compassionate conservation. It also considers new conceptualizations of human/nonhuman animal relationships, particularly as they pertain to the intersections of posthuman rhetorics of compassionate conservation, new materialisms, rhetorics of animal communication, and more recent ideas about multispecies ethnographies (van Dooren; Haraway, *Staying*). In looking ahead, I consider how the confluence of these interdisciplinary ways of knowing can further shape and illuminate our various lived and embodied experiences.

CHAPTER 2

Material Rhetoric in the Midway

Forever—is composed of Nows—
'Tis not a different time—
Except for Infiniteness—
And Latitude of Home—

From this—experienced Here—
Remove the Dates—to These—
Let Months dissolve in further Months—
And Years—exhale in Years—

Without Debate—or Pause—
Or Celebrated Days—
No different Our Years would be
From Anno Dominies—

—Emily Dickinson, "Forever—is composed of Nows"

TO "BEGIN," I feel compelled to note that the material that follows is itself always already an *ongoing agential intra-action of the world.* The ideas conveyed in this chapter, the meaning conveyed *here,* is not confined to the words that compose this chapter. This chapter is one configuration of an "ongoing performance of the world in its differential dance of intelligibility and unintelligibility" (Barad, *Meeting* 148–49). There is no boundary between this chapter, its writer, or this chapter's accounting of this configuration of the world, which, by way of its accounting, takes up other accountings of the configuration of the world. As the writer of this chapter, I participate in material discursive practice but am "neither pure cause nor pure effect but part of the world in its open-ended becoming" (150). Or, following what Barad describes in her acknowledgments to *Meeting the Universe*: this chapter and I, or "'we' have 'intra-actively' written each other" (x). And since there is no singular point of entry into this story—this broader material discursive phenomena by way of ecological dilemma—we may begin where it appears to make "sense": *in the elemental, in place.* So with that, let us descend into the Midway and see where the rhetorical currents take us.

The Midway Atoll comprises three small islands located at the remote, northern end of the Hawaiian archipelago. As part of the nation's largest conservation area, the Midway Atoll provides a near-predator-free habitat for and is also home to the world's largest albatross colony, including the black-footed albatross, the short-tailed albatross, and the more widely recognized Laysan albatross. The International Union for Conservation of Nature (IUCN) currently lists the short-tailed albatross as "endangered" and the black-footed and Laysan albatrosses as "near threatened." Among the threats to albatross populations are longline fishing, predation, and, of particular interest to this chapter, plastic trash in the ocean (Cornell Lab of Ornithology, "Laysan Albatross"). That is, as one BBC news article recently described, "Nearly two million Laysan albatrosses live on the [Midway] islands. Researchers have concluded that every single one contains some quantity of plastic."[1] The BBC article goes on to note that "about one-third of all albatross chicks die on Midway," as parents unknowingly feed their chicks pieces of plastic that they mistake for food (Shukman). When these birds die, their decomposing bodies sadly reveal that they are riddled with plastic debris.

News of this environmental crisis gained a surge of attention in 2011, when National Public Radio (NPR) published a story about photographer and filmmaker Chris Jordan, who, since 2009, has been documenting these deaths of birds in the Midway, both in his film called *Albatross* and in his photo series, *Midway: Message from the Gyre* (see O'Neill). Jordan's photographs, featured in the NPR article and powerful in the gravity they convey, quickly gained the public's attention at the time, and have since continued to circulate in the news media and in museum and art exhibits.[2]

In summer 2016, for example, Jordan's photo series, *Midway: Message from the Gyre,* was featured in an exhibition called *Plastic Fantastic?* at the Honolulu Museum of Art; the exhibit explored "the many facets and uses of plastic through an art lens" and showcased the work of five contemporary artists, including Jordan (Hancock; see also Honolulu Museum). Of particular interest to this chapter, in an artist statement that describes these photographs, Jordan invokes visual metaphors when he states: "For me, kneeling over their carcasses is like looking into a *macabre mirror.* These birds *reflect back* an appallingly emblematic result of the collective trance of our consumerism and runaway industrial growth" (Jordan, emphasis added). That is, part of the work of this chapter is to consider how visual-material rhetorical artifacts, while not impervious to critiques of representationalism and the visual metaphors associated with it, can also help enact the ethical obligations that agential realism may entail. In doing so, I describe how, in the Midway, vulnerable bodies and ecosystems, toxic plastic debris, and the technological apparatuses of visuality and their concomitant visual-material

artifacts, can help configure and reconfigure worlds via their nuanced and paradoxical participation in the intra-activities of matter.

Also around this time, in fall 2016, in another intra-action of material discursive practice, one that was framed as significant for both political history and environmental protection, former president Barack Obama
expanded the boundaries of the Papahānaumokuākea Marine National Monument, which encompasses the northwestern Hawaiian Islands and includes
the Midway Atoll. The Papahānaumokuākea Marine National Monument was
created by former president George W. Bush in 2006 and "already covered
140,000 square miles of ocean around the uninhabited northwestern islands
of Hawaii" (C. Barnett). The boundary expansion "more than quadrupled
Papahānaumokuākea's size, to 582,578 square miles, an area larger than all the
national parks combined" (C. Barnett). With the expansion of the geographic
boundary also came an expansion of the "no-take" area in which mineral
extraction and commercial fishing are prohibited.

On the one hand, the fishing exclusion sparked much debate among the
local fishing industries for its potential to threaten Hawaii's fishing culture. As
Edwin Ebisui Jr., chair of the Western Pacific Regional Fishery Management
Council, put it: "'To the native Hawaiian, access to marine resources is very,
very important and always will be. . . . I don't see how quadrupling the size of
the prohibited fishing area in any way furthers their cultural interests'" (C. Barnett). On the other hand, while deep sea mining and commercial fishing will
be prohibited within the boundaries of the protected area, "recreational fishing
and subsistence fishing by native Hawaiians will be allowed by permit, along
with scientific research" (Hirschfeld Davis). In addition, the Office of Hawaiian Affairs will reportedly participate in the management of the monument,
with the goal of giving "indigenous people a greater say over the steward-
ship of the lands and waters they have inhabited for generations" (Hirschfeld
Davis). Thus, while the boundary expansion of Papahānaumokuākea Marine
National Monument was clearly not without local debate, many lawmakers in
Hawaii felt that the marine-protected area (MPA) could serve as "a model for
sustainability" for the rest of the world's oceans (C. Barnett).

The boundary expansion of Papahānaumokuākea National Monument
was politically and culturally symbolic not only because it leveraged the
100-year-old Antiquities Act, which was first signed by former president The-
odore Roosevelt, but also because the northwestern Hawaiian Islands carry
much cultural significance and are viewed by native Hawaiians as a sacred
place (Hirschfeld Davis). The area is also historically significant, as it is the
site of the Battle of Midway, where Allied forces saw a victory that constituted
a turning point during World War II (Hirschfeld Davis). Foregrounded in
the media accounts, however, was the significance of the boundary expan-

sion as emblematic in working against climate change and protecting oceans and marine life. As Sarah Chasis, director of the oceans program at the Natural Resources Defense Council, put it: "'This act—to build resilience in our oceans, and sustain the diversity and productivity of sea life—could usher in a new century of conservation for our most special, and fragile, ocean areas'" (Hirschfeld Davis). Certainly, these benefits are easily arguable, and the expanded MPA will, in theory, protect marine species like the albatross from the threats of longline fishing; however, the move is not a panacea.

That is, on the one hand, there is no single silver bullet or techno-fix that will undo the anthropogenic effects of climate change; on the other hand, this doesn't mean we ought not to try. President Obama's expansion of the MPA should help protect the region from certain threats like longline fishing and deep sea mining, and it did help garner additional attention around the issue of ocean plastics and vulnerable species in the region.[3] Nonetheless, as this chapter will endeavor to show, a move like the boundary expansion is but one piece of a much larger puzzle. For, while a larger MPA should help protect albatrosses from the threat of longline fishing, for instance, it still does not prevent plastics from washing ashore on Midway Island, or, as one National Geographic article noted: "Being inside a national monument doesn't protect Laysan Island from trash washing ashore, especially on its windward side" (C. Barnett). Put differently, or more agentially (which we will complicate soon enough), ocean currents and the plastics circulating within them are indifferent to the nuances of geographic boundary-making for the purposes of environmental policy and protection. That said, and in keeping with the spirit of this book more broadly, I hardly wish to be dismissive of mapping, itself an enactment of material discursive practice that may comprise the stuff of visual-material rhetorics. As I have argued elsewhere, cartographic practice always already participates in discursive practice and is enmeshed in power relations.

To understand the map as enmeshed in power relations and representative of heterogeneous, contested spaces is compatible not only with Michel Foucault's notion of heterotopias, or heterotopic space, but also subsequently with an understanding of Papahānaumokuākea Marine National Monument as heterotopic. Heterotopic space makes salient the perhaps uneasy relationalities that happen within a site, "which are irreducible to one another and absolutely not superimposable on one another" (Foucault 23). We can try to characterize these sites by "looking for the set of relations by which a given site can be defined," not unlike the designation of prohibitions and affordances of the marine-protected area (23). Such sites have multiple uses and are frequented by various bodies with various sets of sometimes common, sometimes competing goals. In the case of Papahānaumokuākea Marine National Monument, for example, such goals might include mineral extraction; commercial fishing; recreational and subsistence fishing; and the breeding, feeding, and daily activities of marine species.

While the boundary expansion itself does not compose the analytical focus of this chapter, it is relevant in its demonstrating that the marine-protected area bears limited ecological capacity, and that the area is a challenge to try to control. Perhaps the quintessential illustration of this challenge is that enacting new boundaries does not necessarily prevent plastic trash from continuing to wash up on the shores of Midway—arguably one of the most visible ecological crises of this region. The boundary expansion then constitutes one attempt to manage the ecological capacities of this space in a way that serves the perceived interests of all bodies, activities, and ecosystems, albeit in a way that arguably tries to control configurations of worlds and knowledge-making. Thus, the move is obviously not a panacea and not impervious to neoliberal critique.[4] Moreover, compassionate conservation, too, while not necessarily opposed to ecosystem protection via management, would question with critical awareness the role of human intervention in efforts to control, manage, or recuperate the natural world. In this chapter, compassionate conservation becomes relevant as we consider what enactments of ethical obligation might "look like" as we engage with those vulnerable bodies with whom we are inseparably entangled and with whom we share our worlds; it is here that ocean plastic comes to matter, both visually and agentially.

In the case of the Midway Atoll, then, I argue that plastic trash functions as a rhetorical artifact imbued with agential capacities that, by extension, position the albatross body, both living and deceased, as materially rhetorical in ways that we perhaps wish it wasn't. I argue that plastic gains its "thing-power" largely through its toxic, corporeal contact with the bodies that it renders vulnerable. As Judith Butler writes: "We cannot, however, will away this vulnerability. We must attend to it, even abide by it, as we begin to think about what politics might be implied by staying with the thought of corporeal vulnerability itself" (29). Bodies, plastics, spaces, other visual-material artifacts help configure and reconfigure worlds via their participation in the intra-activities of matter—they are entangled in the broader material discursive phenomenon, this ecological crisis of consciousness that is the Midway Atoll and the matter of its vulnerable bodies.

Alive, the albatross is our vulnerable kin, made vulnerable by the consumerism that eventually comes to characterize its naturalcultural body; postmortem, the albatross body becomes a now-decomposing, naturalcultural residue, forensic evidence of the Anthropocene and the toxic consumer culture that gives mobility—some may say agential life—to plastic trash. And so, part and parcel of plastic's mobility is an agential capacity of sorts; that is, while I acknowledge the agential capacities of plastic, I hesitate to position plastic debris as the central protagonist in this story, for I argue that plastic is not some autonomous, anthropogenic trickster or superhero villain that decided to turn up in the Midway and stir up trouble. Rather, it is merely (but not simply) evidence of the geographically far-reaching intra-actions and consequences of human consumerism paired with ocean currents, its agency bound up in and made salient by the material discursive practices that characterize life and death in the Anthropocene.

Subsequently, I argue that Jordan's photos constitute a performative, visual-material rhetorical response to what Rob Nixon refers to as the "slow violence" incurred by vulnerable bodies in an age of anthropogenic environmental degradation. Nixon defines slow violence as "a violence that occurs gradually and out of sight, a violence of delayed destruction that is dispersed across time and space, an attritional violence that is typically not viewed as violence at all" (2). I thus argue that the photos are a visual-material rhetorical response to such slow violence—one that enacts the productive ethical obligations that agential realism may entail—a response that, as Barad describes of writing itself, "is not a uni-directional practice of creation that flows from author to page," but rather entails an "iterative and mutually constitutive working out, and reworking" (*Meeting* x). Thus, I argue that the photos also implicitly understand modes of visuality as materially rhetorical and as bearing the capacity for consequence.

In bearing the capacity for consequence, I argue that artifacts of visual-material rhetoric such as photography, while not impervious to the critiques of representationalist accounts of "reality," can, working in the positive, also help advocate for threatened species and places. Not incompatibly, in the context of her analysis of rape survivors' narratives, Wendy Hesford notes that "material rhetoric is critical for articulating the systematic nature of violence against women and for finding the gaps through which agency can be gained" (197). I agree, and I would also extend this notion to account for the potential of visual-material rhetorics to help articulate the vulnerability of threatened species that happens as a result of the practices that impact environmental degradation. With these ideas in mind, I argue that Jordan's photos also function as a productive means of sharing the elemental, toxic space of the Midway and the bodies that have borne the consequences of its toxicity. They are affective, haptic (Marks), rhetorical inscriptions that make salient the vulnerable albatross and the at-once paradoxically beautiful and toxic world in which it resides, and of which we are all inseparably implicated. Ultimately, I argue that the photos, as visual-material rhetorical artifacts, participate in the intra-actions of material discursive practice and, to borrow some of Haraway's language (*Staying*), help configure a *grieving with* that fosters the *becoming with* necessary for more productive world-making.

ON DATA COLLECTION AND ANALYSIS

In considering the rhetorical work of images, Laurie Gries suggests that we need not think of them as static, but rather consider their potential mobility, transformation, form, and function ("Monkeying"). While I would agree, it is beyond the scope of this analysis to trace the photos' mobilities and transformations in the entirety of their circulatory range, from, say, the NPR story, to the photo exhibit, to Jordan's related film documentary project, *Albatross*.[5] However, these shifting contexts and forms are also important pieces of the larger puzzle of mobility, and they are relevant in the sense that they constitute other possible visual-material rhetorical (re)configurations of the intra-actments of material discursive practice. In fact, I implicitly consider the NPR piece as an initial point of entry into this case, as it was actually the point at which my own curiosity about the photos was piqued; that is, the NPR story was initially sent to me by several of my friends and family members—they and I, then, constituted one possible public audience for the photos. With this, I certainly acknowledge that the NPR piece and the photos' subsequent contexts are all part of the constantly shifting, possible new configurations of the visual-material artifact, bound up in the larger intra-actions of material discursive practice.

While it is beyond the scope of this chapter to explore all the possible contextual twists and turns and workings of these visual-material rhetorical artifacts, I am interested in a specific twist and turn (or diffraction), and one that I feel also provides a suitable point of entry for addressing my research questions. This point of entry involves an exploration of how the images function in relation to the elemental space of the Midway itself and the vulnerable bodies that inhabit it.

For the purposes of this analysis, I am interested in focusing on one aspect of those larger intra-actions, which are always already shaped by and reshaping others. As photos about place and bodies, I am interested, first and foremost, in how the images function in relation to the elemental space of the Midway. To illuminate one piece of the larger workings of material discursive practice attempts a distillation of sorts, one that acknowledges, as I mentioned at the start of this chapter, that the distillation is itself a configuration—an elemental narrative. That is, in trying to better understand how these photos participate in our material becoming *with* the world and in building worlds that can potentially transform knowledge-making about the spaces and bodies that they represent, I am interested in exploring how they help foster "elemental relations," or how they work in relation to the elemental spaces and vulnerable bodies about which they initially set out to communicate (Cohen 55). As visual-material rhetorical artifacts, how do they contribute to and function as part of the larger agential intra-actments of material discursive practice in their knowledge-making and world-making about vulnerable bodies in the Midway? What do they reveal about these bodies and spaces in and of themselves? Again, conversely, this point of entry is also a good match for my research questions. Thus, to explore how images function in relation to the elemental space of the Midway and the vulnerable bodies that inhabit it is one way of exploring the intra-actions of bodies, matter, and environments, but in such a way that illuminates how they matter as environmental accounts in the age of the Anthropocene, or how they help shape a posthuman rhetoric informed by an ethic of compassionate conservation.

While the Midway project comprises not only a photographic series but also a documentary film, I nonetheless feel able to address my research questions by delimiting the parameters of my analysis to that of the still photo. Moreover, while *Midway: Message from the Gyre* is a photographic series, I consider in this chapter just one representative, related photo that circulated in the media: Jordan's image of the albatross, which is also available in the *Honolulu* magazine article "How Albatrosses Taught Photographer Chris Jordan How to Grieve" (Hancock); see figure 1. Thus, when I refer to "the photo," or more broadly to Jordan's photos of the Midway, I am referring to what I understand as this representative photo in figure 1, for the practical sake of clarity in this chapter, while also implicitly acknowledging the importance, beauty, and value of the broader work of the series and its participation in the intra-actions of material discursive practice.

With this framework in mind, this chapter merges ideas about visual-material, environmental rhetorics with questions of agency, affect, and accountability in human/nonhuman animal relationships, in order to consider the impact of the "Pacific Garbage Patch" and plastic ocean debris on the albatrosses of the Midway.[6] It considers not only, first, the embodied bodies of the albatrosses themselves but also, subsequently, the photos that emerged as a form of visual-material rhetorical response to this ecological crisis of consciousness. I argue that these components of the issue—thriving bodies; toxic, deceased, and decomposing bodies riddled with plastic debris; and the photos of those decomposing albatross bodies,[7] set against the elemental backdrop of Midway—all matter and intra-act together; they constitute this material discursive phenomenon, this ecological crisis of consciousness that is the Midway Atoll and the matter of its vulnerable bodies. They are, as both Alaimo and Barad

FIGURE 1. CF010257, Unaltered stomach contents of a Laysan albatross fledgling, Midway Island, 2012. Credit: Photo by Chris Jordan.

might have it, part of the material world, the differential mattering of the universe, and ultimately, as such, the very substance of self, prompting necessary concern for our ethical obligation to the species with whom we share our worlds. Again, this is an obligation that is not only our own, but that agential realism rightly does not exempt us from; as Barad notes: "Particular possibilities for (intra-)acting exist at every moment, and these changing possibilities entail an ethical obligation to intra-act responsibly in the world's becoming, to contest and rework what matters and what is excluded from mattering" (*Meeting* 178). Visual-material rhetorical accounts are one such possibility for ethically intra-acting in our worlds and for such a contesting and reworking of what matters.

THE NATURALCULTURAL MATTER OF VULNERABLE, EMBODIED BODIES

As Katherine Hayles has noted, "the body is always normative relative to some set of criteria" (196). The albatross body has always been marked as remarkable, relative to the normative criteria that define other bird species. It has thus been susceptible to hunting and exploitation, in addition to the threats it has in more recent years faced from plastic ocean debris. To inquire of any naturalist or birding enthusiast what makes the albatross significant as a species is to learn immediately about this seabird's magnificent wingspan: they in fact have "the longest wingspan of any bird—up to 11 feet," which in addition to their aesthetic beauty, allows them to glide right along the surface of the ocean, sometimes for hours, without so much as flapping their wings (National Geographic).

An Historically Vulnerable Body

The albatross's wingspan and unique feathers, however, have also brought the birds unwanted attention historically: "By the turn of the century albatross were slaughtered by the thousands and feathers were sold at high cost to adorn ladies' hats in Europe. . . . As a consequence millions of albatross were killed and the ones that survived were under constant pressure by non-native mammals and human impacts" (U.S. Fish & Wildlife Service, "Wisdom").[8]

Albatross species have reached a documented age of up to fifty years, and are often viewed as quite mysterious because they are "rarely seen on land and gather only to breed, at which time they form large colonies on remote islands" such as, for instance, the Midway Atoll (National Geographic). In addition, their breeding habits have put them at further risk, especially while nesting, as they are "easy to approach because of their instinct to stay on the nest at all cost, making them vulnerable to prey by non-native predators and humans" (U.S. Fish & Wildlife Service, "Wisdom"). Moreover, as philosopher and anthropologist Thom van Dooren describes in his poignant work, *Flight Ways,* for much of the year, "breeding albatrosses at Midway are engaged in a seemingly endless movement between land and water, alternating between egg or chick duties on land and days or weeks at sea in search of food" (24).[9] These challenges necessitate "a very strong pair-bond" between the parents; "if one parent dies or abandons the effort, the chick will not survive" (van Dooren 25).

Albatrosses are also viewed as having spiritual significance among indigenous Hawaiian cultures. As Gerry Miyamoto of Nā Kiamanu and former regent with the Daughters of Hawai'i, explains: "The mōlī [Hawaiian for Laysan albatross] is a high-flying bird, so those feathers were more important because (the birds) fly higher in the sky and were closer to the gods." Indigenous peoples have thus traditionally honored the spirit of the albatross, and the bird is considered the most spiritually significant in ancient Hawaiian history (U.S. Fish & Wildlife Service, "Wisdom"). Attentive to these ideas, the Migratory Bird Treaty Act of 1916, an important effort to protect species that travel across international borders, made it legal to collect albatross feathers but only from deceased albatross on Midway Atoll (U.S. Fish & Wildlife Service, "Wisdom").

The Vulnerable, Embodied Albatross

These aesthetic, cultural, and spiritual factors combined speak to both the albatross's vulnerability and the precarious circumstances of its embodiment. Moreover, while legislation like the Migratory Bird Act and the designation of marine national monuments were ostensibly created to protect vulnerable species, we may also consider their normative power to mark who and what counts as "valuable." For example, Judith Butler, writing in 2003, in the context of her critique of the U.S. response to 9/11, states: "The public sphere is constituted in part by what can appear, and the regulation of the sphere of appearance is one way to establish what will count as reality, and what will not. It is also a way of establishing whose lives can be marked as lives, and whose deaths will count as deaths. Our capacity to feel and to apprehend hangs in the balance" (xx–xxi). Here, Butler not only implicitly describes what is at stake in the practices of visualizing vulnerable beings, but by using the plural pronoun "our" in stating that "our capacity to feel and to apprehend hangs in the balance," she also implies that kinship, interconnection, and ethical obligation are necessary for considering the most compassionate path forward in the face of the slow violence of the Anthropocene that affects vulnerable beings. Implicitly and importantly, Butler also sees the potential loss of compassion for vulnerable others as a consequence of not thinking critically about how we conceptualize vulnerable bodies and the practices of embodiment.

On the one hand, the further regulation and expansion of the boundaries of Midway National Monument, for instance, and by extension, the additional emphasis on the problem of ocean plastics, helps regulate Midway's "sphere of appearance" and thus contributes to how the "reality" of Midway is portrayed and visualized. As a consequence, the body of the albatross is marked as vulnerable and its death portrayed as a loss. Here we see the power of the media and the practices of visualization to normalize what counts as worth protecting; clearly, the practices of normalization are a double-edged sword. On the other hand, as mentioned earlier, a move like the boundary expansion is but one piece of a much larger puzzle and is not a panacea. For, while the boundary expansion should help protect albatrosses from the threat of longline fishing, for instance, it still does not prevent plastics from washing ashore on Midway Island, even though media articles about the expansion also acknowledge the problem of ocean plastics as a threat to the albatross's existence.

Thus, practices of visualization can both reify through normalization as they simultaneously work to illuminate vulnerability and protect vulnerable species. Central to the concerns of compassionate conservation, one question then becomes: What is the most compassionate path forward in considering the best interests of those species with whom we are inseparably entangled and with whom we share our worlds? Moreover, how can representation function in ways that are recuperative, productive, and in integrity with the responsibilities we have to the kin with whom we coexist?

I argue that one path forward entails thinking more critically about these practices of visualization and the consequences of the portrayals of embodiment that they engender and invite; in other words, portrayals of embodiment matter. As Hayles further describes:

> Normalization can also take place with someone's particular experiences of embodiment, converting the heterogeneous flux of perception into a reified stable object. In contemporary scientific visualization technologies such as positron-emission tomography (PET), for example, embodiment is converted into a body through imaging technologies that create a normalized construct averaged over many data points to give an idealized version of the object in question. In contrast to the body, embodiment is contextual, enmeshed within the specifics of place, time, physiology, and culture, which together compose enactment. Embodiment never coincides exactly with "the body," however that normalized concept is understood. (196)

Hayles describes here the potential for visualization to both depict and reify experiences of embodiment. While she speaks of the human experience, and while her example of the PET scan is anchored in human biomedicine, her points are relevant to visual-material, environmental accounts of, in this case, the impacts of ocean plastics on vulnerable seabirds. With this example, she also implicitly summarizes a critique of representation important to feminist science studies: that representation can convert "the heterogeneous flux of perception into a reified stable object" (196). Indeed, the albatross photos can potentially be said to posit an "idealized version" of the subject in question, for as Ulman describes, photography "depicts as much through exclusion as inclusion, constructing narratives and posing questions by inviting us to reflect on what it temporally or spatially crops out of an image as much as what it includes or emphasizes" (43). We can easily make a similar case about cartographic representation and other such modes of visualization that bridge aesthetics with scientific knowledge-making. At the same time, however, we may consider whether, in positing a particular configuration of reality, representations of elemental space and the species inhabiting those spaces might intra-act in ways that bear recuperative power. For as Karen Barad suggests, as this chapter will soon discuss further, "even when apparatuses are primarily reinforcing, agency is not foreclosed" (*Meeting* 178).

In the case of the albatross on Midway, the bird's entanglements with "the specifics of place, time, physiology, and culture" (Hayles 196) configure a vulnerable, naturalcultural, material discursive body. For Jeffrey Jerome Cohen, these entanglements constitute "elemental relations" (55). Through the production and intra-actions of visual-material rhetorical artifacts, we then have the opportunity to know, share, and perform these elemental energies and relations in ways that can remind us or help us understand that we are not the only knowledge-makers in the room; rather, we participate in knowledge-making that is "part of the ongoing reconfiguring of the world" (Barad, *Meeting* 171).

Not inconsistent with thinking on elemental relations, visual-material rhetorical artifacts such as Jordan's photos of the Midway are affectual and sensory; as such, they may constitute what Laura Marks refers to as "haptic images" (2). While Marks describes the haptic image in the context of her study of intercultural cinema, I argue that geographically focused images, especially ones such as the photos of the Midway, in which vulnerable, visceral, decomposing animal bodies are immersed in an elemental setting, can also function in such a way. As Marks describes, some images

> can appeal to a haptic, or tactile, visuality. Haptic images . . . invite the viewer to respond to the image in an intimate, embodied way, and thus facilitate the experience of other sensory impressions as well. These sense experiences are not separate, of course. They combine to form culturally defined "sensuous geographies" . . . or our sensory experiences of place. More fundamentally, they inform each person's sensorium, the bodily organization of sense experience. (2)

Haptic images are related to sensation, in that they facilitate our sensory experiences of place, and are arguably both elemental and rhetorical. In the context of her recent work, for instance, Debra Hawhee invokes the notion of sensation as rhetorical. Drawing on and extending the work of Brian Massumi, Hawhee writes: "The durational intensity that follows a sensory encounter constitutes change. Such dispositional change is the very stuff of rhetoric . . . and such change can happen in an instant" (7). In considering the haptic image as an elemental and as a rhetorical, sensory encounter, I argue in this chapter that haptic images have the potential to participate in "environmental meshworks" that, in the rhetorical configurations they help enact, can also help foster more ethical relations with our worlds.

Cohen implicitly describes environmental meshworks as compatible with material and posthuman rhetorics in many ways. He sees environmental meshworks as active, malleable, elemental, attuned to consequences for human and nonhuman bodies, and immersed in story-telling:

> Within this complicated cosmos, then, we must through narrative and other kinds of action foster ethical relations with humans and inhumans alike: multifold, hesitant, consequence-minded interconnections that thicken, fructify, and affirm. Narrative is the intermediary by virtue of which these environmental meshworks, mangles and networks are articulated, documented, vitalized. (54)

Visual-material rhetorical artifacts can help articulate configurations of these elemental relations, these "environmental meshworks" in which our entanglements with the material world take shape, for better or for worse. As Cohen describes, the elements move us and humble us: "the elements are at once the most intractable, enduring, agentic and fundamental of materials" (55). In an almost poetic description, he adds:

> Thick stone is documentary, the material of our earliest surviving tools and the conveyor of human prehistory. Restless water is that which cannot be inscribed (except as ice), a substance enclosed within our bodies as memory of a briny origin, the force through which we domesticate landscapes. Wind is propulsion, power, spirit, tornado. Fire is obliterative, the partner through which we transform every terrain into which we step. Though they are perilous, even lethal, without elemental confederations we would possess no dwellings. Smaller than gods and larger than atoms, the elements offer a human-scale entry into nonhuman relations. (55)

Merging geographical and rhetorical perspectives, then, the elements provide a point of entry to conceptualizing our relationships and intra-actions with the nonhuman world; they decenter our perspective and remind us that our interventions, manipulations, and practices participate in the larger intra-actions of world-making. But we are given an additional challenge of conceptualization, and our nonhuman kin are prodded and drawn into new elemental relations, when matter becomes elemental in ways unforeseen.

In the case of the Midway Atoll, plastic debris becomes elemental in a less affirmative sense: it becomes part of a toxic, environmental meshwork—materially discursively intra-acting with the albatross's body in ways that are emotionally difficult to try to theorize. Nonetheless, considering early conceptions of material rhetoric, the body of the albatross becomes implicated in a material rhetorical landscape in the sense that the toxic, elemental space of the polluted Midway is enmeshed with and always already poised to negatively impact the body, both while the albatross is living, and postmortem, as its bodily remains biodegrade back into the toxic earth. In this way, the albatross body is inseparable from the products of human consumerism and the subsequently toxic trappings of the material world, its body a material discursive phenomena:

> Bodies are not objects with inherent boundaries and properties; they are material-discursive phenomena. "Human" bodies are not inherently different from "nonhuman" ones. . . . The very practices by which the differential boundaries of the human and nonhuman are drawn are always already implicated in particular materializations. The differential constitution of the human (nonhuman) is always accompanied by particular exclusions and always open to contestation. (Barad, *Meeting* 153)

The albatross body, for better or worse, is quintessentially naturalcultural, but not in any romantic, fantastical way. The albatross body is precariously naturalcultural. Drawing on the work of Anna Tsing, Haraway argues that "precarity—failure of the lying promises of Modern Progress—characterizes the lives and deaths of all terran critters in these times" (*Staying* 37). The precariously toxic body of the albatross is, to borrow from what can be read as one of Haraway's implicit descriptions of naturecultures, "human and non-human, the organic and technological, carbon and silicon, freedom and structure, history and myth, the rich and the poor, the state and the subject, diversity and depletion, modernity and postmodernity, and nature and culture" (*Companion* 4). Alive, the albatross is our kin—our vulnerable, magnificent, naturalcultural kin—always threatened by the potential bodily impacts of the heterotopic, material rhetorical landscape that is the Midway Atoll. It is postmortem, however, that the albatross gains rhetorical momentum in the enactments of material discursive practice and becomes, ironically, a timely catalyst for environmental advocacy and a reference point for ocean conservation and cleanup.

Postmortem, the albatross has shifted from beautiful, vulnerable kin to decomposing natureculture. Its decomposing body now serves as visual-material rhetorical evidence of the consequences of Anthropocene consumerism. As Alaimo has noted, its body is now paradoxically "becoming part of 'nature' again," although not in the uplifting, regenerative sense that we might hope (*Exposed* 130). Moreover, the plastic debris it has ingested does not decompose along with the bird's body—it remains behind, likely to recidivate, to put it in more fully vibrant and anthropomorphic terms. The decomposing body, then, reveals matter from two seemingly distinct but really, always-enmeshed ontologies: the bodily matter of the beautiful creature that once was—the albatross's skeletal remains—and the toxic plastic matter, which together constitute a natureculture of the most unsettling order.

The entangled elements of this naturalcultural specimen—skeleton and plastic—are then parsed out, made visible through the consequences of consumer practice that animate, some may say give life to, the plastic debris that emerges as a salient culprit in this story; that is, it becomes difficult to deny that plastic debris has an agential capacity at this point. Here, I argue that it is possible to retain a view that acknowledges the agential capacities and enactments of, say, plastic ocean debris, while simultaneously maintaining a sharp focus on the consequences of the naturalcultural/consumerist practices that have lent themselves to the agential capacities and trans-corporeal entanglements of that ocean debris in the first place; in other words, we need not swap a focus on matter's agency for an acknowledgment of our own ethical responsibility, for we are all, inseparably, in it together. Clearly, we are inseparable from our nonhuman kin and the worlds in which we coexist with them; plastic, also, a product of human knowledge-making, is an inseparable part of the intra-actions that bear consequences on the environments and bodies with which we are all entangled. But, as discussed in chapter 1, how we talk about or configure agency—what we choose to emphasize and deemphasize—matters greatly, for if agency rests even somewhat within human practice, then it becomes even more crucial that we think critically about whose interests, whose bodies, and whose voices we imagine as affected through that practice.

As Bekoff also acknowledges in conceptualizing compassionate conservation, there may never completely be a way out of human involvement in conservation practice, which only makes an attentiveness to the material discursive practices that we help enact that much more critical. For Bekoff, then, the central question becomes what we choose to make of our worldly involvement—how and to what ends we choose to decenter our perspective and engage a compassionate, posthuman vantage point that acknowledges the implications of our intra-actions. Likewise, as Willey suggests, "we, producers of knowledge, are thus bound to consider the possibilities, both enabling and violent—of interacting with the world by studying it" (1008). While I do favor the intra-activity of agential realism, I would also argue that we must not lose sight of the role of human knowledge-making and thus accountability in the configuration of environments and bodies, and in the consequences of consumerism for vulnerable seabirds; this delicate balance is what makes discussions of agency a critical part of theorizing a rhetoric of posthuman conservation, in which we necessarily shift our perspective from the perceived best interests and outcomes for humans and human needs, to the best interests and outcomes for all of the affected, vulnerable, nonhuman kin with whom we share our worlds. And, in continuing our exploration of the Midway case, I would argue that this is precisely the work that Jordan's photos, as part of ethical, agential practice, help accomplish.

THE MATTER OF VULNERABLE BODIES, REFLECTED AND DIFFRACTED

In this section, I argue that the photos of the Midway are visual-material rhetorical artifacts bound up in the intra-actions that constitute the ecological crisis of the Midway. While the photos are not impervious to the critiques of representationalism, they need not be defined solely by them, either. I argue that, in keeping with the frame of optical metaphor, they can also diffract. It is through the enactment of entanglements and trans-corporeality that diffraction occurs, and ultimately, given the rhetorical work of the photos and their participation in agential intra-action, I argue they can help forward a visual-material, posthuman environmental rhetoric informed by and aligned with some of the tenets of compassionate conservation.

As this section will describe, Jordan's photos are one manifestation of the ethical and agential capacities of matter. As Bennett puts it: "Agency is, I believe, distributed across a mosaic, but it is also possible to say something about the kind of striving that may be exercised by a human within the assemblage" (*Vibrant* 38). As Barad reminds us: "Particular possibilities for (intra-) acting exist at every moment, and these changing possibilities entail an ethical obligation to intra-act responsibly in the world's becoming, to contest and rework what matters and what is excluded from mattering" (*Meeting* 178). Haraway argues that we must learn "to stay with the trouble of living and dying in response-ability on a damaged earth" (*Staying* 2). Jordan's photos of the Midway may be read as exemplifying and interrogating these ideas well. They are part of the agential assemblage that constitutes the crisis of plastics in the Midway, as Bennett might have it. His work enacts a specific possibility for the world's becoming, and with it, invites us to consider alternatives. That said, the rhetorical work of photography is not uncomplicated, and thus the photos are paradoxical in the possible readings and interpretations that they perform and invite—in the stories they help tell.

ON THE PROBLEMATICS OF REPRESENTATION: REFLECTIONS AND DIFFRACTIONS

As Wendy Hesford acknowledges: "At the heart of the critical project of constructing a material rhetoric of violence and trauma is the crisis of representation, prompted in part by the poststructuralist argument that there is no unmediated access to the 'real'" (196). Subsequently, Hesford argues that "in formulating a material rhetoric of violence, trauma, and agency," we need to acknowledge that narratives, both textual and visual, "re-present trauma. In addition, we need to consider how these representations are sustained by realist conventions of documentation and interpretation and the intimate and institutional networks that uphold them" (196). As Ulman similarly acknowledges, the predominant understanding of photography as mediated not unproblematically requires

> a representing subjectivity—the photographer; an object of representation such as a landscape, plant, or animal; and a medium of representation such as a digital photograph. The act of making a photograph separates its subject visually and temporally from its surroundings, translates it into a different physical form . . . and rejoins it with other photographic representations . . . presumably redefining to some degree viewers' relationships with and capacity to experience the object(s) depicted in the photograph by influencing how we expect a landscape or animal or wildflower to appear. (27)

Scholars of feminist science studies, including Haraway, Harding, Hayles, and Barad, have likewise conveyed their critiques of mediation and representationalism and the power of images to ratify and reify; moreover, Barad's agential realism and her notion of the *apparatus* (as I will soon discuss further) address these issues and blur the boundaries between a representing subjectivity and its object of representation. As Barad argues, "to the extent that concepts, laboratory manipulations, observational interventions, and other human practices have a role to play, it is as part of the larger material configuration of the world" (*Meeting* 171). Thus, the photos of the Midway, while not impervious to representationalist critique, need not be denounced on representationalist grounds, either, for as I will describe, they may also be read as part of embodied world-making and as such, illuminating and performing nontoxic practices that we might engage in and with, that both "disclose trans-corporeality," as Alaimo has noted (*Exposed* 130), and that help give voice to the marginalized, vulnerable kin, now victims, of the Anthropocene.

Given these ideas, I understand nature photography as part of material discursive, embodied practice that is also a manifestation of the agential intra-actments of matter. This embodied practice, while not impervious to critique, also constitutes a nontoxic, recuperative, rhetorical practice that paradoxically helps share the elemental, toxic space of the Midway and the bodies that have borne the consequences of its toxicity. As Carole Blair has written, "we must ask not just what a text means, but more generally, what it does; and we must not understand what it does as adhering strictly to what it was supposed to do" (23). Thus, as rhetorical, haptic, environmental accounts, these photos participate in the material becoming of the worlds of which we are an inseparable part.

In the sections that follow, I will first briefly summarize some of the critiques of representational practice, as they pertain specifically to this analysis. I will then describe why the photos of the Midway, while not impervious to critiques of representationalism, do not merely reflect back another realist version of the object of their representation; I will argue that through their paradoxical anthropomorphizing, they also bear the capacity to convey partial perspectives, and in their disclosing of trans-corporeality (Alaimo, *Exposed*), they do more than reflect—they also diffract, thus participating in more productive, nontoxic, and compassionate practices of world-making. Put differently, the photos of the albatross, in serving as a mirror of our collective, toxic consumerism, have the function of anthropomorphizing through the reflections they invite; these anthropomorphizations disclose trans-corporeality, and trans-corporeality produces diffractions. As Stormer and McGreavy aptly note, in drawing also on the work of Deleuze: "We cannot avoid anthropomorphism. Critical anthropomorphism is not appropriative, not colonization by representation. Unlike anthropocentrism, anthropomorphism is humanity as mutable form and makes possible 'a comparison of powers that leads us to discover more in the body than we know, and hence more in the mind than we are conscious of' (Deleuze 1988, 90)" (9). I thus argue that to understand rhetorical responses such as Jordan's photos as embodied knowledge allows visual-material rhetorics to participate in productive and compassionate modes of knowledge-making and thus world-making.

As Barad and Haraway have noted, optical metaphors such as reflection have long been used to talk about knowledge-making and to critique representational practice; "the physical phenomenon of reflection is a common metaphor for thinking" (Barad, *Meeting* 29). Optical metaphors and analogies, as well as anthropomorphizations, are also arguably accessible to nonspecialist, public audiences, and are thus often invoked in science communication. Thus, it is intriguing but not necessarily surprising that, with regard to the photos of the Midway, the albatross is described using a metaphor of reflection. While I will soon complicate this idea, Barad, however, like Sandra Harding and others, critiques metaphors like reflection and representationalism for their tendency to perpetuate more "realist" versions of reality, especially in the sciences. As Barad describes:

> Mirrors reflect. The mirror is something to provide an accurate image or representation that faithfully copies that which is being mirrored. Hence mirrors are an often-used metaphor for representationalism and related questions of reflexivity. For example, a scientific realist believes that scientific knowledge accurately reflects physical reality, whereas a strong social constructivist would argue that knowledge is more accurately understood as a reflection of culture, rather than nature.[10] (*Meeting* 86)

Instead, Barad argues for a more critically aware, performative notion of discursive practice when she argues that "unlike representationalism, which positions us above or outside the world we allegedly merely reflect on, a performative account insists on understanding thinking, observing, and theorizing as practices of engagement with, and as part of, the world in which we have our being" (133). Barad contends here, like Haraway and Harding, that a performative understanding of discursive practice eschews representationalism and can produce more situated, local, partial perspectives.

Harding similarly understands the totalizing practices of modern technoscience as problematic in this regard, and thus questions whether science has the capacity to generate the knowledge-making practices necessary to sustain our worlds (16). For Harding, modern technoscience often finds itself at odds with local knowledge-making practices; that is, "representations of nature, society, and maximally effective knowledge production in the sometimes more effective 'local knowledge systems' conflict with those in modern technosciences" (17). Haraway likewise takes issue with the potential lack of accountability inherent in scientific visualization and ultimately calls for more partial perspectives and a "doctrine of embodied objectivity" (*Simians* 188).

For Haraway, "feminist objectivity means quite simply situated knowl-edges" (*Simians* 188). Haraway is quick to clarify that situated knowledges and partial perspectives are not antidotes to the dilemma of the totalizing vision in the sense that they offer instead endless relativism; rather, for Haraway: "Rela-tivism and totalization are both 'god-tricks' promising vision from everywhere and nowhere equally and fully, common myths in rhetorics surrounding Sci-ence. But it is precisely in the politics and epistemology of partial perspectives that the possibility of sustained, rational, objective inquiry rests" (*Simians* 191). Partial perspectives thus entail and are about embodied knowledge:

> We need to learn in our bodies, endowed with primate colour and stereo-scopic vision, how to attach the objective to our theoretical and political scanners in order to name where we are and are not, in dimensions of men-tal and physical space we hardly know how to name. So, not perversely, objectivity turns out to be about particular and specific embodiment. . . . The moral is simple: only partial perspective promises objective vision. This is an objective vision that initiates, rather than closes off, the problem of responsi-bility for the generativity of all visual practices. (*Simians* 190)

Partial perspectives, then, do not shy away from the difficult work of grap-pling with new and unfamiliar mental and physical terrain that we struggle to conceptualize, as Latour critiques of our seeming inability to comprehend the gravity and events of the Anthropocene. Written over two decades ago, Haraway's doctrine of embodied objectivity and partial perspectives emerges as even more relevant today than ever before.

As I have argued elsewhere, partial perspectives require "compassion and empathy," and are about "achieving a sort of objectivity that is rooted not in the claims of an allegedly neutral or utilitarian science, but of understand-ing and advocacy" ("Cartographic" 124). Partial perspectives, in their atten-tiveness to compassion, empathy, and embodied knowledge, are thus better attuned to "patterns of difference" (Barad, *Meeting* 29). And patterns of differ-ence, say Barad and Haraway, are more closely aligned with diffraction than reflection. As Haraway describes:

> Diffraction patterns record the history of interaction, interference, reinforce-ment, difference. Diffraction is about heterogeneous history, not about origi-nals. Unlike reflections, diffractions do not displace the same elsewhere, in more or less distorted form. . . . Rather, diffraction can be a metaphor for another kind of critical consciousness . . . one committed to making a dif-ference. . . . Diffraction is a narrative, graphic, psychological, spiritual, and

political technology for making consequential meanings. (*ModestWitness* 273)

Summarizing Haraway, Barad notes that "a diffractive methodology is a critical practice for making a difference in the world. It is a commitment to understanding which differences matter, how they matter, and for whom" (*Meeting* 90). Likewise, Barad notes: "We need to understand diffraction effects. How are differences constituted and enfolded? What differences matter, how do they matter, and to whom?" ("Invertebrate" 236).

Thus, if we are to understand nature photography as participating in material discursive, embodied practice that is also a manifestation of the agential intra-actments of matter, it is critical that we understand how such visual-material rhetorical artifacts constitute and take up differences. And it is here that we must acknowledge the paradox—we must be aware of how the photos participate in knowledge-making that may very well transform, but, as Hesford notes, may also simultaneously be "sustained by realist conventions of documentation and interpretation and the intimate and institutional networks that uphold them" (196). I argue that the photos of the Midway indeed do both, and in doing so, operate paradoxically: on the one hand, they operate within those normative structures of photographic, visualizing practice; on the other hand, they do far more than reflect. Through their anthropomorphizing, they can be said to reflect in a way that also beautifully diffracts.

THE PHOTO AS EMBODIED, VISUAL-MATERIAL RHETORIC: REFLECTIONS AND DIFFRACTIONS

Jordan's photos provide a cautionary tale about the consequences of neglecting to understand our interconnectedness with our nonhuman kin; these consequences are made salient through the body of the deceased albatross, which now serves as a "macabre mirror," reflecting back to us, in stark relief, our toxic, corporeal consumerism (Jordan). In doing so, these photos, a configuration of material discursive practice, anthropomorphize, or, as Bennett defines the term, they interpret "what is not human or personal in terms of human or personal characteristics" (*Vibrant* 98).

On the one hand, anthropomorphizing is often viewed more critically for its perceived tendency to privilege the human perspective and thus perpetuate human exceptionalism; that is, we can only ever get a handle on the issue if it is somehow placed in terms that we can relate to more personally. On the other hand, as Bennett describes, anthropomorphism can also function more productively to draw our attention to the mundane in more meaningful ways; thus, as she describes:

> In a vital materialism, an anthropomorphic element in perception can uncover a whole world of resonances and resemblances—sounds and sights that echo and bounce far more than would be possible were the universe to have a hierarchical structure. We may at first see only a world in our own image, but what appears next is a swarm of "talented" and vibrant materialities (including seeing the self). (*Vibrant* 99)

I argue that this is precisely the case with the albatross photo; that is, where we may first be prompted only to look in the mirror, we ultimately recognize more than just ourselves—we see the vulnerable, toxic, elemental body and the consequences of our cultural undertakings. The anthropomorphizing of the albatross body, via the rhetorical artifact, thus enacts a paradoxical configuration in which anthropomorphizing moves us from reflection into more entangled ways of knowing.

Paradoxical Reflections

Thus, in thinking back to Barad's words, if the mirror, as an optical metaphor, "is something to provide an accurate image or representation that faithfully copies that which is being mirrored" (*Meeting* 86), then the photograph of the albatross, as mirror, is said to provide an accurate image or representation of who we are; we see, in the albatross's body, riddled with plastic, the products of human consumerism—evidence of our human condition. That is, most visibly salient within the albatross's body are bits of plastic. The photos provide a caution about the consequences of neglecting to understand our interconnectedness with our nonhuman kin. Plastic debris is the most visibly salient feature of the photos, and clearly out of place among the otherwise organic elemental features of body, space, and landscape. This version of material discursive, embodied practice configures a toxic, corporeal, elemental landscape.

In this exploration of the interconnectedness of our worlds, then, we are the albatross and the albatross is us. This is our worldly, human condition, and it is, by toxic extension, theirs. In this configuration, bodily boundaries dissolve into toxic, elemental space. The albatross is a toxic body; we are all toxic bodies. Interestingly, here, while mirrors are meant to reflect, and while we would critique reflection for its problematic assumption of a separation between image and observer, these photos become complicated in their hesitant embrace, for they depict interconnection, but in a complex way that also reveals the consequences of not understanding our actions as having blowback or perhaps unintended ramifications for our kin and the worlds we share.

The photos paradoxically reveal interconnection via the consequences of thinking in terms of a separate "us" and "them," or perhaps in terms of not thinking of "them" at all. That is, the deceased body of the albatross, its skeletal remains intermingled with the bits of plastic once ingested by the bird, reflects the consequences of slow violence that we have not yet come to terms with. The photo reveals the hegemony of human exceptionalism—that power that humans hold and wield, unwitting or not, over nonhuman animals through our consumer practices. It makes salient the unequal outcomes and consequences of those consumer practices. Thus, in the photo's revealing of a separateness that is also a toxic interconnectedness, we begin to see that this mirror, or reflection, is more complicated than we thought.

Trans-Corporeal Diffractions

The photos are thus more than just a mirror. This mirror, as Alaimo brilliantly states, also *discloses*. And that disclosure, as we will see, constitutes a diffraction. In her chapter "Oceanic Origins," from her recent work, *Exposed*, Alaimo briefly invokes Jordan's photos and describes them as participating in more than just the representationalist practice of reflection; rather, she aptly describes them as "disclosing trans-corporeality" (130). As Alaimo eloquently puts it when she briefly addresses the "Pacific Garbage Patch" and acknowledges Jordan's work: "These photographs disclose trans-corporeality—animal bodies invaded by terrestrial, human consumerism, revealing the swirling natural-cultural agencies, the connection between ordinary terrestrial life and ocean ecologies, and the uneven distribution of harm" (130).

Merriam-Webster defines the verb "disclose" as "to make known (as information previously kept secret)" ("Disclose"). To disclose, then, is to make known—to make visible—to share. To disclose is to share information or something that was not previously visible or knowable prior to the sharing. Disclosure often implies the sharing of private or personal information; we might associate the verb with a sentence like "I don't feel comfortable disclosing that information," or something similar. In this case, the photos disclose the very personal consequences of toxic, elemental embodiment—a kind of toxic trans-corporeality, as Alaimo might have it. Trans-corporeality is conceptually consistent with agential realism, and agential realism is allied with diffraction.

In disclosing trans-corporeality, then, the photos do more than reflect—they also diffract. As mentioned earlier, they make salient a specific, toxic, corporeal configuration, in which humans, nonhuman animals, matter, and environment are interconnected via a paradoxical inability to reconcile the interconnectedness of our worlds. That is, the photos reveal the differences or inequalities in these bodies, "how they matter, and for whom" (Barad, *Meeting* 90). I would add here that diffraction also recognizes and acknowledges vulnerability. The photos diffract by dramatically recognizing vulnerability, but paradoxically by reflecting back to us, through anthropomorphization, the consequences of human exceptionalism as they have manifested in our vulnerable kin. As Bennett adds: "A touch of anthropomorphism, then, can catalyze a sensibility that finds a world filled not with ontologically distinct categories of beings (subjects and objects) but with various composed materialities that form confederations" (*Vibrant* 99). The photos thus reveal the history of toxic interactions, interferences, and the "variously composed" vulnerable bodies that have borne the consequences of these now-toxic, elemental spaces.

The photos thus reveal the naturalcultural, paradoxical body, but they themselves are also part of the mattering of the material world, and thus part of all of us. Again, it is through these rhetorical, environmental accounts that, via Alaimo, "the material world becomes the very substance of self" (*Bodily* 3). The photos are visual-material rhetorical artifacts—agential cuts that enact specific possibilities for "the world's becoming" and "contribute to the differential mattering of the world" (Barad, *Meeting* 178). Moreover, in producing a specific configuration of the mattering of our worlds, it becomes possible that they also help enact others.

VISUAL-MATERIAL, EMBODIED, NONTOXIC PRACTICES THAT SHARE TOXIC, ELEMENTAL SPACE

How, then, do the photos participate in or help forward a posthuman ethic of compassionate conservation? On the one hand, posthumanism is about decentering the human perspective, and these photos were quite literally taken by and portray a human perspective and vantage point. On the other hand, through their paradoxical anthropomorphizing, they prompt us to consider our impact on the individual lives of other vulnerable species. The photos are part of the material discursive practices that participate in the mattering of our worlds—in their disclosure of trans-corporeality, the photos are elemental themselves.

Cohen argues that we must "compose our stories and our ethics not from the elements (as if all that is inhuman were inert) but with them (as agency-exerting partners possessed of unsounded depths and innate dignity)" (58). The photos indeed compose and disclose with the elements; they share elemental space—they are haptic images, bound up in the intra-actments of bodies (subjectivity and object of representation: photographer and albatross), elements, environments, artifacts. Subsequently, the elemental narrative is how many of us first learned of the issue via the journalistic context of the NPR story. Such ideas are compatible with Rickert's notion of an ambient rhetoric, whereby "ambience grants not just a greater but an interactive role to what we typically see as setting or context, foregrounding what is customarily background to rhetorical work and thereby making it material, complex, vital, and, in its own way, active" (xv). Rickert argues, then, "that we must come to see that 'the human' or human arts cannot exist in a manner ontologically distinct from material and information spaces, including technology. Doing so necessitates an ecological shift in what it means for rhetorical agents to inhabit and interact in an environment" (xv). So then, Jordan's photographs of the albatrosses of the Midway, these elemental products of the human arts, are enmeshed with and enact the surrounding environment and context—and it is this agonistic situation, or this specific exigency, enmeshed with the practices of visualization and their inscriptions, that constitutes these (re)configurations of our worlds.

AFFECTIVE INSCRIPTIONS AS PART OF MATERIAL DISCURSIVE PRACTICE

In this section, I will describe Latour's notion of the inscription and how it makes room for affect; moreover, I argue that the inscription is subtly different from but not incompatible with Barad's notion of the apparatus. The inscription then becomes both affectual and part of the material discursive practices of agential intra-action. Conversely, affect becomes compatible with the material discursive practices of agential intra-action.

For Latour, inscriptions take shape through writing and imaging procedures and are "part of a whole process of mobilization" ("Drawing" 40). Significantly, the inscription is but one component of this process of mobilization and is capable of shaping our interpretations of and interactions with the world. Moreover, it is important to note that Latour distinguishes, in the quote that follows, between images themselves and imaging procedures. Implicitly drawing on a rhetorical approach, Latour asks, for example: "Everyone agrees that print, images, and writing are everywhere present, but how much explanatory burden can they carry? . . . First, [he says,] we must consider in

which situations we might expect changes in the writing and imaging procedures to make any difference at all in the way we argue, prove, and believe"
(23). Here, Latour implicitly invokes ideas about understanding photography,
for instance, as material rhetorical, embodied practice, in which we must be
attentive to the implications of inclusions, exclusions, and so on. For, to use
Barad's terms, each instantiation enacts a specific agential cut. Thus, we might
consider that agential intra-actions and the affective articulations underpinning material discursive practice, of which inscription is a part, can help enact
difference in particular configurations of knowledge-making.

In describing affect, it is first important, as Jenny Edbauer Rice notes, to
distinguish between "emotion" and "affect," as the two terms are easily con-
flated. As Rice conveys, emotions have a "narrativized content that is shaped
through specific cultural, social, and political contexts," whereas affect "does
not necessarily have a narrative" (201). Debra Hawhee similarly describes the
"distinction between affect and emotion as riding a line of cognitive awareness
(where knowable concepts of emotion organize otherwise inchoate though no
less visceral affective intensities)" (6). In other words, affect can, through the
moments and forces of intensities to which it gives rise, then configure more
specific feelings and emotions. Hawhee favors "the imprecision of feeling,"
as it can account for a broader range of embodied and cognitive experiences
(6). Likewise, Hawhee notes that "feeling" may be a reasonable translation for
pathos, which, as she points out, "indicates disposition or state as well as—and
as formed by—experiences and incidents" (6). While Hawhee does not explicitly use the term "affect" for reasons pertinent to her study, she draws on Brian
Massumi's related notion of sensation, which arises out of affect, and which
Massumi writes, "pertains to the dimension of passage, or the continuity of
immediate experience," and, therefore, "to a direct registering of potential"
(Massumi 258–59). Pertinent to this analysis is the idea that affect, or the force
of intensity to which it gives rise, "constitutes change" (Hawhee 7). Moreover,
writes Hawhee, "Such dispositional change is the very stuff of rhetoric . . . and
such change can happen in an instant" (7).

As Gregory Seigworth and Melissa Gregg describe, affect is not "invested
in us . . . [or] sutured into a progressive or liberatory politics" (10). Drawing also on Massumi, Rice notes that affect "is like a degree of intensity that
is prior to an indexed or articulated referent. Affect describes an energetics
that does not necessarily emerge at the level of signification" (201). Further
engaging the idea of affect as energy, but from a subtly different perspective,
Rice outlines Teresa Brennan's more relational notion that "affects and energies are transmitted between bodies" (202). In this way, "affects emerge across
bodies both physically and biologically. These transpersonal affects are the
social-material elements of 'personal' thoughts and feelings" (202–3). Or, as

Seigworth and Gregg similarly describe an approach to affect rooted in science studies: "affect is the hinge where mutable matter and wonder . . . perpetually tumble into each other" (8). Such a view is consistent with a more posthuman understanding of affect, whereby, as Roelvink and Zolkos note, in borrowing from Braidotti, "affective attachment acquires a more affirmative expression of forming connections to 'non-anthropomorphic organic others'" (3, qtd. in Braidotti 103).

Additionally, in drawing on Sara Ahmed, Rice notes that an "affective element" (211) can underpin public discourse, and that public spaces, both physical and online, can "comprise numerous articulations between images, discourses, and feelings" that are adhered in a "loose collective" (210). Moreover, Rice adds that "theories of affect suggest a process of disarticulation, or an unsticking of those figures that seem to be glued together, followed by a rearticulation, or a new way of linking together images and representations that is less oppressive" and perhaps more empowering or productive (210). I agree with Rice that this sort of public discourse seems more associational than deliberative (210). I would also add that thinking of affect in this way, combined with the notion that the forces of intensities to which it gives rise can then configure more specific feelings and emotions, not only situates affect within the realm of rhetoric but also then seems compatible with the workings of agential intra-action and its material discursive practices. In this conceptualization, affect is thus bound up in material discursive practice.

Given these ideas, I understand affect as intersecting with Jordan's photos in this way: Affect does not necessarily have linear, narrativized content, but neither does it function outside of discourse. It is also relational, emerging across bodies; transmitting bodily energies; tapping into the intra-actions of bodies, matter, and environments; and participating in the shaping and reshaping of discursive practices. In this way, affect may influence the enactments of our ethical responsibilities to our worlds, and the material discursive intra-actments that constitute those enactments. The albatross photos are haptic images that are part of the agential intra-actions that constitute material discursive practices surrounding the ecological crisis of ocean plastics. If an affective element underpins discourse, and if the photos are part of the discourses about ocean plastics, then the photos bear affective elements. One question then becomes: What are the implications of these affective elements? I thus argue that to view the photos as bearing affective elements can help illuminate the capacity of visual-material artifacts to prompt an ineffable *becoming with*, to borrow again from Haraway's language (*Staying*), that transcends a human-centered vantage point. Material discursive enactments can configure haptic, visual-material artifacts that provide a means of sharing elemental experience—they are part of the agential intra-actions that, when considered also affectual, are "at once intimate and impersonal" by way of the specificity of their always-shifting, affective moments (Seigworth and Gregg 2). Put differently,

> affect *accumulates* across both relatedness and interruptions in relatedness, becoming a palimpsest of force-encounters traversing the ebbs and swells of intensities that pass between "bodies" (bodies defined not by an outer-skin envelope or other surface boundary but by their potential to reciprocate or co-participate in the passages of affect). (Seigworth and Gregg 2, emphasis in original)

Moreover, and importantly: "affect marks a body's *belonging* to a world of encounters" (2). In describing affect as "a palimpsest of force-encounters" that "pass between bodies," it again becomes easy to conceptualize affect as participating in the intra-actions of agency.

Affect, then, is bound up in material discursive practice; it is part of the configuring of agential cuts; specific agential cuts can produce specific but always shifting responses; our responses depend upon our interpretation, and our interpretation is always already reconfigured in the intra-actions of material discursive practice and the "larger agonistic context," as Latour puts it. To understand the practices underpinning knowledge-making, Latour says, means thinking not only about writing and imaging but also about the larger, agonistic context: "We have to hold the two eyepieces together," he says, in order to get a "real binocular," which "takes time to focus" ("Drawing" 24). In other words, it is not the mere fact of the photograph in itself, but also its intra-actions, what the photo musters, what it instills in its viewer, or, as Latour describes, "it is the inscription as the fine edge and the final stage of a whole process of mobilization, that modifies the scale of rhetoric" ("Drawing" 40). Not only, then, may we understand the inscription as part of material discursive practice and as bearing affectual weight, but also, for Latour, while he may distinguish between image and imaging procedure, the inscription is enmeshed with the agonistic situation and its apparatuses; it is not merely a product of the devices of scientific instrumentation. Or, put another way, the affectual and the merely instrumental are incompatible to think together.

Barad's view of the apparatus, while not inconsistent with Latour's, goes a step farther, in describing even more explicitly that apparatuses "are not mere instruments or devices that can be deployed as neutral probes of the natural world," and neither are they merely human manifestations or human/nonhuman assemblages; rather, they constitute "specific material reconfigurings of the world" (*Meeting* 142). For Barad, "apparatuses are themselves phenomena"

(170). Again, the mediated act of making a photograph becomes a murky proposition, and the boundaries between representing subjectivity (read: photographer) and object of representation (read: albatross), and the photograph itself, begin to dissolve. In this working, "apparatuses are not bounded objects or structures; they are open-ended practices" that are always already reconfiguring our worlds (170). Subsequently, "in an agential realist account, human subjects are neither outside observers of apparatuses, nor independent subjects that intervene in the workings of an apparatus, nor the products of social technologies that produce them" (171). Here, then, images, imaging procedures, human bodies, animal bodies, elemental space, are, quite elegantly, bound up in *"material-discursive practices—causal intra-actions through which matter is iteratively and differentially articulated, reconfiguring the material-discursive field of possibilities and impossibilities in the ongoing dynamics of intra-activity that is agency"* (Barad 170, emphasis in original). Latour's process of mobilization, within which the inscription is enmeshed, is then part of "the ongoing dynamics of intra-activity that is agency" (Barad, *Meeting* 170).

I appreciate Latour's conceptualization of the inscription for its more overtly rhetorical approach and for the way that it can potentially account for affect; Barad's notion of the apparatus, not incompatibly, but more explicitly, incorporates Latour's inscription into the "ongoing dynamics of intra-activity," within which affect can also circulate (*Meeting* 170). Thus, in returning to my thoughts at the start of this chapter, where I consider the idea of visualizing albatross bodies via the practices of photography, or when I refer to the photos of the Midway, or albatross bodies, or when I refer to Jordan, as photographer, I am imagining not only that specific point of reference but also more broadly, though implicitly, the larger dynamics of intra-activity and knowledge-making in which they are all enmeshed, and of which affect is a component. The material discursive practice that constitutes these photos participates in specific cultural, material configurations of and knowledge-making about our worlds. This material discursive practice may be underpinned by affect, and we might glimpse these shifting affective moments as they play out in circulation, contextualization, and interpretation.

The apparatus of material discursive practice—not excluding, but rather, enmeshed with the bodies of the albatrosses and the body of the photographer—is marked by and transmits affect. The photos, too, share elemental space, and in doing so, constitute haptic images that transmit affect across bodies. *The transmission of affect underpins and helps shape the discursive processes of mobilization that, in this configuration, also enact a moment of ethical response-ability.*

AFFECTUAL, MATERIAL DISCURSIVE PRACTICE:
THE WORK OF THE PHOTOS

Thinking on representation and responsibility, animal studies scholar Nigel Rothfels notes that "the stakes in representing animals can be very high. . . . [How] we talk or write about animals, photograph animals, think about animals, imagine animals—represent animals—is in some very important way deeply connected to our cultural environment" (xi). Through their participation in material discursive practice, Jordan's photos have much to say about our cultural environment. They reveal inequality, vulnerable bodies—they simultaneously enact the need for understanding the interconnectedness of our worlds and the consequences of not doing so. That is, they acknowledge the ecological imbalance and even violence that occurs as a result of not thinking *with* or becoming *with*. Thus, on the one hand, the photos run the risk of making our kin vulnerable in a new or different way, through material discursive practice that amplifies imbalance and the subsequent consequences of human consumerism. On the other hand, however, perhaps in making salient this imbalance, the photos also provide an opportunity for new knowledge-making; this new knowledge-making then involves an acknowledgment—an acknowledgment of loss—and with that, as this chapter will soon describe, an opportunity for transformation, an opportunity to grieve *with,* in order to think *with* (Haraway, *Staying*; Ballif).

Thus, despite the possible representationalist critiques of the photos as reifying a specific physical reality or uncritically positioning us "above or outside the world we allegedly merely reflect on" (Barad, *Meeting* 133), I do not at all denounce the knowledge-making work in which these photos participate. Rather, I align with the work of feminist and animal studies scholar Kathryn Gillespie, who understands Jordan's work as performing geographer John Silk's concept of "caring at a distance."

The concept of "caring at a distance" extends the notion of "care and caring" from the more traditional face-to-face encounter to more distanced interaction. Visual culture and imagery may then play a role "in extending the scope of beneficence beyond our 'nearest and dearest' to embrace distant others" (Silk 165). Gillespie suggests that "caring at a distance for the Midway albatrosses represents a mode of connecting to distant others whose lives and deaths are shaped by plastic waste." In this way, caring at a distance involves a mode of seeing "distinct from observation," eschews voyeurism, and prompts instead action and transformation; moreover, part of that transformation involves grieving (Gillespie). As Butler notes: "To grieve, and to make grief into a resource for politics, is not to be resigned to inaction, but it may be understood as the slow process by which we develop a point of identification with suffering itself" (30). To consider the vulnerability of others allows us to "critically evaluate and oppose the conditions under which" some lives are deemed "more grievable than others" (Butler 30). As I argue in this chapter, part of that transformation happens through the grieving catalyzed by the elemental, haptic, affectual qualities of the image. Barthes, for instance, not only critiques the ontological certainty posited by the photo, as "its essence is to ratify what it represents" (85), but also acknowledges its materiality, ephemerality, and its always-shifting nature—its "certain but fugitive testimony" (93). In doing so, he acknowledges the photo's affectual momentum.

Through their material discursive enactment, the albatross photos transmit affect, and in doing so, they constitute, share, and transmit the transcorporeal intra-actions of material bodies, terrain, matter, and meaning. The boundaries between human observer, embodied bodies, technologies, and artifacts dissolve, bound up in material discursive practice. The photos, as specific enactments of material discursive practice, provide a means of sharing elemental experience—they participate in the intra-activity of agency by revealing the consequences of human exceptionalism, not in theory, but in practice. They visualize the consequences of consumerist cultural practices that uncritically understand our kin as *out there*. Thus, as Alaimo puts it, when drawing on the work of Barad: "We are always on the 'hook'—on innumerable hooks—ethically speaking, always caught up in and responsible for material intra-actions" (*Exposed* 133).

Affect is bound up in the practices of intra-action and moves from, between, and among bodies. The photos, caught up in material discursive practice and never outside of discourse, bear and transmit affectual weight. As visual-material rhetorical artifacts, they are an instantiation, a configuration, of these intra-active practices. As part of material discursive practice, then, these artifacts, the photos, can affect us. They participate in shaping discourse about the issue. How we are affected, and to what extent, varies based on instantiation and interpretation.

The photos of the Midway convey the albatross as reflecting the toxic implications of human consumerism; in doing so, they seemingly take the viewer to task. Alaimo, Bennett, Barad, and Haraway would agree that moralism and blame are not a productive means for enacting material discursive practice or "staying with the trouble" (Haraway, *Staying*). And yes, this material discursive configuration now runs the risk of sliding into moralism, though it does not stay there—it is always in flux, always full of interpretive possibility, given an agential realist account anchored in material discursive practice. These photos reveal a necessary forensics of the Anthropocene—

this configuration is, on the one hand, a manifestation of human knowledge-making, but on the other hand, an agential realist account would suggest that the photos also participate more broadly in world-making. As such, they are part of the ongoing articulations of material discursive practices. The photos are one version of what ethical obligation "looks like," by making salient the consequences of its absence; as such, they are, paradoxically, one contribution to an attempt at ethical world-making.

As Jordan describes in a recent interview (Hancock), the photos' affectual transmission also invites us to grieve *with*, and perhaps move through grief and mourning, into beauty. There is still a way forward. There can be more to this story. Thus, perhaps that way forward is also through the move from reflection toward diffraction. The way forward involves seeing in ourselves, anthropomorphically, another; the way forward involves compassion and empathy—it involves seeing in a way that makes a difference in the world. Perhaps the photos help get us started; if they move us uneasily toward moralism through their revealing of a mirror, then they also reveal an opportunity for engagement with our more-than-human world through their disclosure of trans-corporeality—through their disclosure of an opportunity to be "accountable for marks on bodies" (Barad, *Meeting* 178). If reflection can tend toward moralism, then perhaps diffraction can tend toward ethical responsibility.

Paradox: In Shimmer, Love

That is, if the photos *only* mirrored, if they only ratified and reified, they might stall at moralistic judgment. But they are part of the entanglement—the substance of self—they disclose trans-corporeality. In their affectual weight, in their haptic intensities, they have the potential to constitute change. In this case, in doing so, they are part of the mattering of the universe, and they circulate with life, with death, and as Barthes describes in an interesting analog, with love.

In an ironic twist (relative to our larger focus on ocean plastics, that is), Barthes, in describing the paradoxical ephemerality and mortality of the photograph, says that the only way to transform the photograph is to dispose of it—to throw it away. To do so, however, accelerates not only the transformation or disintegration of the photo but also the loss of life, and love, that comes with it:

The only way I can transform the Photograph is into refuse: either the drawer or the wastebasket. Not only does it commonly have the fate of paper (perishable), but even if it is attached to more lasting supports, it is still mortal: like a living organism, it is born on the level of the sprouting silver grains, it flourishes a moment, then ages. . . . Attacked by light, by humidity, it fades, weakens, vanishes; there is nothing left to do but throw it away. (Barthes 93)

Still, again, there is no escaping the photo and its "certain but fugitive testimony" (93); it posits certainty, but paradoxically it is always on the move, in flux, in motion that marks the ephemerality of life. Barthes asks: "What is it that will be done away with" as the photo fades, weathers, and ultimately becomes debris once again? "Not only 'life,'" says Barthes, "but also, sometimes—how to put it?—love" (94).

That is, in describing a photograph of his parents, Barthes expresses that the image embodies their love for one another. He says: "In front of the only photograph in which I find my father and mother together, this is a couple who I know loved each other, I realize: it is love-as-treasure which is going to disappear forever; for once I am gone, no one will any longer be able to testify to this: nothing will remain but an indifferent Nature" (94).

Interestingly, Seigworth and Gregg note that in a collection of lectures called *The Neutral,* Barthes "calls for a 'hyperconsciousness of the affective minimum, of the microscopic fragment of emotion . . . which implies an extreme changeability of affective moments, a rapid modification, just a shimmer'" (10, qtd. in Barthes 101). For Barthes, "the neutral" is not actually neutral but rather about the potential energy of intervals, or the relations between two moments, spaces, or objects: "In these in-betweens or blooming intervals, intensities are continually divulged in the supple relations between a world's or a body's interleavings and their vectors of gradience" (Seigworth and Gregg 10). Here, too, binaries do not apply or hold up; rather, significantly, Barthes was interested in the progression of these intensities and how they could stretch in ways that would afford him, more kinetically, "'a free manner—to be looking for my own style of being-present to the struggles of my time'" (Seigworth and Gregg 11). As Barthes then described, and as Seigworth and Gregg convey, "What should follow as critical practice . . . is a neutrally inflected, immanent pathos . . . that would be an 'inventory of shimmers, of nuances, of states, of changes' . . . as they gather into 'affectivity, sensibility, sentiment,' and come to serve as 'the passion for difference'" (11). As Seigworth and Gregg then describe, affect theory is "an inventory of shimmers," but it is more than that—it is also "a matter of affectual composition" (11). Here they mean "composition" both in the sense that it is an "ontology always coming into formation," but also in the sense that it is a "creative/writerly task . . . a passion for differences . . . making an inventory (of singularities). And in the interval, is the stretching: unfolding a path-ology (of 'not-yets')" (11). In this way, this inventory of shimmers has a paradoxically ephemeral staying power. Significantly, these shimmers and interactions and energetic transmissions manifest in configurations that gather into sentiment and material discursive instantiation (11). As Hawhee mentions, again, they are the "stuff of rhetoric" (7). The affectual shimmer is bound up in material discursive practice and can gather, through configurations, into specific sentiments, passions.

In the above passage from *Camera Lucida*, Barthes grieves anticipatorily for the inevitable loss of the "love-as-treasure" that constitutes the photo of his parents and the love they shared, and the love he felt for them; his grieving marks a mythopoetic movement and relation between worlds and temporalities—it marks a past and an anticipatory, eventual loss of the love that the photo configures and embodies. This eventual loss of love is at once anticipated and fleeting-in-advance; it is known only to him and to nobody else—it is a treasure that he has found and that will soon enough be lost; it carries with it affectual articulations that play out in the acknowledgment of this rapidly changeable moment that gathers into sentiment, into passion, and dissolves into shimmer.

Gathering into Sentiment(s)

Barthes' photograph of his parents, not unlike the albatross photo, embodies relationship and attachment—it conveys and enacts life, and love, and loss in our worlds. And as part of the mattering of the universe, it is an embodied, affectual visual-material, rhetorical articulation in the moment, its meaning and interpretation part of ongoing intra-actions. Its meaning is subject to shifting interpretation and depends on the contextual, embodied, elemental configurations of knowledge-making in which it is immersed, and for which we are always already responsible.

Jordan's photos paradoxically reveal interconnection by making salient the consequences of thinking in terms of a separate "us" and "them." That is, the albatross body reflects consequences that we have not yet come to terms with. It reveals the power humans hold and wield, unwitting or not, over nonhuman animals. The photos reveal vulnerabilities and inequalities, and in ways configure, through the interpretation they invite, moments of grieving *with* in order to become *with*. Put differently: Spaces produce intensities—elemental reverberations. Worlds are affectual. Affects circulate, and they give rise to particular emotions, feelings, sensations. As Jordan has similarly described, the affectual intensities of the Midway produced in him visceral feelings of disgust, grief, respect, and love (Hancock).

IN MATERIAL DISCURSIVE PRACTICE, MOURNING AND WORLD-MAKING

In a recent interview that helped publicize the photos that were included in the 2016 *Plastic Fantastics?* exhibit at the Honolulu Museum of Art, Jordan discusses some of his own experiences on Midway Island. In the interview, he describes the visceral, cognitive, and emotional experiences of his photographic work that took place over the course of eight trips to Midway Island (Hancock). In conveying some of these experiences, I feel compelled to note that I am not thinking here of Propen-as-author relaying the ideas of Jordan-as-photographer; rather, I imagine my own participation, through the broader work of this chapter, as an intra-actment that further reconfigures these ongoing material discursive practices of knowledge-making, or, more simply (or maybe just more concisely), perhaps I am telling a story about telling a story. Moreover, as Barad reminds us, in an agential realist account, "human subjects are neither outside observers of apparatuses, nor independent subjects that intervene in the workings of an apparatus, nor the products of social technologies that produce them" (*Meeting* 171). Importantly, this does not relinquish us, or our human vantage point, from accountability for the knowledge-making projects in which we participate or our roles as researchers; rather, we are always already part of the larger phenomenon of material discursive practice.

In describing in a recent interview (Hancock) his own process, experiences, and even how he imagines viewers might interpret his work, Jordan arguably conveys his own subjectivity; however, in an agential realist account, this subjectivity is also bound up in larger intra-actions. As Barad reminds us, "even when apparatuses are primarily reinforcing, agency is not foreclosed. Furthermore, the space of agency is not restricted to the possibilities for human action" (*Meeting* 178). Jordan implicitly seems to understand his own process in a likewise manner—as transformative and enacting moments of interconnectedness through shifting feelings of sadness and grief, love and appreciation; as he says, "Grief reconnects us with our love for all beings" (Hancock). In this way, subjectivity is not absent, but neither is it fixed in such a way that precludes other possibilities for intra-action. As Jordan implicitly describes, he participates in and enacts a visual-material rhetorical configuration—an agential cut that constitutes an ethics of interconnectedness and "love for all beings" (Hancock).

Jordan describes the albatrosses as embodying an elemental narrative; as he puts it, they are "a kind of poetry coming from the earth" (Hancock). He experienced the photos as "transformative" in the grief they provoked and in terms of how they helped him to "connect more deeply with what's going on in our world"; likewise, he imagines that the photos can create new opportunities to "help other people connect with themselves and the world more deeply" (Hancock). When asked about his personal connection to his work and the Midway project, Jordan describes his personal experience as "a transformational, healing experience" that was also "a way to reach a kind of universal experience" (Hancock). That is, he describes the process of photographing the albatrosses as a healing that unfolded over time.

Over the course of the eight trips he made to the island, Jordan says: "The first several trips were just dark experiences of death. . . . It wasn't until several trips in that I began to really experience the beauty of these birds, as kind of the antidote to the horror" (Hancock). He describes this process as "the shape of the journey," as he "slowly found" his way "to love these creatures" and to realize, through the difficulty of this experience, "just how amazing and beautiful and magnificent they are" (Hancock). Jordan further describes the Laysan albatross as "a spiritual being," and imagines visitors to the exhibit to understand the project as "a kind of grief ritual":

> That is really the heart of the project for me. . . . I did a lot of grieving on Midway . . . and I've come to believe that it's actually a transformationally powerful experience. There's something really important about grief. It's different from despair and sadness. Grief is the same as love. It's a felt experience of love for something that we're losing or have lost. And maybe at no other time do we feel our love for something so much as when we're losing it, be it a person or anything that we love. In that way, feeling our grief for what's being lost in our world reconnects us with our love for the world, and helps us to feel our love for something that we might not even have known that we cared about. It's kind of a transformational shock for me to realize that I love albatrosses, because I've never thought about albatrosses in my life. I didn't know that I cared about them at all. Grief reconnects us with our love for all beings. (Hancock)

Through participating in the intra-actions of material discursive practice, Jordan shares the grief that arises out of the elemental spaces of the Midway, and in doing so, "shares the love," to borrow from Nathaniel Rivers ("Serial"). Through practices of visuality, he is arguably "building the world he wants to make," by participating in the disclosure of a vulnerable world potentially lost (Rivers, "Serial"). Himself enmeshed in material discursive practice, he prompts us to do better—this is his version of ethical responsibility enacted. Here, haptic transmissions of elemental energies enact momentary material discursive configurations that then circulate through journalistic environmental accounts. Bodies, worlds, matter, are bound up in material discursive practice, all related to this labor of love. The photos of the Midway are an environmental exposé of sorts, an exposure through their disclosure of trans-corporeality. This material discursive practice, through the agential intra-actions of those inscriptions, transmits affect.

As audiences immersed in our own contexts and worlds, we encounter these configurations, maybe through an NPR article, or perhaps at an art exhibit—the configurations reverberate further, producing new moments of intensities, shimmers, and in those shimmers, sentiments, feelings. We are then picked up and interwoven into broader material discursive practice, which transmits its intensities continuously, again. Here, spaces, bodies, subject, object, and technologies dissolve to reveal trans-corporeality in these new interpretive, visual-material rhetorical configurations of material discursive practice. The images provide an invitation to engage, not to walk away—they are an invitation to "stay with the trouble," via Haraway (*Staying*), and in doing so, to configure new opportunities for world-making.

Through his grief, Jordan participates in material discursive practice that constitutes a configuration of ethical responsibility by way of these visual-material rhetorical artifacts. I argue that to participate in these knowledge projects by way of these photographic visualizations helps enact partial perspectives. That is, the photographer, and the photographs—in this instantiation of knowledge-making—do not shy away from the difficult work of grappling with new and unfamiliar mental and physical terrain that we struggle to conceptualize; they face head-on the gravity and events of the Anthropocene. They endeavor "to name where we are and are not, in dimensions of mental and physical space we hardly know how to name"; thus, the knowledge-making work in which they participate is thus about "particular and specific embodiment" (Haraway, *Simians* 190). These visual-material affectual, rhetorical artifacts are not mere products or reflections of human intentionality; they constitute "a performative account [that] insists on understanding thinking, observing, and theorizing as practices of engagement with, and as part of, the world in which we have our being" (Barad, *Meeting* 133). Likewise, they are about more than the mirror; more deeply, they are about the diffractions—the grief, the mourning, the beauty, and the love that are bound up in these intra-actments of material discursive practice.

Mourning as Ethical Obligation and Necessary for Becoming With

As Haraway writes: "Grief is a path to understanding entangled shared living and dying; human beings must grieve *with*, because we are in and of this fabric of undoing. Without sustained remembrance, we cannot learn to live with ghosts and so cannot think" (*Staying* 39, emphasis in original).[11] In participating in the material discursive practices that transmit the affectual, haptic energies of elemental spaces, then, Jordan's photos not only disclose transcorporeality, but in doing so, they also help enact and configure inscriptions imbued with grief, mourning, and, ultimately, love. Thus, as I argue here, these photos paradoxically enact Derrida's notion of the "haptic eye."

In enacting the "haptic eye," to apply and extend the ideas of Michelle Ballif, this agential, material discursive practice, of which the photos are a part, performs a paradoxical mode of "ethical relation" that dissolves the distinction between the living and the dead, and in doing so, performs a becoming *with* by way of grieving *with*. Moreover, I argue that this mode of ethical relation can help enact an ethical obligation that can participate in the material becoming of the world. The work of mourning, via the photos of the Midway, then constitutes "the ethical relation between the self and the other, the otherness of the self, and the otherness of the other" (Ballif 456).

Ballif questions how we might "mourn the other—as *other*" (462, emphasis in original). That is, the act of mourning is always "doomed to fail" because, says Ballif, "the dead other sets up the conditions for the impossibility of mourning. Precisely because . . . the dead other is *always already* with/in the self in a preoriginary way" (462, emphasis in original). To circumvent this double bind thus requires an unconventional move—that of believing in ghosts, in the paradox of the specter (Ballif 463).[12] At first glance, this notion seems to run counter to the idea of the haptic image, as the specter is technically "invisible," and, as such, not privy even to feminist critiques of representationalism so often levied on the image; however, we could argue similarly of the haptic image, in its paradoxical ability to facilitate a sensory experience of place that is at once rhetorical and elemental. The paradox of the spectral other likewise is in its haptic sensibility—in its barely tangible but highly visceral materiality. The specter manifests "a 'spectral asymmetry' that 'interrupts' 'all' 'specularity'" (Derrida qtd. in Ballif 464). As Ballif heart-wrenchingly puts it, "We sense the spectral look" (464). This, Ballif says, is the "primoridial ethical relation: we do not see who looks at us, but we respond to the look" (464). This idea captures the heartbreak of mourning as well as the paradox of intra-acting ethical obligation through visual-material discursive practice. The idea of the specter captures the affective nature of material discursive practice as well as the paradox of mourning through the practices and intra-actments that attempt visual-material rhetorical address.

Paradoxically, as Ballif describes, we are posed with the challenge of considering how to regard the invisible other "from a position of blindness" (464–65). Or, put differently, in a slight appropriation: How might we learn to get on together in the worlds we share with vulnerable, disregarded bodies, when we ourselves struggle to reconcile the gravity of the events unfolding before us, or to conceptualize our interconnectedness with those worlds? Or, how we might learn to become *with*? This requires more than god-tricks and views from nowhere; rather, it requires embodiment, visceral stories, the transmission of elemental, haptic energies that help enact configurations—perhaps haunted configurations—that grieve *with*, feel *with*, to become *with*. As Marks describes: "When verbal and visual representation is saturated, meanings seep into bodily and other dense, seemingly silent registers" (5). Here, Ballif conveys the not incompatible notion of Derrida's "haptic eye: 'Can eyes manage to touch, first of all, to press together like lips?'" (Derrida qtd. in Ballif 465). This kiss constitutes a type of haptic understanding, and an enactment of mourning, thus "structured by impossibility and 'spacing' as well as delay. . . . As with all relations, the 'kiss' is haunted" (Derrida qtd. in Ballif 465). As Ballif writes, "Such a 'kiss' is precisely a response to the ethical responsibility of, for, and to the dead" (465).

CONCLUSION

Thus, to become *with*—to engage in an ethic of compassionate conservation, requires more than just being an "eye-witness" (Ballif 464). It requires the grieving *with* that the haptic eye affords—it requires the open-endedness of being haunted in, by, and of the world. Arguably, then, Jordan's photos are imbued with the shimmers of hauntings—the haptic eye enacts the shimmering configurations of grief, beauty, and love through which we encounter the transmissions of elemental energies that haunt this instantiation of material discursive practice. I argue, then, that the haptic image and the haptic eye enable a grieving *with*, via Haraway (*Staying* 39), that can potentially open the door to more productive knowledge-making and world-making.

As I have argued in this chapter, bodies, plastics, environments, and visual-material artifacts such as photos help configure and reconfigure worlds via their participation in the intra-activities of matter; as such, they are entangled in the broader material discursive phenomenon, this ecological crisis that is the Midway Atoll. Photos such as Jordan's constitute a performative, visual-material rhetorical response to the slow violence that characterizes this issue of the inadvertent impacts of technoscience on environment and species—a response that then enacts the ethical obligations that agential realism can entail.

Moreover, I have argued that a visual-material, posthuman environmental rhetoric informed by the principles of compassionate conservation—in this case, especially the tenet that all bodies matter—can help make salient these rhetorical entanglements, and ultimately, prompt enactments that can help shape productive intra-action and policy-making. I have likewise argued that in enacting this posthuman performative response, Jordan's photos also function as a productive means of sharing elemental, toxic space and the bodies that have borne the consequences of its toxicity. Considered in the context of Spinoza's ethics, plastic makes contact with albatross bodies in ways that are harmful and toxic—that are "decompositional" and unethical (Deleuze 19). The photos seek to enact a more compositional, recuperative ethics, in part through their work as affective, haptic, rhetorical inscriptions that make salient the vulnerable albatross and the at-once paradoxically beautiful and toxic world in which it resides, and of which we are all inseparably implicated, and in part through the grieving they enable.

Subsequently, I argue that the haptic image and the haptic eye enable a "grieving *with*," to borrow again from Haraway, that paradoxically opens the door to more productive knowledge-making and world-making. More significantly, and finally, I argue that to view the photos of the Midway as bearing affective elements can help illuminate the capacity of visual-material artifacts to prompt an ineffable becoming *with* that transcends a human-centered vantage point and potentially allows for more productive world-making. As we head east, next, back to California's central coast, we will encounter variations on these themes, as vulnerable marine species yet again find themselves entangled in the material discourses of Anthropocene technoscience.

CHAPTER 3

===========

Seismic Risks and Vulnerable Bodies

Freer
          than most birds
     an eagle flies high up
                              over San Francisco
                         freer than most places
          soars high up
                    floats and glides high up
          in the still
                    open spaces

          flown from the mountains
          floated down
                              far over ocean
                    where the sunset has begun
                    a mirror of itself

He sails high over
                         turning and turning
     where seaplanes might turn
          where warplanes might burn

He wheels about burning
                              in the red sun
          climbs and glides
               and doubles back
                         upon himself
          now over ocean
               now over land
     high over pinwheels stuck in sand
     where a rollercoaster used to stand

          soaring eagle setting sun

All that is left of our wildness
—Lawrence Ferlinghetti, "Seascape with Sun & Eagle"

WOULD IT be heavy-handed to suggest that the literal shifting of tectonic plates makes for the figurative quintessential player in the agential realist account? As an East Coast native doing my best to become *with* the West Coast, I can safely say that nothing so quickly configures world-making as an earthquake or the threat thereof. Perhaps that is why, upon moving to central California in 2012, the ongoing debate about seismic testing first caught and held my attention. Initially living only about ten miles from the Diablo Canyon nuclear plant, I tuned in with even greater interest to a seemingly local debate about seismic testing, which I have since come to understand more broadly as epitomizing and challenging larger questions about agency and human/nonhuman animal relationships in an age of technoscience. No longer in the Midway, then, we now find ourselves about 3,000 miles east, back on the mainland, where yet another agential tale of the Anthropocene unfolds.

In 2009, the California power company Pacific Gas and Electric Company (PG&E) applied for a twenty-year license renewal for the Diablo Canyon nuclear power plant, which is located about halfway between Los Angeles and San Francisco. In the summer of 2011, just after the March earthquake and tsunami that caused the nuclear disaster in Japan, PG&E asked the Nuclear Regulatory Commission (NRC) to delay issuing the license renewal until they could complete the necessary seismic testing to assess earthquake faults near the plant. Following the Fukushima disaster, the NRC had required all nuclear plants in the United States to conduct additional "seismic hazard evaluations" (Sneed, "Diablo Canyon"). Citing the "much more dynamic seismic situation west of the Rockies," the NRC granted PG&E's request for additional time to research, plan, and conduct the tests (KCBX Newsroom).

Diablo Canyon sits on an eighty-five-foot cliff overlooking the Pacific Ocean and is situated within three miles of two fault lines (D. Baker). The Hosgri Fault lies several miles offshore of the plant, and was originally discovered in 1969, when the plant was near completion (Koenen; *Tribune* Staff). Then, in 2008, geologists discovered the Shoreline Fault, which runs less than one mile offshore of the plant (Sneed, "Diablo Canyon"). While Diablo Canyon was designed to withstand a 7.5 magnitude earthquake, there was new concern, based on understandings of what the Hosgri Fault is *potentially* capable of, that the two faults could work in tandem to produce a much larger earthquake than the plant could potentially withstand (D. Baker). Further complicating the issue, and a main focus of this chapter, is the fact that the planned seismic testing itself was perceived as presenting a risk to coastal life and marine mammals in the region. Interestingly, even though many stakeholders agreed that the faults must be assessed prior to Diablo's license renewal, there has been much debate—perhaps even equal or greater debate—over the potential impacts of the seismic testing itself, particularly on marine species.

With this, it is also important to note that this chapter specifically does not view any single actor in this story in a critical light, for, as Bennett reminds us: "In a world of distributed agency, a hesitant attitude toward assigning singular blame becomes a presumptive virtue" (*Vibrant* 38). That is, my goal in this chapter is not *at all* to identify any one actor or technology or institution as the cause of any one effect or potential effect, for, as Bennett describes, there are myriad scenarios, technologies, and contexts in which "humans and their intentions participate, but they are not the sole or always the most profound actant in the assemblage" (37). Rather, part of the work of the agential realist account is to consider the ways that *all* humans, nonhumans, environments, and technologies intra-act in the material discursive practices of world-making.

Nonetheless, there is no circumventing the fact of public debate surrounding the seismic testing debate, and so part of this chapter's goal will be to consider the function of such debate in the agential assemblage. A material feminist, agential realist account of the seismic testing debate thus provides an opportunity to explore the various emergent rhetorical configurations that arise through these intra-actions—configurations that often incorporate the vantage points of various stakeholders with varied backgrounds and rationales—configurations that I argue signal the potential for a posthuman conservation ethic. That is, ultimately, I demonstrate how the rhetorical artifacts associated with this debate paradoxically signal a move away from human exceptionalism and toward an interest in a more posthuman conservation ethic.

As mentioned above, part of the public debate over the proposed seismic testing had to do with potential risk to marine species in the region—most notably, the California sea otter and the harbor porpoise.[1] Seismic testing involves the use of sound cannons that are thought to disturb local marine life, including seals, sea lions, and sea otters. While PG&E planned to implement mitigation measures to monitor the effects of the testing on marine mammals like sea otters, stakeholders and members of the public were nonetheless skeptical that marine life as well as local industries would avoid harm (Sahagun, "PG&E Plan"). Moreover, the U.S. Fish and Wildlife Service requested that PG&E track and monitor the otters and porpoises, in order to gauge whether the seismic testing would impact their feeding, breeding, and migration patterns (Sneed, "Research"). This mitigation measure itself drew critical public response, as citizens and environmentalists viewed tracking as yet another possible disturbance to species, and questioned the value of further harassing these species in order to then gauge how they would respond to the already potentially disturbing seismic tests.

In recent years, in fact, there has been so much local and statewide debate about the potential impacts of the seismic tests on marine life, that in November 2012, the California Coastal Commission (CCC) voted to deny PG&E's permit for seismic testing, stating that the company did not provide enough information about the effects or adequately mitigate for them, thus putting a temporary halt to the seismic tests.[2] Thus there existed an already-skeptical public, and one that seemed to value marine species on both intrinsic and extrinsic levels. Notably, as cited in several media outlets, "the concern that crystallized opposition to the sonic blasting was the harm it could do to marine life. Two of the most vulnerable species are sea otters and harbor porpoises, both of which are territorial and most vulnerable to harm if displaced by the loud noises or exposed to them for an extended period" (Sneed, "PG&E May Still Pursue"). Central to some of the ideas in this chapter is the public's perception that the threat to marine species from seismic testing overrides the potential threat to the public from not conducting the tests near Diablo Canyon. Such public perceptions are rooted in varying, sometimes aligned, sometimes divergent rationales for and ideas about why humans should value and protect vulnerable species.

Given these questions about the impacts of seismic testing on marine species and the various rationales for protecting them, and grounded in an analysis of emergent texts and media articles about the debate, this chapter explores how human/nonhuman animal relationships are configured and constituted through the material discursive practices of technoscience, which work against the modern tendency to create distinct ontological boundaries between humans and nonhuman animals, in this case, relative to arguments about seismic testing.

Like ocean plastics in chapter 2, I understand, for instance, fault lines as neither indifferent to the concerns of technoscience or environmental advocacy, nor as the central protagonist in the story, but as mattering nonetheless in this accounting of technoscience in the Anthropocene. Thus, I view the seismic testing debate, not unlike Bennett's figuring of the 2003 blackout, as allowing for an agential accounting of how bodies—both human and nonhuman—ecosystems, technologies, and other more explicitly or "traditionally" rhetorical artifacts like maps and texts intra-act in broader material discursive practices that, following Barad, participate in the ongoing reconfigurings of the world and illuminate points of entry into knowledge-making. Thus, seismic testing emerges as a material discursive phenomenon that participates in the configuring and reconfiguring of enactments of ethical obligation that have important consequences for world-making.

Moreover, because this book also operates from a rhetorical perspective, I have an additional, related focus within these agential accounts: I am most interested in exploring those more overtly rhetorical, visual-material artifacts and how, as part of broader material discursive practice, they themselves participate in and help configure instances of world-making. In other words, while there are always myriad "things" at play in the agential realist account, I am most interested in holding a lens to how visual-material rhetorical artifacts like maps and emergent texts matter (in both senses of the word) in the seismic testing debate. I thus argue that they participate in and perform the larger intra-actments of material discursive practice, and in doing so, help enact configurations of ethical obligation in a risk society.

Interesting about such emergent texts and environmental accounts is that, on the one hand, it is possible to suggest that they illuminate a human-centered vantage point, via the perspectives about environmental issues that they convey on the part of stakeholders or concerned groups, for instance. On the other hand, however, drawing again on ideas from Alaimo, Barad, Bennett, and others, my goal is to consider a more agential realist, posthuman, material feminist accounting of the seismic testing debate that understands visual-material rhetorical artifacts as constituting specific configurations of knowledge-making that enact the sort of ethical obligation and questions of power and accountability that agential realism does not preclude but that does not necessarily happen solely via the efforts of the individual.

We may recall, as Bennett says, that distributive agency "does not posit a subject as the root cause of an effect. There is instead always a swarm of vitalities at play. . . . This understanding of agency does not deny the existence of that thrust called intentionality, but it does see it as less definitive of outcomes" (*Vibrant* 31–32). Diane Davis similarly advocates for the "posthumanist notion that human beings are always already functions of other functions. . . . Human agency is problematic indeed in the face of this realization: if human beings are routinely and unceremoniously possessed by outside forces or 'rhythms' . . . they can hardly fancy themselves in control either of their lives or of the course of human events" (23). At the same time, Bennett suggests that it is "also possible to say something about the kind of striving that may be exercised by a human within the assemblage" (*Vibrant* 38). Similar to Bennett, Boyle argues: "Less important for a posthumanist account is how an individual's agency, as evidence of a consolidated and intentional agent, is developed and sustained. This is not to say that necessary political action cannot be undertaken" ("Writing" 544). Also positing a more relational orientation, Barad argues that an agential realist take on technoscientific practice would suggest that "we are not outside observers of the world. Neither are we simply located at particular places *in* the world; rather, we are part *of* the world in its ongoing intra-activity" (*Meeting* 184). Moreover, as Nathaniel Rivers argues, "environmentalism specifically needs a more intense rhetoric—one engaged not simply in human discourse, but in the nonhuman, in the object," to which I would also add the nonhuman or more-than-human animal ("Deep" 422). I thus argue that the seismic testing debate reveals a trans-corporeality aligned with what might be akin to a posthuman environmentalism that considers our participation in the ongoing intra-actions of the world.

Holding a lens to visual-material rhetorics, I will describe, for instance, how stakeholders in this debate often voice a sense of responsibility for marine species and seek to recover marginalized voices, in a sense conveying what Davis has referred to as a posthumanist "ethics of decision . . . [that] begins with straining to hear the excess that gets drowned out" (19). I argue, then, that visual-material rhetorical artifacts enact and participate in a posthuman ethics that helps make salient otherwise vulnerable, marginalized voices—that helps reveal the role that humans can play within and among the agential assemblage to help enact a posthuman, trans-corporeal ethical obligation, or as I will argue, the beginnings of a posthuman conservation. Perhaps most interesting about this case is again its paradox: that humans participate in material discursive practice in ways that paradoxically call into question the very role of the human. In essence, then, by attempting to recover marginalized voices and "open up the flow," to borrow from Davis (19), humans participate in a kind of posthumanism that moves us incrementally closer to a posthuman conservation ethic. Such a posthuman conservation ethic neither endorses humanism nor slides into antihumanism; rather, it constitutes a "becoming with" that might characterize more productive world-making in the Anthropocene.

To this end, I argue that merging ideas about compassionate conservation with a visual-material rhetorical approach can help us better understand how rhetoric informs ideas about conservation and compassion for living creatures in an age of technoscience and the posthuman. Moreover, I argue that an analysis of the seismic testing debate and its emergent texts and contexts further illuminates how we perceive our relationships with and potential responsibilities to nonhuman species. Consistent with these ideas, this chapter (and chapter 4, even more so) also explores the role of monitoring and GPS-type tracking[3] in environmental conservation; that is, what is it about our current cultural moment that legitimates knowledge-making borne out of technologies of observation as applied to nonhuman animal bodies? I thus view technoscience endeavors like GPS tracking and seismic testing as products and programs of human consciousness and awareness whose associated risks, goals, and potential outcomes help enact specific configurations of worlds in which we are not outside observers but active participants. Likewise, I argue that emergent texts including media articles about the debate, opposition let-ters, public memos, and position statements—rhetorical artifacts in and of themselves, sometimes more typically textual, other times predominantly visual—intra-act in material discursive practice in ways that illuminate larger questions about agency and uncertainty in a risk society, and how humans value and imagine their relationships with other nonhuman animal species.

Understanding the posthuman as also concerned with animal studies and "more-than-human" ways of knowing also allows for a more "embodied com-munication" (Haraway, *When* 26). In other words, such a rhetoric would stem from a relational embodiment that considers bodies in the world in terms of our relational intra-actions with one another. Haraway describes embodied communication as "communication about relationship, the relationship itself, and the means of reshaping relationship and so its enacters" (26). In describ-ing this idea, she also references the work of Gregory Bateson: "This [embod-ied communication] is what human and nonhuman mammalian nonlinguistic communication fundamentally is, that is, communication about relationship and the material-semiotic means of relating" (Haraway, *When* 26). To explore the goals, entanglements, and consequences of human and nonhuman animal communication and relationships is not incompatible with ideas about com-passionate conservation.

As described also in chapter 1, compassionate conservation is a "rapidly growing international and cross-disciplinary movement" that promotes peace-ful coexistence with nonhuman animal species and understanding wild ani-mals as sentient individuals, with regard to conservation practice (UTS). As Marc Bekoff, well-known scholar of ecology, evolutionary biology, and animal behavior, describes, compassionate conservation is mindful of the paradox of conservation practice: that while there may never fully be a way out of human intervention into the environment, we must think and act with conscious and compassionate regard for the lives of our nonhuman kin. Thus, compassion-ate conservation eschews human exceptionalism and seeks to work against the tendency toward human mastery and control of nature in conservation prac-tice, foregrounding instead attentiveness to issues of power and accountability and principles of coexistence and "do no harm"; such views are not incompat-ible with ideas about material feminisms and posthumanism. As Bekoff notes, for instance: "Usually, our own needs are our main concern whenever we con-sider how we influence—that is, manage and control—the lives of billions of animals. It's easy to think this way because we have, or think we have, more power, and it seems as if we can dominate other forms of life and landscapes as we want. In reality, as global climate change has made clear, we are in less control than we'd like to believe" (*Animal* 17).

While Bekoff's compassionate conservation advocates for as much of a hands-off approach as possible, he also recognizes that at the end of the day, humans are still in a position to make these decisions "on behalf of" non-human species. Compassionate conservation necessarily challenges these entrenched belief systems by requiring "trade-offs among different values" in an effort to help reduce harm to species: "Finding ways to compassionately and practically share space (coexistence), via trade-offs among different values, is vital if we are to reduce harm to animals" (UTS). A compassionate conservation approach would thus view wildlife as both intrinsically and extrinsically valuable. These questions form much of the inquiry underpinning this chapter and this book more broadly, as well as the stuff of a visual-material, posthuman environmental rhetoric attentive to our sense of relationship with other species.

A focus on embodied relationship, the human sense of kinship with other species, and ideas about agency as they pertain to human and nonhuman animal relationships in and through technoscience is not to set aside but rather to extend approaches to visual-material rhetorics. Such approaches may still involve an exploration of, say, the map-as-text's rhetorical value as viewed through the lens of a material rhetoric framework, coupled with Foucault's notion of space as heterotopic, which I have advocated for elsewhere (*Locating*), and which I reviewed in chapter 1 and invoke briefly in this chapter as well. That is, the texts analyzed in this chapter are artifacts of visual-material rhetoric in many of the ways that we have become familiar with, or that we have come to expect from such a rhetorical lens: they make arguments about contested space, and to varying extents, they rely on visual information and they describe or advocate for the immediate need to protect the vulnerable bodies of marine species. But they do more than that: they reveal the various agencies at play in this story. As Alaimo says, environmental accounts "often reconceptualize material agencies—the often unpredictable and always interconnected actions of environmental systems, toxic substances, and biological bodies" (*Bodily* 3). Texts like position statements, opposition letters, media articles, maps, and memos similarly help illuminate our trans-corporeal entanglements in ways that more explicitly reveal the need to resist hierarchical and binary modes of understanding and communicating about nonhuman animal species.

Importantly, then, I argue here that the texts analyzed in this chapter are visually materially rhetorical not in the sense that they are carved from stone or made of fabric per se, but in a way that merges the concerns of both material rhetoric and new material feminisms, through their role in performing and making salient the intra-activity of bodies, technologies, and environ-

ments, and subsequently, through the role they play as agential rhetorical artifacts in recovering the marginalized voices of vulnerable species—through
their active role in "opening up" the dialogue about vulnerable bodies. Essentially, I argue that these visual-material artifacts help perform a posthuman,
material discursive practice—one that, again, does not understand ethical
obligation as stemming from an individual subject, but that does not preclude
broader, more complex considerations of ethical obligation in material discursive practice, either. Thus, to understand visual-material rhetorical artifacts as
participating in agential, environmental accounts in such ways can help move
us incrementally closer to a visual-material, posthuman conservation.

ON DATA COLLECTION AND ANALYSIS

To help address these issues, I conducted an interpretive, qualitative study that
involved collecting, triangulating, and analyzing several types of data. I first
learned of the seismic testing debate and began following the issue in local
media coverage around 2012. My primary source of media coverage was the
local newspaper, the *San Luis Obispo (SLO) Tribune,* which has followed and
covered the issue thoroughly over time and continues to do so, most recently
reporting on PG&E's announcement to shut down Diablo Canyon by 2025
(Sneed, "PG&E Agrees"). I also followed other local and national news coverage and analyzed memos, position statements, and opposition letters published by local nonprofit and environmental organizations. I have avoided
relying on "niche" media, social media, or any obviously biased online sources
that might represent an extreme or less balanced point of view.

In addition to researching media articles about the debate, I also studied many of the documents available publicly online, including environmental impact reports and project descriptions, with accompanying charts and
maps; memos; position statements; and opposition letters authored by local
and national nonprofit environmental organizations.

As one might imagine, myriad online texts, documents, and reports exist
chronicling various perspectives and aspects of the seismic testing debate.[4]
Thus, I had to make decisions about how to delimit the parameters of the texts
that I would analyze in this chapter; that is, I considered what kind of focus,
analysis, and discussion would allow me to capture the nature of the debate
and its key arguments and concerns as they pertained to the scope of this
chapter. As noted above, this analysis and chapter are focused predominantly
on the aspects of the seismic testing debate most related to human/nonhuman
animal relationships.

Specifically, a guiding research question underpinning this chapter is: How does the seismic testing debate and its emergent texts and contexts help further illuminate the ways in which we value species and the reasons or rationales for why we may want to protect, advocate for, or feel a sense of kinship with them? I thus read and analyzed texts with a focus toward this area. Additionally, in selecting texts to analyze and reference, I wanted to try to include a representative range of types of materials. Given these considerations—*topical,* with a focus on human/nonhuman animal relationships, and *scope,* in terms of representing a range of materials—I have chosen to reference, when relevant to the discussion, the following documents:

- Media articles about the debate, spanning roughly from 2012 to the present.
- A project description, titled "Offshore Central Coastal California Seismic Imaging Project: Updated Expanded Project Description," which was prepared by Pacific Gas and Electric Company and submitted in 2012 to the California Coastal Commission (PG&E, "Updated Expanded"). This document is publicly available on the CCC website. When referencing this document within this chapter, I cite it as (PG&E, "Updated Expanded").
- Maps depicting the intended seismic survey area, which are publicly available on PG&E's website (see survey maps in PG&E, "Seismic Safety and Advanced Seismic Testing"), or included in the project description mentioned above, as well as referenced or adapted in some of the documentation prepared by other environmental groups.
- A publicly available, infographic-style flyer prepared by PG&E to communicate with the public about the exclusion and safety zones that would be maintained while conducting the seismic tests (see PG&E, "Seismic Survey Safety" and "Seismic Safety and Advanced Seismic Testing").
- A publicly available memo from the Monterey Bay National Marine Sanctuary (MBNMS) Advisory Council, which describes the seismic survey project (Michel). This memo was prepared for an October 2012 meeting of the MBNMS Advisory Council and was made available to readers as an online attachment in the *SLO Tribune* article "More Critics Decry Seismic Testing off the Central Coast" (Etling), and thus circulated widely in the popular media at the time.
- An opposition letter from Surfrider Foundation, a prominent national nonprofit environmental organization with a local chapter in San Luis Obispo, California, that voiced opposition to the proposed seismic testing (Surfrider Foundation, "Opposition").

- Position statements and related online letters or statements from several prominent local and national environmental groups opposing seismic testing.

I analyzed and coded quotes from media articles and other documents like memos, opposition letters, and position statements for themes that emerged. These themes were generally related to the following areas: types of perceived risk (to humans, marine species, ecosystem, economy), skepticism of technology, references to available documents such as maps, weighing the risk-benefit ratio, mitigating risk, rationales for and attitudes about valuing marine species, and attitudes implicitly aligned with compassionate conservation. These themes in many ways guided my organization of the chapter. Finally, it is important to note that I do not necessarily rhetorically analyze these documents in full, nor do I undertake a formal genre analysis in my analyses of them or in this chapter, per se; rather, I reference sections of these materials as they pertain to my larger focus on arguments about visual-material, posthuman environmental rhetorics and human/nonhuman animal relationships.

These themes, and this range of perspectives, then begin to illuminate not only the various ways that the public perceives their relationship to marine mammals but also how the public perceives and articulates the potential risks of technology relative to the benefits it would yield. In this case, the risks and benefits of technology are understood largely through the lens of potential impact on marine species. Again, as I will show, this debate reflects a public that implicitly understands the concerns of human and nonhuman species as enmeshed with one another.

RISK AND DISCOURSE IN TECHNOSCIENCE

It is important to note that skepticism about the seismic safety of Diablo Canyon predates this most recent debate. That is, local publics already perceived risk from the Diablo Canyon facility, given some controversial points in the plant's early history related to design and architectural issues, as well as the discovery of the Hosgri Fault in 1969 (*Tribune* Staff). More recently, in 2012, the plant was temporarily knocked offline when jellyfish-like creatures called sea salp clogged the plant's cooling water intake cove (CalCoast News). Thus, based on past and more recent history, many already-skeptical stakeholders questioned whether the benefits of conducting the seismic testing would outweigh the risks.[5] As one member of the MBNMS Advisory Council noted during the October 2012 council meeting (for which the above-referenced memo was prepared), there was great concern that the negative impacts for marine life "far outweigh any beneficial information" that the seismic testing would reveal (Etling).

At the same time, some have argued that the potential benefits of the testing have not received enough attention. A marine mammal expert and former program director for National Science Foundation (NSF) ocean sciences environmental operations, for instance, had noted that for all the "hype on risks to [marine species] from seismic research," the benefits get little attention, and "the risk to people for not pursuing this type of research is simply not part of the story" (Zaragovia). Further, state senator Sam Blakeslee, "who has expressed concerns about the techniques" used in the testing, has noted that "we don't know when stresses on these faults will cause them to fail, with potentially devastating results" (Lambert).

Weighing the Risk-Benefit Ratio

Nonetheless, despite sometimes conflicting perspectives, "a common theme among opponents is the belief that the damage the sonic blasts will do to the ocean outweighs whatever new earthquake fault information the process will generate" (Sneed, "Nearly"). One concerned citizen also voiced a pervasive theme in the debate when, during the October 2012 MBNMS Advisory Council meeting, she said: "This feels like a runaway train. I have a lot of concern the negative impacts would outweigh any beneficial information the testing would yield. . . . We have no information that this will change what they do at Diablo. No way to evaluate the risk/reward" (Etling). This statement reflects a kind of cost-benefit analysis, in which seismic testing may be viewed as a runaway train, not worth the risk for *any actors*—human or nonhuman.

This perceived risk for all actors blurs the boundaries between human and nonhuman animals, thus addressing Rivers's concern that "environmentalism and its concomitant rhetorics . . . frequently draw a bold line between humans and nonhuman nature: the animate and the inanimate, and the animal, vegetable, and mineral. Nature, it is presumed, is that which is free from human contact and intervention" ("Deep" 422). Such questions about the perceived need for human intervention in nature, and to what ends, seem precisely what is at stake in the seismic testing debate. Concerned stakeholders and publics are implicitly establishing a "more intense rhetoric" through their own debates over and acknowledgment of the interplay of human intervention, technology use, and marine species (Rivers, "Deep" 422). The seismic testing debate has effectively blurred the once-bold line between these human and nonhuman natures. These themes of weighing the risk-benefit ratio and the impacts of risk for humans and marine species then underpin the analysis in this chapter.

Mitigating Risk in a Risk Society

As sociologist Ulrich Beck has described, a "risk society" occurs when the "speeding up of modernization has produced a gulf between the world of quantifiable risk in which we think and act, and the world of non-quantifiable insecurities" ("The Terrorist Threat" 40). I suggest that the seismic testing debate reflects such a risk society and falls within the space of this gulf. That is, recent events in Fukushima, coupled with the proximity of Diablo Canyon to existing fault lines and the potential for seismic activity in the region, created an exigency that gave rise to the perceived need to further quantify or assess the risk of damage from earthquake activity. However, the as-yet-nonquantifiable but potential risks to marine species, as a result of that risk assessment, are not necessarily viewed as safe or worthwhile risks among many stakeholders.

Moreover, the scientific community has just recently begun to acknowledge the growing but still perceived as lacking empirical evidence of the adverse effects of sonic tests involving sound cannons or air gun noise on marine mammals. That is, "significant gaps" in knowledge still exist in this area, and the adverse impacts for hearing and other physical or behavioral disturbances are still understood largely in terms of their "potential biological effects" (Gordon et al. 14). In many cases, then, the evidence for strandings, beachings, or marine mammal deaths as a result of these sonic testing technologies is still seen as less tangible or visible and thus considered a challenge to confirm. Such technologies are, then, in many ways perceived as enacting a potentially risky or unknown "slow violence" (Nixon). As Nixon describes, "violence is customarily conceived as an event of action that is immediate in time, explosive and spectacular in space, and as erupting into instant sensational visibility" (2). Slow violence, on the other hand, "is neither spectacular nor instantaneous, but rather incremental and accretive, its calamitous repercussions playing out across a range of temporal scales" (2). In February 2012, for example, a mass stranding of dolphins on the northern coast of Peru made the national news, largely because the cause was unknown; many speculated, however, that nearby seismic testing could be the cause (Polom). It is also important to note that sonic testing technologies are used not only in the context of seismic risk assessment but also in other matters related to natural resource extraction and oil drilling (see Jasny; Natural Resources Defense Council). Organizations like the Natural Resources Defense Council (NRDC) continue to argue against the use of these technologies in many settings, whereas this chapter considers one such context for their potential use.

Thus aware of a skeptical public, then, PG&E tried to demonstrate low risk to marine species with reports that described the seismic tests and the mitigation measures that would be undertaken to ensure limited harm or harassment to vulnerable species. There was specific concern related to the sound emitted by the planned high-energy, offshore seismic surveys, which, as described in the local media at that time, could potentially "harass" up to "2,830 whales, dolphins and seals of 25 different species" (Sneed, "Nearly").

The term "harassment," with regard to marine mammals, is language based on criteria set forth in the Marine Mammal Protection Act (MMPA) that describes the ways in which organizations may interact with marine species throughout the course of research or data collection. To harass implies a disturbance but not injury or death. In areas like Morro Bay, California, surrounding Diablo Canyon, harbor porpoises and California sea otters would potentially feel the impacts of these tests the most.[6] As Helen Golde, acting director of the Office of Protected Resources of the National Marine Fisheries Service (NMFS) at the time noted, regarding possible risks to harbor porpoises: "This small-bodied species has a high metabolic rate requiring regular caloric intake to maintain fitness and health; therefore there is a potential for adverse health effects if an animal were forced into an area offering suboptimal habitat for an extended period of time" (Sneed, "Nearly"). Sea otters would also potentially be impacted by the tests, and the U.S. Geological Survey (USGS) planned an extensive study to tag, monitor, and gauge the impacts of the seismic surveys on the otters. I discuss some of the responses to and rhetorical implications of the sea otter tagging program in more detail later in this chapter.

In response to the perceived risk and disturbance to these and other species from the high-energy seismic tests, PG&E would commission the NMFS and other agencies to implement additional mitigation measures during the tests to ensure the safety of marine species. These measures included:

- Increasing the loudness of the sound cannons incrementally to give marine mammals an opportunity to swim away from the area, and keeping "sound emissions at lower levels" when the research vessel emitting the noise is "turning and not actively surveying";
- "Observing protocols for shutting survey work down if marine mammals are close to the research vessel or if there is evidence that marine life is

being injured or killed." To this end, trained spotters or "observers" would also be on the research vessel "to watch for and alert the survey vessel if marine mammals are in the vicinity";

- "Conducting aerial, acoustic and beach monitoring before, during and after the survey work" to discern the location of marine mammals and look for any behavioral changes that reflect stress "or the possibility of animals beaching themselves"; and
- Conducting surveys during November and December 2012, when biologists said the "impacts would be minimized" (Sneed, "Nearly").

In addition, PG&E described on their website and in a project description report submitted to the CCC the nature of the "safety" and "exclusion" zones that would be maintained while conducting the seismic tests. Based on available research, they had determined that marine mammals should not enter a 1.2-mile radius around the research vessel conducting the sound tests, or what was called the "exclusion zone," within which sound levels were estimated to be above 180 decibels (see PG&E, "Seismic Survey Safety" and "Updated Expanded" 9).

PG&E also created graphics and an accompanying infographic-style, downloadable PDF flyer that appears on their website and uses a combination of text and visuals to describe this information to a public audience in a user-friendly manner (see PG&E, "Seismic Survey Safety"). Ann M. Penrose and Steven B. Katz understand a "public audience" to "imply a wide range of listeners and readers with a variety of interests, needs, and educational backgrounds" (198). PG&E's infographic flyer indeed reflects an attempt to appeal to such a wide range of potential readers who may be wary of perceived risk. As such, it employs several rhetorical strategies to adapt scientific and technical information to a public audience immersed in a risk society.

The "Seismic Survey Safety" Infographic

The "Seismic Survey Safety" infographic flyer appeals to a public audience primarily by adapting to that audience through the use of definition, example, analysis, and graphics (Penrose and Katz 214–20). Most prominent on the page is the document's title, "Seismic Survey Safety," which is followed by a brief introduction and argument stating PG&E's dedication to conducting the seismic survey in such a way that minimizes environmental impact and ensures the protection of marine mammals (PG&E, "Seismic Survey Safety"). This introduction implicitly acknowledges a public audience immersed in a risk society, and attempts to allay concerns about risk to environment and marine species. Moreover, the flyer implicitly approaches the issue from an ecologistic vantage point that sees impact to environment as synonymous with impact to marine species.

Following the title header, most prominent are the headings "Exclusion Zone" and "3.8 mi Safety Zone." These headings adapt to the audience by using definitional strategies. Based on the focus of the public and media's concerns, the flyer aptly deems explanation of the exclusion and safety zones as essential to the concerns of the audience, and therefore defines each term textually and also sets the textual definition within a graphic that defines the same term using visual information (Penrose and Katz 215). For example, the flyer defines "3.8 mi safety zone" as an area in which audio levels are within 160 decibels. If marine mammals are known to be within this zone, then the research vessel would change its route ("Seismic Survey Safety"). This definition is placed within a blue concentric circle that visually, symbolically represents a 3.8-mile safety zone within the ocean; however, since this is not a map drawn to scale, the placement of text within the visual is meant to aid more with general conceptualization than to provide exact data to scale.

The flyer also adapts to its audience through examples; for instance, it includes a visual example of the survey vessel that would carry out the seismic tests. The image of the vessel includes descriptive labels of its features, such as acoustic receivers, perhaps in order to help explain how the ship operates and to help demystify its role in the survey process, should citizens or beachgoers see the ships on the water during the testing.

In addition to examples, the flyer adapts to its audience through analysis, in which "division, not classification, is the primary strategy used to unpack a concept" (Penrose and Katz 216). The flyer "breaks a whole into constituent elements" by unpacking the mitigation measures into component processes, which are scenario-based (Penrose and Katz 216). For example, the header "Mitigation" describes how impacts to marine species will be lessened through the implementation of a specific contingency plan ("Seismic Survey Safety"). The section then includes a bulleted list that breaks the mitigation measures into their constituent elements (Penrose and Katz 216). One such element describes the use of acoustical and infrared equipment to monitor marine mammal activity, while another such element describes the gradual ramping up of air gun usage, with an attentiveness to the distance of marine mammals from the research vessel ("Seismic Survey Safety").

The flyer is visually and textually clear in terms of the technical information it provides. As a social semiotics approach would suggest, artifacts of visual communication may be understood as reliable only to the extent that readers trust the information that they receive. Readers place trust in an image based on the "modality markers" in the image or message, and based on "textual cues" for what may be deemed credible or questionable (Kress and van Leeuwen 159). These markers and cues, which here take the form of definitions, examples, and visuals, constitute "motivated signs—signs which have arisen out of the interest of social groups who interact within the structures of power that define social life, and also interact *across* the systems produced by various groups within a society" (Kress and van Leeuwen 159, emphasis in original). Thus we might understand the flyer as a product of the institutions of technoscience, and having arisen out of a cultural moment that defines social life at least partially through an interest in seismic testing. Subsequently, the flyer interacts, in this case through visual communication, across the additional knowledge systems produced by stakeholders opposing that seismic testing. Moreover, from the perspective of social semiotics, "truth is a construct of semiosis, and as such the truth of a particular social group, arising from the values and beliefs of that group" (159). As long as the message, in this case the infographic flyer, adequately expresses these beliefs, communication happens without issue (159). However, as Kress and van Leeuwen acknowledge, such a theory of modality "has to account for a complex situation: people not only communicate and affirm as true the values and beliefs of *their* group," but they also communicate and legitimate "the values and beliefs of other groups" (160, emphasis in original).

The flyer implicitly reflects such a complex situation. It affirms the values and beliefs of this institution of technoscience—an institution with an interest in carrying out seismic testing in a manner deemed credible across social groups. It also implicitly acknowledges, through its markers and cues, the values and beliefs of a public audience immersed in a risk society. This risk society is focused predominantly on questions about the safety of the seismic surveys and accompanying mitigation measures, largely as they pertain to the welfare of marine species. In this sense, the flyer has aptly assessed its audience. The trickiness arises with the flyer's attempts to address and allay these concerns by acknowledging the public's concern for marine species in such a way that suggests there is no real need for concern, given the safety and exclusion zones and mitigation measures that would be put in place. Thus, the flyer reflects social groups in tension—groups who may be aware of each other's concerns and interests on the one hand, but whose values are nonetheless not fully aligned on the other hand.

The Track Line Map

In addition to the infographic flyer and other Web-based information, PG&E also included in their 2012 project description submitted to the CCC a "Proposed 2012 Project Survey Track Line Map" (PG&E, "Updated Expanded" 5). The "Track Line" map depicts the survey area called "Box 4," and essentially illustrates the planned path of the research vessel within this survey area Box 4.

The MBNMS's memo appears to include adaptations of the "Track Line" map as well as the "Survey Area (Zone 4)" map (see PG&E, "Seismic Safety and Advanced Seismic Testing"). For example, page 4 of the MBNMS memo appears to depict the Zone 4 survey area, but with a 160-decibel "safety radius" drawn around it (Michel). The map included in Surfrider's opposition letter, which was submitted to the CCC, also appeared to show the survey area Box 4 with buffer zone radii superimposed upon it, in order to argue that some beaches would receive sound impacts beyond the levels considered safe for those recreating in certain areas ("Opposition"). I argue that these technical descriptions of the impact of higher decibel levels, coupled with their potential effects, evokes in the reader a visceral experience while also seeking to advocate for vulnerable bodies.

In the next sections, I argue that, similar to the analysis in chapter 2, the maps and emergent texts associated with the seismic testing debate are artifacts of visual-material rhetoric that participate in and perform the larger intra-actments of material discursive practice. In doing so, I also consider how such rhetorical artifacts can help enact configurations of ethical obligation related to marine species and ecosystem protection by incorporating the marginalized voices of vulnerable marine species. Ultimately, I argue that these emergent texts signal an implicit interest in a posthuman conservation ethic.

More specifically, I argue that the maps, coupled with information about safe exposure levels for the sonic tests and the debate about those safety zones, not only played a role in the debate and the CCC's eventual decision to deny the high-energy offshore surveys, instead allowing instead the low-energy offshore surveys, but also reflect a risk society interested in protecting marine species. In doing so, the maps illuminate the differing values and interests of these institutions and social groups. I thus argue that these maps and emergent texts have larger rhetorical implications for ideas about human/nonhuman animal relationships and for forwarding a posthuman conservation ethic informed by the tenets of a compassionate conservation.

The Monterey Bay National Marine Sanctuary (MBNMS)
Advisory Council Memo

As mentioned earlier, concerns about seismic testing were not specific solely to San Luis Obispo, Morro Bay, or the areas immediately surrounding Diablo Canyon. Farther north, in areas like Cambria and Monterey, California, organizations were also concerned about possible harm to species. The MBNMS Advisory Council especially weighed in, citing concern about the testing in a 2012 memo that preceded their October meeting on the same issue. Their memo, authored by council superintendent Paul Michel, was included as a publicly available attachment in the *SLO Tribune* article "More Critics Decry Seismic Testing Off the Central Coast" (Etling).

The MBNMS memo noted that while the proposed testing would happen south of the MBNMS boundary, and while models predicted that sound levels near the sanctuary's southern boundary "would likely not be high enough to affect sanctuary resources," levels may nonetheless approach the "threshold values used by NOAA [the National Oceanic and Atmospheric Administration]" (Michel 1). This possibility led to an "interest in validation of model predictions and in comprehensive monitoring of sound levels and marine mammal distributions and densities before, during and after the survey" (Michel 1). NOAA had also stated that if the seismic testing were authorized, the MBNMS should be included in any of PG&E's mitigation and monitoring plans; thus, because the MBNMS's and NOAA's concerns both pertained to "the impacts of sound on marine mammal and fish species," offices within NOAA helped "identify and recommend appropriate mitigation and monitoring" (Michel 2).

After establishing that the MBNMS and NOAA would work together to recommend mitigation and monitoring plans, the memo went on to describe some of those plans, which included "fishery resource assessments, . . . shoreline stranding response, . . . aerial surveys," and "'listening' based monitoring which uses three types of passive acoustic technologies" (Michel 2). Finally, the memo referenced its attached maps, mentioning first that, "currently, PG&E is seeking approval from the California Coastal Commission for its revised seismic survey focused on the area referred to as 'Box 4,'" and next, that PG&E had initially planned to conduct seismic testing "in two of the four 'boxes' or zones outlined on the project map," but that it now "only plans to survey Box 4 off the coast of Morro Bay, postponing the testing in Box 2, which ranges from Morro Bay to northern Santa Barbara County" (Michel 2).

Similar to the "Track Line" map (PG&E, "Updated Expanded" 5), the first map included in the MBNMS's memo depicts the Box 4 survey area, as well as the borders of marine protected areas (MPAs) along the Central Coast, including the boundaries of the MBNMS. Both of these maps, from PG&E's "Updated Expanded Project Description" and the MBNMS memo, depict the relatively close proximity of the southern boundary of the MBNMS to the Box 4 survey area, now the primary area of concern for those groups opposed to the seismic testing. In addition, the MBNMS's version of this map also depicts with a blue line the location of geophones, which, as mentioned in the MBNMS memo (Michel 1), are recording devices, or "ocean bottom sensors," that would help create a geologic and seismic profile of the region (see also PG&E, "Updated Expanded" 12).

The second map included with the MBNMS memo appears to be based on PG&E's "Survey Area (Zone 4)" map (see PG&E, "Survey Maps: 2012 Survey Area (Zone 4)"). This map in the MBNMS memo appears to show Box 4, but with the 160-decibel "safety radius" drawn around it, depicted with a bright red dotted line ("MBNMS Memo" 4). The primary purpose of this map, then, seems to be to clearly depict the safety radius around the Box 4 survey area. Interestingly, this safety radius, or "safety zone," also appears in the public flyer created by PG&E ("Seismic Survey Safety"), but is presented there with a design and color scheme that is arguably more calming and visually appealing and less alarming than the thick red dotted line used in the MBNMS's memo attachment. I argue, then, that the presentation of the safety radius in the MBNMS's map more directly reflects a risk society concerned for the welfare of marine species relative to seismic testing.

The MBNMS's (and Surfrider's, as I will describe below) use or adaptation of the "Track Line" map reflects the different values and interests of these social groups. That is, PG&E initially included the "Track Line" map in their "Updated Expanded Project Description" to depict and describe the path of the research vessel that would carry out the seismic tests within the safety zones; their description of the track lines, while implicitly conveying concern for marine mammal protection, was primarily technical in nature. On the other hand, the manner in which the MBNMS memo discusses and contextualizes these maps more explicitly reflects their concern about marine species' exposure to sound from the seismic tests. Finally, the MBNMS's seeming adaptation of the Zone 4 survey area map to include the red outline of the 160-decibel safety radius also emphasizes the perceived risk to marine species on the part of stakeholders.

While the primary concern of the MBNMS pertains to marine mammals and fish species, other organizations, like Surfrider Foundation, a national organization with a strong San Luis Obispo chapter, focuses their mission more broadly on "the protection and enjoyment of the world's ocean, waves and beaches" (Surfrider Foundation, "Our Mission"). Thus, the opposition letter written by the San Luis Obispo chapter and submitted to the CCC focused their arguments primarily on the impacts of seismic testing on the ecosystem and recreation, while also addressing concern for marine species. Their opposition letter and others submitted to the CCC also included a combination of textual and visual arguments in the form of maps.

Surfrider's Opposition Letter

Surfrider's opposition letter, also a discursive artifact that enacted perceptions of risk about the seismic testing debate, was addressed and submitted to the CCC in October 2012. Their letter identified two main categories of potential impact related to the high-energy seismic tests: recreational impacts and ecosystem impacts. Based on Surfrider's inclusion of "existing documentation, analysis of expert testimony and discussions with expert geophysical researchers," they concluded in their letter that "the Project is unlikely to provide the information necessary to improve seismic safety estimates for DCPP [Diablo Canyon Power Plant] and will not advance worst-case scenario modeling or address the most serious risks" ("Opposition" 7). Moreover, they noted that the project would have "devastating effects on ocean ecosystems and impact coastal and ocean recreation, tourism and the local economy" (8). The seismic survey, they maintained, would also jeopardize "marine life and ocean users while hoping to create a seismic profile that will not conclusively reduce uncertainties regarding earthquake hazards at DCPP" (8).

Referencing an environmental impact report from PG&E, Surfrider's letter also expressed concern that the seismic tests could impact ocean users[7] such as divers and swimmers, and contended that while PG&E had made provisions for divers, they had not adequately or specifically done so for other ocean users such as swimmers or surfers ("Opposition" 2). Surfrider did not feel that the information from PG&E's environmental impact report satisfied their questions about the proximity of the "vessels/air guns" to the shore, and the "instantaneous decibel (dB) exposure levels" to "nearshore environments," and thus asked the CCC to provide further clarification, at which point, according to Surfrider's opposition letter, the CCC provided the maps and table that then appear in Surfrider's letter ("Opposition" 2).

The first map included in Surfrider's letter shows the Box 4 survey area and appears to be based on the map included in PG&E's "Updated Expanded Project Description" (5). In addition, the "Box 4" map in Surfrider's letter also depicts, using green, brown, yellow, black, and red concentric circles, the different buffer zones for the air gun arrays superimposed over the Box 4 area. The buffer zone information appears to be based on the table included on the following page of their letter, which comes from PG&E's "Updated Expanded Project Description" (10, table 1.2). Surfrider also included a second map that showed the postponed Box 2 survey zone and the buffer zones for those air gun arrays superimposed over the Box 2 area. This map also depicts the different buffer zones, using the same set of concentric circles, presumably based on the same information from the 2012 project description submitted by PG&E to CCC.

Surfrider included the maps primarily to support their argument that the seismic testing was, in their view, considered unsafe for human ocean users. They also supported this point with evidence from a study that the U.S. Navy conducted on divers, which concluded that 145 decibels is a safe level of sonar exposure for humans ("Opposition" 3; see also U.S. Department of the Navy). Thus, superimposed with concentric colored circles that showed the buffer zones, and based on information from the "Calculated Radii" table 1.2 in the "Updated Expanded Project Description," Surfrider argued that the "Box 4" map in their letter "illustrate[s] [that] some beaches will receive 160dB (yellow circles). Since dB ratios are logarithmic, 160dB is **30 times above the safety threshold** the Navy identified at 145 dB" ("Opposition" 3, emphasis in original).

While Surfrider's primary focus was the matter of safe exposure levels to the sonic tests for human ocean users and the question of whether adequate safety measures would be taken, their opposition letter also mentioned concern about "harm to sensitive habitats and marine mammals" ("Opposition" 5). With this, they also cited research studies documenting the harmful impacts of ocean noise on marine mammals (see Engås, Løkkeborg, and Soldal; Green). Thus, through the combination of factors—cited research; the inclusion of mapped data that, in their view, showed that some beaches would receive higher decibel levels during seismic tests than is considered safe for human exposure; and their own statements of concern for the well-being of humans, marine mammals, and ocean ecosystems—Surfrider concluded, again, that the seismic study could have "devastating effects" on ocean ecosystems and "ocean recreation, tourism and the local economy," as well as jeopardize "marine life and ocean users" while not reducing uncertainty about earthquake hazards at Diablo Canyon ("Opposition" 7).

The Initial and Larger Rhetorical Implications of the MBNMS's and Surfrider's Maps

Given the nuanced implications of the MBNMS's and Surfrider's maps, I argue that these subtly different appropriations of the "Track Line" map not only illustrate an example of critical cartography at work and exemplify the idea of the map as a visual-material rhetorical, heterotopic artifact, but more importantly, they also signal a larger, perceived need to value and protect marine species—a perceived need aligned with compassionate conservation, as implied through these texts' focus on the potential risk to marine species and ecosystems from seismic testing. As such, these emergent texts also enact perceptions of accountability and ethical obligation related to the issue. Cartographic practice, for instance, when considered from the perspectives of both rhetoric and new material feminisms, easily aligns with critical cartography, which understands mapping as always already participating in discursive practice and "reflective of, and productive of, power" (Harris and Hazen 63). Subsequently, as I have argued elsewhere (*Locating*), to view the map as power-laden, fraught with multiple meanings in tension, or representative of heterogeneous, contested spaces, is compatible with Michel Foucault's notion of heterotopias, or heterotopic space.

Foucault states that we all reside in heterogeneous spaces—that "we do not live in a kind of void, inside of which we could place individuals and things"; rather, "we live inside a set of relations that delineates sites which are irreducible to one another and absolutely not superimposable on one another" (23). We can try to characterize these sites by "looking for the set of relations by which a given site can be defined" (23). Such sites have common but multiple uses, and are frequented by various bodies with various sets of sometimes common, sometimes competing goals. In particular, Foucault is interested in those sites "that have the curious property of being in relation with all the other sites, but in such a way as to suspect, neutralize, or invert the set of relations that they happen to designate, mirror, or reflect" (24). On the one hand, then, I argue here that the maps involved in the seismic testing debate indeed count as a version of heterotopic space, as they are representations of a particular "real" territory, from which multiple arguments or ideas about a place and the actions happening within that place may be inferred. Such ideas are often borne out of knowledge claims that result in competing or contested discourses about what counts as the most "accurate" representation of a single territory. Maps can then be understood as both visual-material and heterotopic rhetorical artifacts. On the other hand, however, in considering also the clear interconnectedness of human and more-than-human species as exemplified through this case, it becomes necessary to take visual-material rhetorics even further—to acknowledge the need for and conceptualize a rhetorical approach that accounts more explicitly and even foremost, for nonhuman animals, beyond just the immediate work of rhetorical texts. To view the map as both rhetorical and heterotopic is thus a first step toward a *larger* focus on embodied relationship, the human sense of kinship with other species, and ideas about agency as they pertain to human and nonhuman animal relationships through technoscience and the risk society in which they are enmeshed.

Risk as Perpetuated and Sustained through Discourse

The risk society reflected and perpetuated through the seismic testing debate is a product of discourse. Once included with the *San Luis Obispo Tribune* article, for example, the MBNMS's memo and the maps, as discursive artifacts reflective of a risk society, arguably gained further discursive momentum and visibility within the public sphere. Likewise, Surfrider's opposition letter, once submitted to the CCC, served as a public text voicing formal opposition to the seismic surveys. As Jeff Grabill and Michelle Simmons have noted, "The 'truth' about risk is also a product of disputes within the public arena, in which experts make a bid for citizen approval" (423). And for Ulrich Beck, risk is a cultural construct, where "the *perception* of threatening risks determines thought and action" ("Risk" 213). In the seismic testing debate, the cultural values of local communities along California's Central Coast, and the intrinsic and extrinsic value of marine species for those communities, influences perceptions about whether seismic testing is worth the risk.

Risk then becomes part of a larger discourse in which concerned citizens are at the center of knowledge claims. In this sense, risk has Foucauldian overtones that stem from Michel Foucault's idea of governmentality. Policy theorist Daniele Navarra sees Foucault's concepts of governmentality and risk as compatible. Navarra notes, for example, that since the sixteenth century, knowledge about the public has been gained through demographic statistics and used to calculate life expectancy, mortality rates, and birth rates, and "to deploy and prioritise resources, assign tasks and produce technologies aimed at the well-being of the population. Therefore, Foucault's idea of governmentality, even if not directly aimed at explaining risk, understands it as a 'discourse' which places the citizen at the centre of a net of expert systems of knowledge" (Navarra). These knowledge systems then perpetuate the "language of [what counts as] socially appropriate or risk-free behaviour" (Navarra). How citizens might respond to or interpret what counts as the most appropriate or risk-free behavior related to seismic testing, then, is tied to discourses about perceived risk to human and nonhuman animals from the seismic surveys. This is not to say, however, that in this configuration, agency or autonomy is situated squarely within the realm of the human; if anything, it seems quite the opposite.

In this risk society, borrowing from Davis, "life, language, and Being are in motion and we are not in charge of the flow" (17). And as Alaimo describes: "Citizens within risk society not only experience their own inability to properly assess danger, but they suspect that even the authorities do not, in fact, have everything under control. More broadly, risk society renders the Enlightenment quest to master nature an absurdity" (*Bodily* 93). The maps and associated project descriptions likewise did not ultimately help convince concerned citizens, stakeholders, and eventually the CCC that the benefits of the high-energy surveys would outweigh the risks. Moreover, Surfrider had recommended in the conclusion of their letter that, rather than conduct new tests, PG&E should

> synthesize existing data . . . utilize recent data (collected by PG&E both terrestrially and through offshore low energy testing) to better understand seismic risks, seek further independent review of the need for additional study, and only then propose a project using state of the art techniques that minimize harm to estimate earthquake hazards. ("Opposition" 8)

Surfrider's recommendation here is also compatible with the aims of compassionate conservation, which would similarly advocate for a "do no harm" approach to conservation and environmental management and policy.

Ultimately, the CCC denied the high-energy offshore seismic tests, and PG&E was able to complete their study in 2014 after adjusting its testing methods to forego the controversial high-energy surveys and incorporating a range of data from other low-energy surveys and other sources (Sneed, "Diablo Canyon"; D. Baker; see also note 2). We might consider, then, that the most compassionate choice was to opt instead for the low-energy surveys. While the institutions of technoscience might not have framed or phrased the decision in exactly those terms, or with the tenets of compassionate conservation expressly in mind, concerned citizens and stakeholders prompted a public discourse that arguably helped achieve such a compromise. Moreover, I suggest the texts and contexts related to the debate can help illuminate the various ways in which humans value species and the reasons or rationales for why we may choose to advocate on their behalf. In the next section, I begin to delve into these broader implications of visual-material, environmental rhetorics for human/nonhuman animal relationships.

ARGUMENTS AND ATTITUDES ABOUT VALUING
MARINE SPECIES IN THE CONTEXT OF SEISMIC TESTING

The seismic testing debate provides a unique window into the various ways that stakeholders perceive risk to and value marine species. These rationales then shape ideas and communication about how marine species may be impacted by seismic testing and the roles they play in the issue and ultimately in our lives more broadly. Communication scholar Julia Corbett, for example, considers and complicates the different types of attitudes that humans have regarding our relationships with nonhuman animals. Corbett cites utilitarian attitudes, involving the "practical and material value" of an animal's habitat; naturalistic attitudes, involving an "interest and affection for wildlife and the outdoors"; ecologistic attitudes, involving concern for the environment as a system and the interrelationships between wildlife and habitats; and moralistic attitudes, which would involve "concern for right/wrong treatment" (190).

I appreciate Corbett's overall framework, and I additionally understand what she describes as moralistic attitudes, above, as not necessarily aligned with questions of blame but more so with the compassionate conservation tenet of "do no harm." Following Deleuze and Spinoza (see chapter 1), we may then understand "do no harm" not as anchored in an opposition of transcendent values (Good-Evil) but rather as related to "the qualitative difference of modes of existence (good-bad)," or right/wrong or humane treatment of animals, for instance (Deleuze 23). Thus, I understand and adapt Corbett's formulation in this analysis as referring to questions of "do no harm," which then mesh with ideas about perceived ethical obligation and compassionate conservation.

Likewise, Bekoff, too, feels that "we shouldn't let anger guide us. . . . We need to be kind and empathic and cooperate with one another, so that we can define and work toward common goals, even when we disagree on the exact path" (*Animal* 199). Moreover, it is important to note, again, that neither Barad's agential realism nor Bennett's agential assemblage align with moralistic questions of blame, nor do they conflate moralism with ethical obligation. Subsequently, neither of their agential understandings preclude considerations of ethical obligation within the assemblage or within material discursive practice. With nuance, however, Bennett also reminds us that situating agency explicitly within the realm of the human does not resolve matters, either.

Bennett acknowledges that even though humans can form intentions and have the capacity for self-reflection, nonhuman forces nonetheless have much influence in the equation. Barad, too, reminds us that ethics is "not about right response to a radically exterior/ized other, but about responsibility and accountability for the lively relationalities of becoming of which we are a part" (*Vibrant* 393). Alaimo sees and acknowledges the deep challenge of such an agential conceptualization—one that also underpins much of this book's thinking on what ethical obligation "looks like" in this age of technoscience and the Anthropocene.

As Alaimo describes, Barad's theory of intra-action "supplants the human subject as the locus of both 'knowing' and 'ethicality'" (*Bodily* 111). Moreover, Barad's ethics is "about responsibility and accountability for the lively relationalities of becoming of which we are a part" (393). In other words, we are always in flux as we intra-act in the material becoming of worlds in which we also have little to no control; Bekoff, Bennett, and Haraway argue likewise. As Alaimo acknowledges: "Attending to our ontological entanglements and 'lively relationalities,'" which cannot be circumscribed or defined in advance, is a rather formidable ethical/epistemological enterprise that reconfigures commonsensical conceptual landscapes" (*Bodily* 111). Alaimo sees what she calls "material memoirs"[8] as offering a "glimpse" of what such an ethics might look like. Building on this idea, I similarly understand the work of visual-material rhetorical artifacts and emergent texts in this debate as providing a point of entry—a way forward, in helping us to understand, as Alaimo says, "what it means to know, to be, and to act, when one is literally part of the emergent material world" (*Bodily* 111). I thus argue in this section that these various attitudes and ideas about how we value wildlife signal an overall interest in moving toward a posthuman conservation ethic.

The rationales described below, then, tend to focus on the following themes and attitudes, which emerged during my reading and analysis of texts about the debate, and which are based on but also adapt some of Corbett's categories, as described above: (1) utilitarian and extrinsic concerns; (2) ecologistic concerns; and (3) implicit concerns of "do no harm," which then reflect ideas about ethical responsibility and compassionate conservation. Moreover, these themes and attitudes do not constitute discrete entities or categories; in fact, to place each of these themes within their own subheading is a bit of a textual construction devised for the sake of clearer organization. Thus, I acknowledge within each subheading the ways in which these attitudes indeed overlap to form a spectrum of rationales, ranging from utilitarian to ethical, with an ultimate, implicit concern for recovering the marginalized voices of these vulnerable species in such a way that signals a move toward a posthuman conservation ethic.

Utilitarian and Extrinsic Rationales as
Also Qualified with Ecologistic Concerns

The range of perspectives invoked when considering the potential impacts of seismic testing on marine mammals include both extrinsic and intrinsic rationales for valuing species, and demonstrate that the lives of human and nonhuman species are highly intertwined. Some concerns are clearly more utilitarian and extrinsic, as one media article described: "Opposition to the seismic surveys is steadfast among environmentalists, fishermen, and county residents, who fear the surveys could harm the local economy" (Sneed, "Nearly").[9]

While some stakeholders cite more immediately utilitarian and humanistic concerns that acknowledge impacts to local fishing and tourism industries, even those stakeholders seem to acknowledge the interconnectedness of humans, marine species, and the environment; in other words, predominantly utilitarian arguments are also qualified with long-term ecologistic concerns. For example, one environmental impact report prepared by the State Lands Commission "concluded that plans by PG&E to emit extremely loud sounds into the ocean to map earthquake faults could have a significant impact on commercial fishing" (Sneed, "Offshore"). In addition, fishermen would not be able to work in the survey areas while the tests would be conducted (Sneed, "Offshore"). Also citing setbacks related to the establishment of sustainable fisheries in the area, the State Lands Commission's report noted that "the disruption would occur at a time that the local fishing industry is in transition toward establishing a sustainable fishery. . . . Cumulative effects are potentially significant because the local commercial fishing industry has been weakened by other factors, and the proposed seismic surveys may contribute to multiple disruptions over consecutive seasons" (Sneed, "Offshore").

Moreover, a spokesperson for Surfrider Foundation expressed both utilitarian and naturalistic, as well as more ecologistic concerns, respectively, regarding seismic testing: "This section of coast offers expansive stretches of beach and reef breaks. . . . This proposed high-energy seismic testing project threatens the sporting experience and the biodiversity of the Central Coast" (Sneed, "Nearly"). The nonprofit organization Save the Whales also weighed in, citing both utilitarian and ethical concerns. As they noted, "Tests would last 24 hours for 33 days and would kill or injure marine mammals (some of them endangered species), including whales, dolphins, porpoises, seals and otters. A deaf marine mammal is a dead one as this is the sense they rely on to communicate, navigate and find food. Seabirds and other species such as endangered sea turtles, could be affected as well, with little or no way of mitigating the impacts" (Sidenstecker). Citing more utilitarian concerns, the organization also noted, "Fishermen are concerned about the detrimental effects on their livelihood" (Sidenstecker). As I also describe below, Save the Whales voiced additional concerns in their online statement about threats to marine species that align even more explicitly with some of the guiding principles of compassionate conservation. Again, while some groups do cite utilitarian and more extrinsic arguments related to impacts on tourism, fishing, and recreation, these arguments are typically qualified with ecologistic acknowledgments of the interconnectedness of humans, marine species, and the environment.

Ecologistic Concerns as Considered Part of Larger Concerns of "Do No Harm"

In an online statement published on the weblog of the Northern Chumash Council, the Barbareno Chumash Council (BCC) of Santa Barbara refers to marine species as their own relatives—a view grounded in an ecologistic view and also aligned with ideas about compassionate conservation: "Our Barbareno Chumash Council (BCC) of Santa Barbara denounces all Federal, State and local bodies and especially PG&E of the possible, forthcoming or future destruction of our relatives off the coast in our waters" (Northern Chumash Tribal Council). Moreover, they argued, "What happens in the Ocean and on the Coast is an affair that matters to the Chumash Nation territory and our Turtle Island and our relatives; such as the Dolphins and Whales as well as other Ocean relatives" (Northern Chumash Tribal Council). Here, the reference to "our Ocean relatives" directly conveys a sense of kinship with marine species that not only reflects ideas about compassionate conservation but likewise demonstrates an explicit concern for vulnerable bodies through an appeal to do no harm.

The organization San Luis Obispo Coastkeeper also voiced ecologistic rationales for opposing seismic testing.[10] Describing themselves in their position statement as "an advocate for fishable, swimmable, drinkable water," they noted both an understanding of the need to assess earthquake risk and skepticism about the risks involved given the current intended approach: "While our organization understands the importance [of] a more complete examination of possible earthquake risk is to public health and safety, we are very concerned about the long-term risk [to] marine life off our coast as well as the serious impacts to the Central Coast Network of Marine Protected Areas likely to occur from the study as proposed" (Hensley, "Position").

Interestingly, geophysicist and San Luis Obispo County supervisor Bruce Gibson implicitly acknowledged the interconnectedness of marine species and technology in the seismic testing debate when he stated: "When you have whales and nuclear power in the same conversation, you need to proceed with caution" (Cuddy). Additionally, in this context, Gibson had noted that while San Luis Obispo County does not have "regulatory authority" over the seismic testing, "it has the responsibility to listen to and protect its citizens" (Cuddy). The combination of these statements speaks to the interconnectedness of species, environment, and technology.

Through the analysis above, it becomes possible to discern a public that is concerned about potential harm to species and interested in protecting marine mammals from what is perceived as a risky technological endeavor. Moreover, it becomes clear that concerns about "doing no harm," and feelings of responsibility toward species, are the predominant rationales cited in opposition to the seismic tests. Thus, we may see emerging a subtle progression from utilitarian and humanistic to more compassionate concerns, which, as I will describe further, then illuminates a rhetoric of compassionate conservation.

The Principle of "Do No Harm" as Aligned with Compassionate Conservation

While many of the concerns voiced in these position statements are grounded in utilitarian or ecologistic arguments, these rationales typically move into a focus on doing no harm, and are implicitly aligned with some of the guiding precepts of compassionate conservation. That is, many scientists and environmentalists were concerned with the well-being of marine mammals and the potential disturbances to species, suspecting, still, that sound cannons can cause marine mammals to experience "acoustical trauma," become confused and strand themselves, or look for other areas in which to feed (Polom). As one veterinarian with the Monterey Bay Aquarium described when referring to the potential harassment of sea otters: "When you are handling wildlife, it's a tricky proposition, especially with carnivores and endangered species. . . . You don't want to take any shortcuts. The otters deserve better" (Sneed, "Research"). Consistent with the principles of compassionate conservation, this veterinarian's statement clearly reflects a perceived need to act in the best interest of this vulnerable keystone species.

The local nonprofit organization San Luis Obispo Mothers for Peace, which is "concerned with the local dangers involving the Diablo Canyon Nuclear

Power Plant, and with the dangers of nuclear power, weapons and waste on national and global levels," also voiced concerns about potential harm to species in their opposition to seismic testing (Mothers for Peace, "Welcome"). In a 2013 statement on their website, Mothers for Peace (MFP) noted that they agree that "seismic studies are imperative"; however, they wrote, "MFP opposes the technology of high energy acoustic blasting as proposed by PG&E in 2012. That technology would have caused great harm to all sea life in the vicinity" ("2013 Mothers for Peace"). Citing views compatible with compassionate conservation, Save the Whales also voiced concern in their online statement about the possible suffering and death of vulnerable species like harbor porpoises. As they put it, "It is feared that testing could seriously damage a small population of harbor porpoises in the Morro Bay area. This species is most sensitive to loud man-made sound and is the mammal most vulnerable to habitat abandonment and hearing loss" (Sidenstecker).

COMPASSIONATE CONSERVATION MEETS POSTHUMAN TECHNOSCIENCE

Finally, the entanglement of bodies, environments, and technology, expressed implicitly through an interest in compassionate conservation, was perhaps no clearer than when, in many position statements, organizations recommended the adoption of technologies less harmful for marine life. In an online position statement that cited "grave and valid" concerns about the impacts of seismic testing on marine life, Mothers for Peace advocated exploring less harmful earthquake risk assessment technologies: "Because of the grave and valid concerns voiced by the fishing and environmental communities, Mothers for Peace advocates that the seismic testing be delayed to allow time to thoroughly explore other technologies less harmful to marine life, and baseline studies of marine life must be completed and analyzed before any testing begins" ("Position").[11]

Also citing a risk-benefit ratio that did not seem to pan out, the Sierra Club likewise asked PG&E and the CCC to examine alternative approaches to the seismic surveys: "In light of the doubts voiced by geologists and seismologists about the degree of usefulness of the proposed project, we would ask PG&E and the Commission to examine the potential for a suite of less harmful alternative methods to determine the seismic risk surrounding Diablo Canyon Power Plant [DCPP]" (Christie). The Sierra Club's position statement went on to question whether less harmful alternatives had been adequately researched: "A combination of more sophisticated modeling, low-frequency testing, or use of new technology currently in development were not fully examined in the Environmental Impact Report as alternatives" (Christie). Based on these questions and critiques, they proposed additional possible alternatives and recommended that the CCC "deny the permit . . . and work with the applicant to fully examine alternatives that have the potential to produce more valuable data and greatly reduce impacts on the marine environment" (Christie).

Finally, the San Luis Obispo Coastkeeper also recommended delaying the seismic surveys until "an environmental baseline study has been conducted and alternative methods such as low-impact studies or other technology currently in development have been fully examined" (Hensley, "Position").

The requests and recommendations of Mothers for Peace, the Sierra Club, and Coastkeeper to research and employ alternative, less potentially harmful seismic risk assessment technologies all reflect the idea that compassionate conservation involves trade-offs and the need to make alternative choices "about how we conduct research to learn about the natural world" (Bekoff, *Animal* 1). Or, as Bekoff also describes from an ecologistic vantage point: "We lessen our negative impact on animals when we increase our compassion for them and strive to make the planet a peaceful, sustaining place for all beings" (3). Aligned in varying ways with the principles of compassionate conservation, and implicitly acknowledging the connections between humans, animals, and technoscience, then, these groups advocate for a potentially less harmful and risky approach to seismic testing.

Similar to the work of photography in chapter 2, I understand these emergent texts as artifacts of visual-material rhetoric that participate in and perform the larger intra-actments of material discursive practice. In doing so, they help enact configurations of ethical obligation in a risk society. Through their participation in this agential accounting, they help reveal a risk society that is always already a product of discursive intra-actions that emerge with and against paradoxical performances of mastery over nature and a simultaneous questioning of whether such control is even possible. In this agential realist environmental account, control of bodies and ecosystems becomes a double-edged sword that threatens to potentially harm and exacerbate uncertainty, as it simultaneously offers to do no harm and protect.

Indeed, part of the significance of the seismic testing debate is this multiplicity of voices, bodies, and artifacts being represented through what ultimately seems to be a clear focus on vulnerable bodies through the lens of a risk society. Enactments of ethical obligation then reveal a sense of responsibility for these species, reflecting the implicit values of these local communities, conveying again what Davis refers to as a "post-humanist ethics" (19). That is, as Davis has noted, "an ethics of decision in a world that has lost its criteria for responsible action begins with straining to hear the excess that gets drowned out, sacrificed for the clarity of One voice, One call, One legitimate position. A post-humanist ethics ought not be about shutting down the flow but about opening it up, pulling back the stops" (19). Building on these points, I suggest that the dissolving boundaries between human and nonhuman animals reflect a qualitative, palpable shift in the form and scope of this agential landscape—we see a shift in what counts as perceived risks and for whom. And the whom, here, becomes especially significant—no longer are we dealing with a primarily human "whom"; rather, a posthuman advocacy emerges in the form of a risk society that explicitly incorporates and accounts for the perceived needs of vulnerable marine species.

Geographers who study human/nonhuman animal relationships likewise explore the immersion and distribution of nonhuman animals within society, often citing the tensions produced by such sharing of space (Michael 281). As Mike Michael describes in his cultural study of roadkill, for example, humans have long been enculturated to understand animals as having certain places or purposes within society: "As pets, or as laboratory, wild or feral, and as farm animals, they culturally and physically are situated in particular ways: There are, in other words, some quite standardized views about what sort of animal belongs in what sort of space. . . . Animals move across . . . spaces in a number of ways" (281–82). In moving across spaces, animals create what geographers Jennifer Wolch and Jody Emel call "borderlands," in which "humans and animals share space, however uneasily" (xvi). I suggest here that the seismic testing debate illustrates such uncertainty, perhaps unease, in negotiating these shared spaces—the need and want to coexist but an uncertainty or a lack of consensus on the best way to do so, an implicit interest in embodied communication complicated by the encumberments of a risk society. On the one hand, there is clear interest in "opening up" the conversation to include and account for the welfare of marine species; on the other hand, ideas about how to best account for their welfare vary among stakeholders. A public mistrustful of Diablo Canyon and nuclear power rejects the idea that seismic testing is worth the risk; state officials and scientists who support the idea of seismic testing must then address concerns about potential harm to marine species—the focal point of the risk.

Compassionate Conservation in an Age of Technoscience: The California Sea Otter

If there is one marine species that exemplifies not only Wolch and Emel's point that "humans and animals share space, however uneasily" (xvi), but also the tensions that characterize the seismic testing debate, it is the California sea otter. The most recent research into the effects of seismic testing on sea otters drew much public critique. Overseen by the USGS, the project involved the capture, tagging, and tracking of otters in an attempt to gauge the effects of the testing on their breeding and migration habits. The tracking, proposed as a mitigation measure, drew negative public response, as it was viewed as yet another possible disturbance to species. Again doubting whether the benefits of tracking the otters would outweigh the risks, concerned publics questioned the value of further harassing this species in order to gauge how they would respond to the already disturbing seismic tests. Thus the perceived need to track and monitor the otters in the context of the seismic testing debate also reflects implicit ideas about how we understand, value, and interact with non-human species co-implicated in a risk society.

The California sea otter in particular is a vulnerable species, protected within California, after having been hunted to near extinction in the 1800s (Sneed, "Research"). As a keystone and sentinel species,[12] the status of the sea otter is often considered the benchmark of what is considered an acceptable impact on the environment. While this tagging project arose in the context of the seismic testing debate, research into the health of otter populations in California has been ongoing for decades (Sneed, "Research"). Moreover, organizations like the Monterey Bay Aquarium have since the 1980s been studying sea otters with the goals of "understanding threats to the population" and helping promote their recovery (Monterey Bay Aquarium). Within the context of the seismic surveys, a team of veterinarians and scientists would monitor otters along the Central Coast in an attempt to learn how they would respond to the tests. The monitoring plan, a mitigation measure proposed by PG&E, was viewed as controversial by some, largely because of the context in which it was deemed necessary. The plan involved the capture of about sixty otters, during which scientists would take blood samples and implant the otters with tracking devices to record their daily activities and responses to the seismic tests (Sneed, "Nearly").[13]

While PG&E had obtained a permit from the State Lands Commission to carry out the seismic studies, they still needed permission from the CCC, who ultimately denied the request for the high-energy offshore surveys. Even though those surveys were eventually canceled in favor of the low-energy surveys (see note 2), biologists continue to monitor the otters who were tagged for the study, in an attempt to further understand the issues impacting their population (Sneed, "PG&E May Still Pursue").

While acknowledging the risks of the capture and tagging procedures, some scientists and stakeholders nonetheless convey an interest in the knowledge gained through monitoring otter and porpoise populations, and see a value in better understanding these species' responses to what they view as the inevitable task of seismic testing—whether it happens now or down the road. As the director of the organization Friends of the Sea Otters in Monterey stated, "If these surveys are [eventually] going to get green-lighted, it's important to have in place something that will measure the effects" (Sneed, "Research"). And interestingly, Friends of the Sea Otter, while opposed to the seismic testing itself, "supports capture-and-tag research in order to learn more about the animals" (Sneed, "Research"). Likewise, while acknowledging the challenge of tagging otters and the care with which the process needs to be carried out, one veterinarian with the Monterey Bay Aquarium expressed that tagging is "the best way to get the best information" about "these hard-to-study creatures" (Devitt). Interestingly, a research biologist with the NMFS similarly described what she perceived as an unintended benefit of tracking harbor porpoises in the context of seismic testing: "It increased awareness of a cryptic species. . . . You can't appreciate something you don't see" (Sneed, "PG&E May Still Pursue"). On the one hand, we see a main tenet of compassionate conservation present in this statement—a perceived interest in learning more about a "cryptic species," and the perception that technoscience can help us close this knowledge gap. On the other hand, as Haraway reminds us, and as chapter 4 explores in greater depth, our ability to see and assumedly appreciate this cryptic species is a complex undertaking in which "animals, humans, and machines are all enmeshed in hermeneutic labor . . . by the material-semiotic requirements of getting on together in specific life-worlds. They touch; therefore they are. It's about the action in the contact zones" (*When* 262–63). This ability to visualize the heretofore unvisualizable is a complicated form of material rhetoric and embodied communication in which vulnerable bodies are simultaneously made more vulnerable through practices of revealing, and yet perceived as more easily protected through those very practices—a double bind, perhaps, brought on by an interest in knowing through seeing and tracking.

Indeed, these rationales for tracking the otters, and the perceived benefits of doing so, in many ways situate scientists as advocates for a species that would otherwise be unable to advocate for themselves. This advocacy, however, is complicated in its embrace, for it reflects a need to make visible that which we do not explicitly know needs or wants to be made visible. And in doing so—in advocating through processes of seeing and revealing—the lives of these nonhuman species are subject to our control yet again.

Ostensibly, to track the body of the sea otter helps work against distinct ontological binaries of human and nonhuman, fostering what Latour refers to as social hybridities. According to Latour, as Michael describes, "we moderns have kept separate society and nature: In contrast to premodern cultures, modernity fundamentally has been concerned with purifying what [Latour] sees as the constitutive hybridity of the social. Thus, we moderns routinely have indulged in dualism" that tends toward continued binaries but also contains "multitudes of hybrids" (Michael 282). Animal bodies are the quintessential example of the hybrid, as they are "at once material, symbolic, physical, technological, and cultural" (Michael 284). The role of the otter in the seismic testing debate portrays well the paradoxical intra-actions of embodied bodies in technoscience, in its configuring of the animal body as vulnerable, embodied hybrid. The best way to advocate for the needs of the otter then involves some form of technological, embodied mediation and intervention into the world of the nonhuman animal—a paradoxical knowledge project that makes salient vulnerable bodies as it simultaneously seeks to enact ethical obligation on their behalf. Such a view perhaps raises more questions than it answers, in terms of responsibility, accountability, and as Haraway puts it, "hermeneutic agency" (*When* 262).

CONCLUSION

On the one hand, then, we may consider these questions of coadaptation raised by Haraway and ask, for instance, whether inducing marine mammals to adapt to us (by way of tracking) then requires that they make themselves visible in order to be justly appreciated. On the other hand, interestingly, the seismic testing debate also signals an adaptation to the perceived needs and welfare of marine species. Does this adaptation then signal a shift toward a more explicit acknowledgment of hybridity and the co-construction of human/nonhuman animal agency, as we will also consider in chapter 4? If so, then we are, remarkably, beginning to see a value shift, signaled by local communities who understand marine species as both valuable and vulnerable on multiple levels. Not incompatibly, this shift may also be a by-product of the public's skepticism for the speeding up of modernization, as expressed through a risk society that views nuclear technology as outpacing more ethical concerns and that ultimately wants to see Diablo Canyon decommissioned. Likewise, we might question the broader rhetorical and cultural implications about what is reflected in the perceived need to mark nonhuman animal bodies with technologies of visualization in an effort to best advocate on their behalf.

The seismic testing debate, then, emerges as a phenomenon that participates in the configuring and reconfiguring of enactments of ethical obligation that have important consequences for world-making. These enactments of ethical obligation illuminate posthuman leanings through their decentering of human interests and experience, and their calling into question the human domination of nature through the institutions of technoscience and the reach of its reverberations.

The vibrational intensities of sonic testing reverberate throughout the assemblage—they affect bodies, they inform and inspire rhetorical artifacts, they affect relationalities. On the one hand, this naturalcultural, technological practice would appear indifferent to consequence; yet it is cast into the spotlight, paradoxically made relational and rhetorical when considered in light of the agential cuts it always already helps configure. These rhetorical configurations then reveal vulnerabilities through their enactments of ethical obligation. From the vantage point of Spinoza's ethics, sonic testing emerges as potentially corporeally harmful and traumatic—as "decompositional" and not productive of thriving bodies (Deleuze 19). The emergent rhetorical accounts that describe such trauma then seek to advocate—to enact a more compositional, recuperative ethic. In doing so, they help enact configurations of ethical obligation in a risk society, where control is a contested entity. Rhetorical artifacts emerge and reemerge in the context of shifting perceptions of risk and seismic testing; they participate in and perform the larger intra-actments of material discursive practice. On the one hand, these emergent accounts may arguably represent human belief systems and values, but on the other hand, they do so in a paradoxical way that calls into question the very role of humans, technologies, and institutions. In this way, they help configure what ethical obligation might look like in the agential realist, environmental account.

In this account, issues of control emerge as paramount: questions of and quests for control become paradoxical markers that may make vulnerable as they simultaneously seek to protect or advocate. There is no either/or in this environmental account; rather, what emerges is, again, a paradox. In this agential accounting, fault lines, through no fault of their own, constitute risky terrain upon which institutions of technoscience stake their claims of reassurance via technologies of exploration. Institutions of technoscience work to allay subsequent and seemingly inevitable perceptions of risk, to which concerned stakeholders continuously respond.

As Bennett aptly reminds us, "the notion of a confederate agency does attenuate the blame game, but it does not thereby abandon the project of identifying . . . the sources of harmful effects. To the contrary, such a notion broadens the range of places to look for sources" (*Vibrant* 37). We may look to "long-term strings of events" (37) and be reminded that the seismic testing debate in central California arguably has its roots in much broader and vaster patterns of energy consumption, infrastructure pressures, and, following Bennett, "the assemblages they form" (37). When these macro-level issues percolate and become visible at the regional level, we get a glimpse into the local, public discourses that emerge from them. These emergent discourses and texts reveal and illuminate the agencies at play: human, nonhuman, spatial, technical.

A rhetorical analysis of some of these emergent texts has thus revealed the prevalence of attitudes that are predominantly skeptical of the benefits of seismic testing and opposed to it for reasons of its potential risk to the economy, ecosystems, and marine life. At the same time, however, many local and regional organizations have voiced support for related, ongoing research of species such as the California sea otter, which includes tracking them, in order to learn more about their habits with the goal of being able to further advocate for their protection.

These varied perspectives illustrate some of the complexities of the question of what counts as environmental rhetoric, or how we ought to understand its purview, and the role of human intervention to protect vulnerable species in an age of technoscience. As Rivers describes, environmental rhetoric, in "traditional terms . . . attempts two things: convince an audience of the connection between human agency and efficacy and current environmental events or conditions. . . . Second, such rhetoric must persuade the same audience that other human agencies must be employed to produce amelioratory effects" ("Deep" 426). Interestingly, the debate about the value of seismic testing illustrates a public that sees the connection between human agency, but not necessarily human efficacy, relative to achieving a better understanding of earthquake risk at Diablo Canyon; as a result, concerned publics and stakeholders are not convinced that employing human agencies in pursuit of such knowledge will produce amelioratory effects.

I would argue that part of the public's resistance or pushback on this front has to do with a larger but nuanced issue that Rivers identifies in these two traditional aims of environmental rhetoric: "the stress on and drive toward human mastery of the environment" ("Deep" 427). These concerned publics and groups implicitly express discomfort with the ways that seismic testing becomes a multilayered, nuanced project of human mastery over the environment and species. For instance, there exists both support and opposition within the scientific and environmental communities for tracking the California sea otter. Support for tracking the otters is related to an interest in learning more about the species to further advocate for their protection—also arguably a project of human intervention, as compassionate conservation would have it. Opposition to tracking the otters, however, is not necessarily about the *practice* of tracking, per se; rather, it is about risk perception, or the idea of tracking as a mitigation measure developed in response to the separate, deemed-too-risky project of seismic testing. So again, we see a risk society at work, continuously weighing the risk-benefit ratio of human/nonhuman animal/technoscience relationships and assessing the appropriateness of human intervention given what is perceived to be our potential responsibility to environment and species.

I argue that to grapple with such questions about how we perceive our relationships with and responsibilities toward nonhuman animal species in an age of technoscience signals a shift toward a posthuman conservation ethic—one that may not be *fully* realized through the seismic testing debate, but that we see as taking shape through its enactments of ethical obligation made salient in emergent texts and discourses. With the seismic testing debate, then, concerned publics and stakeholders seem to be implicitly acknowledging the problematics of human intervention in the environment and questioning the degrees to which, and the circumstances around which, intervention makes sense. Finally, this agential, environmental account, imbued with the themes of new material feminisms and informed by rhetorical analysis, has allowed for a window into these immediate arguments and rationales about seismic testing; however, this chapter has also raised larger questions about our interest in, curiosity about, and perceived responsibilities to marine species.

Part of the work of this chapter has been to consider the function of emergent texts in the agential assemblage, and how the enactments of these rhetorical artifacts, through their participation in more productive worldmaking, indicate a shift away from human exceptionalism and toward a more posthuman "becoming with" through their questioning of human control and intervention into bodies and ecosystems. These larger questions will continue as we proceed into chapter 4. For example, is concern for species by way of tracking them the new "technoscience version" of compassionate conservation? Can such philosophies and practices align with the overarching goals of compassionate conservation, or perhaps begin to constitute a posthuman conservation? As we head south now, to the Patagonian Sea, we will explore some of the additional ways in which technoscience participates in marine species and ecosystems advocacy through practices that involve visual-material rhetorics.

CHAPTER 4

Tracking to Sea (in the Anthropo-scene)

Do not say that I'll depart tomorrow—
even today I am still arriving.

Look deeply: every second I am arriving
to be a bud on a Spring branch,
to be a tiny bird, with still-fragile wings,
learning to sing in my new nest,
to be a caterpillar in the heart of a flower,
to be a jewel hiding itself in a stone.

I still arrive, in order to laugh and to cry,
to fear and to hope,
the rhythm of my heart is the birth and death
of all that are alive.

—Thich Nhat Hanh, from "Please Call Me By My True Names"

IN 2009, the conservation organizations Birdlife International and Wildlife Conservation Society (WCS) partnered to produce a digital text called the *Atlas of the Patagonian Sea: Species and Spaces.* The *Atlas* was created to aid in policy decisions related to fisheries management and the designation of transportation routes within the Patagonian Sea, which ranges from southern Brazil (on the Atlantic side) to southern Chile and is increasingly threatened by development and overfishing. Significantly, the *Atlas* is also the first-ever such work created largely by tracking the movements of seabirds, marine mammals, and sea turtles in the area. These marine species were outfitted with remote tracking devices for a ten-year period, and the resulting satellite data were then used to help compile the *Atlas.*

In this chapter, I analyze the *Atlas,* understanding it from the related perspectives of material rhetoric and new material feminisms. That is, similar to the analysis in chapter 2, I understand the *Atlas* as an artifact of visual-material rhetoric that participates in and performs the larger, relational intra-actments of material discursive practice. In doing so, and in using the *Atlas* as an illustrative case, I also consider how cartographic practice, when understood as a rhetorical knowledge-making endeavor that is part of larger material discursive practices, can help enact configurations of ethical obligation and marine species and ecosystem protection by advocating for nonhuman animal bodies residing in the spaces represented through the map. Ultimately, I argue that the *Atlas* helps move us incrementally closer to visualizing a post-human conservation.

In arriving at these broader conclusions, I explore an approach to environmental rhetoric that is located at the intersections of animal studies,[1] critical cartography,[2] and visual-material rhetorics, or an approach to visual rhetoric attuned not only to the persuasive components of visual artifacts but also to the ways in which considerations of spaces, bodies, and materiality specifically influence the rhetorical analysis of the visual (Propen, *Locating*). Further yet, to consider the intra-actions of spaces, bodies, technologies, and elemental environments that constitute the *Atlas,* or this specific configuration of material discursive practice, then raises questions of agency, or how and to what extent these various agential components, including the bodies of marine species, participate and intra-act in the material discursive practices of world-making. In referencing the notion of "intra-action," I again draw on Barad, who notes that "in contrast to the usual 'interaction,' which assumes that there are separate individual agencies that precede their interaction, the notion of intra-action recognizes that distinct agencies do not precede, but rather emerge through, their intra-action" (*Meeting* 33).

To arrive, then, at these conclusions about how visual-material rhetorical artifacts like the *Atlas* constitute specific configurations that participate in the intra-actions of material discursive practice requires a few steps along the way. Drawing on Michel Foucault's theory of heterotopias and Carole Blair's theory of material rhetoric, I first situate rhetorical artifacts as not merely textual but also visual and material—as spatial. It is here that I also describe the related textual work of the *Atlas* with more specificity. Subsequently, from the vantage point of new material feminisms, in situating the *Atlas* as a visual-material rhetorical artifact, I likewise understand it as one component of the broader material discursive practices underpinning efforts to protect the Patagonian Sea and its marine life—one that not only involves the intra-actions of scientists, technologies, marine species, and ecosystems, but that also foregrounds questions of power and accountability in knowledge-making practices. I thus understand humans, nonhuman animals, environments, and technology as intra-acting in the co-construction of knowledge-making related to the *Atlas.* They constitute the entangled components of material discursive practice that, following Alaimo and Barad, are part of the material world, the differential mattering of the universe, and ultimately, as such, the very substance of self, prompting necessary concern for our ethical obligation to the species with whom we share our worlds.

Following Barad, Braidotti, and Wolfe's notions of posthumanism, I also argue that a posthuman "co-presence" helps make possible these specific configurations of knowledge-making that are also attentive to the lives of nonhuman animals. Moreover, I argue that a visual-material, posthuman environmental rhetoric informed by the principles of compassionate conservation, especially the tenet that *every body* matters, can help make salient the implications of these discursive practices and subsequently prompt additional consideration of the implications of agential realism for nonhuman marine species who participate in material discursive practice in ways that *matter very much* to the shape of these knowledge-making projects. Ultimately, this chapter endeavors to conceptualize what a posthuman conservation might look like.

THE *ATLAS* AS VISUAL-MATERIAL RHETORIC

For Carole Blair, material rhetoric involves looking beyond a text's symbolic meaning to also consider its broader consequences on bodies in the world. In redefining what counts as a text, Blair considers the impacts and consequences that texts can have in the rhetorical situation. To this end, she questions "the significance of the text's material existence," its "degrees of durability [and] modes or possibilities of reproduction or preservation," and most important, how the text impacts bodies in the world (30).

While Blair refers to the text's impacts on people specifically, I extend her inquiry to consider the text's influence on nonhuman bodies as well. Based on these ideas, I understand "text" not only in the more traditional sense of printed words on the page but also as multimodal, or as combining visual, material, auditory, or digital information. Many forms of visual rhetorical texts, like memorials and maps, are also material, in terms of the broader consequences they can have in the world—not only in terms of the potential physicality of the text itself, say, as a marked path that guides visitors' experiences of a park, but also in the ways that their knowledge claims have the capacity to affect bodies through their portrayals of space or their involvement in policy-making, for instance.

Cartographic practice, when considered as both a rhetorical endeavor and a conservation effort, can provide a clear lens through which to understand the role that visual-material artifacts can play in environmental and wildlife conservation efforts and policy-making. In particular, conservation mapping is one area of cartographic practice that implicitly understands mapping as a rhetorical activity compatible with the considerations of visual-material, environmental rhetoric. Likewise, to pair Blair's earlier theory of material rhetoric with Foucault's theory of heterotopias helps us to understand rhetoric's purview as not constrained to the realm of the textual but rather as open to the realm of the visual and material—of the spatial. From here, we move more easily toward intra-action. That is, as I argued in chapter 3, to understand the map as both rhetorical and heterotopic is a first step toward a *larger* focus on embodied relationship and ideas about agency as they pertain to human and nonhuman animal relationships in Anthropocene technoscience.

Conservation mapping refers to spatial practices that designate "geographical areas as relevant for conservation" (Harris and Hazen 52). The reliance on maps to designate conservation areas may inadvertently perpetuate the idea that human and nonhuman animals should be viewed as separate, overemphasize boundaries, or perpetuate "an overly-fixed and static approach to conservation" (Harris and Hazen 56–57). Conservation mapping, like critical cartography, understands mapping as always already "reflective of, and productive of, power" (Harris and Hazen 63). As discussed also in earlier chapters, to view the map as power-laden, fraught with multiple meanings in tension, or representative of heterogeneous, contested spaces, is compatible with Michel Foucault's notion of heterotopias, or heterotopic space.[3]

To briefly review, Foucault states that we all reside in heterogeneous spaces—that "we do not live in a kind of void, inside of which we could place individuals and things"; rather, "we live inside a set of relations that delineates sites which are irreducible to one another and absolutely not superimposable on one another" (23). We can try to characterize these sites by "looking for the set of relations by which a given site can be defined" (23). Such sites have common but multiple uses, and are frequented by various bodies with various sets of sometimes common, sometimes competing goals. In particular, Foucault is interested in those sites "that have the curious property of being in relation with all the other sites, but in such a way as to suspect, neutralize, or invert the set of relations that they happen to designate, mirror, or reflect" (24). I argue here, initially, that the map counts as a version of heterotopic space in that more representational sense, as it makes salient a particular "real" territory, and often juxtaposes and conveys multiple arguments or ideas about a place. Such ideas are often borne out of knowledge claims that result in competing or contested discourses about what counts as the most "accurate" representation of a single territory.

More importantly, however, to understand the map as heterotopic is also to understand it as always already intra-acting in material discursive practice.

Thus, we may conceptualize maps and images not merely as depicting the "reality" they set out to represent, but also as participating more agentially and intra-actively in the relational enactments of world-making. Thus, to understand heterotopias as materially rhetorical allows for an understanding of heterotopic space as *intra-active* and as affecting the bodies inhabiting that space.

With these ideas in mind, this chapter takes the *Atlas of the Patagonian Sea* as its primary artifact of analysis, with a specific focus on how mapping projects implicitly portray particular species and places, and how such mapping practices, in configuring and perpetuating rhetorical, heterotopic representations, can impact the lives and futures of the nonhuman animals represented through them. Subsequently, I consider the questions of agency that arise when humans, nonhuman animals, and technology intra-act and communicate in the co-construction of knowledge-making related to the *Atlas,* and ultimately consider what this might mean for how we might conceptualize a posthuman conservation.

ON DATA COLLECTION AND ANALYSIS

The *Atlas* is a complex heterotopic representation of the Patagonian marine ecosystem and the species that reside within it. Available to the public online at http://atlas-marpatagonico.org/, the site's message is presented through a combination of text and images that work together to argue for the conservation of the Patagonian Sea and its marine species. As the editors of the *Atlas* explain: "The Patagonian Sea . . . is a unique, highly productive ocean which is plentiful in species of high aesthetic, ecological and economic value" (Falabella et al., "The *Atlas*"). This statement speaks to the value and interconnectedness of ecosystem, humans, and nonhuman animals, and also provides a rationale for the *Atlas*'s inclusion of the two distinct but interconnected primary sections, "Species" and "Spaces."

In addition to these two main sections, the *Atlas* includes nine additional links that appear at the bottom of every page within the site. Five of these nine pages provide context related to the "Spaces" and "Species" sections, and are titled "The *Atlas,*" "The Maps," "GIS," "Threats to Biodiversity," and "Important Marine Areas." The other four pages provide copyright and supporting information. These additional sections also convey explicit and implicit arguments about the value of the Patagonian marine ecosystem and its resident species that are, in many cases, rooted in a combination of ethical, ecologistic, and naturalistic attitudes.

While I consider the information provided throughout the *Atlas* as integral to the rhetorical power of the work as a whole, it is beyond the scope of this chapter to analyze the *Atlas* in full. Thus, I have chosen to delimit the parameters of my analysis to what I understand as representative sections of the work. I focus specifically on the first page of the "Species" section, "Wandering Albatross," and material from the "GIS" page that speaks to the relationships among humans, marine mammals, and remote satellite technologies. Finally, I invoke ideas and concepts from throughout the rest of the *Atlas* as they are relevant to my overall discussion or help to contextualize points made in the *Atlas* itself. I feel that such a focus adequately allows for an exploration of the concerns central to this chapter; namely, it allows for an exploration of the questions of agency that arise when humans, nonhuman animals, and technology intra-act and communicate in the co-construction of knowledge-making, and ultimately, the implications of such knowledge-making for how we might come to conceptualize a posthuman conservation.

THE RHETORICAL WORK OF MAPS AND PHOTOS IN THE "SPECIES" SECTION

The "Species" section describes the "use of the Patagonian Marine Ecosystem by seabirds and marine mammals" (Falabella et al., "Home"). The editors implicitly convey an ecological perspective that understands the natural world as a system in which humans, wildlife, and habitats are interconnected when they note that "these top predators require considerable space and resources and are vulnerable to many human activities. This makes them good indicators of the status of conservation of the ecosystem" (Falabella et al., "The Atlas"). In this view, the ecosystem is not seen as separate from the lives, uses, and needs of marine mammals and seabirds, nor is it seen as impervious to the impacts of human use.

The marine species described in this section fall within the five main categories: albatrosses, petrels, penguins, pinnipeds (seals and sea lions), and marine turtles. Each category contains between one and five species. For example, listed under the first category of "Albatross" are the wandering albatross, northern royal albatross, black-browed albatross, grey-headed albatross, and light-mantled albatross. Each species is given its own page, which typically includes two to five visual representations (such as photographs and maps) and one textual description of the species being described. I describe the wandering albatross page here, to provide a sense of how pages in this section are organized and the arguments they make.

The wandering albatross page contains a photograph[4] of the albatross, followed by four maps that describe nesting sites, principal feeding areas, and distribution and usage data from spring to summer, and autumn to winter, respectively (Falabella et al., "Wandering Albatross").

The photo depicts a portrait of the wandering albatross in flight above the ocean (Suter). Clicking on the image enlarges the photo, revealing the entirety of the bird's body as it soars beautifully above the ocean, making salient its impressive wingspan. The albatross is pictured thriving in its natural environment, and through the photo's composition, which provides a view of the bird soaring over the ocean with its wings fully extended, viewers get a sense of the bird's uniquely impressive aesthetic characteristics.

Drawing on concepts from W. J. T. Mitchell's *Picture Theory* and Barthes's *Camera Lucida,* Quinn R. Gorman suggests, in his essay in the collection *Ecosee,* that environmental photographs such as the albatross one depict nature in terms that encapsulate or embody both realist and social constructionist perspectives. That is, not unlike Ulman in chapter 2, Gorman complicates the rhetorical work of nature photography when noting two seemingly polarized positions related to the representational work of photography. He describes those who advocate "scientific or literary realism who believe that with the proper care there can be a more or less mimetic relationship between signs and 'natural' referents, [and] social constructionists who believe in the inevitably arbitrary, cultural, and constructed character of signs and sign systems, however carefully crafted or functional" (241). This creates a double bind. Either, he says, we "allow the world to be captured by the discourse of realism, which asserts the competence of representational mimesis to reproduce the world in words, or we allow it to be captured by the discourse of textuality, which claims that the interests of a natural Other are inevitably and utterly invaded by our own cultural baggage" (241). Instead, Gorman argues that photography "can supply the ground for a representational ethics that resists the very *possibility* of a complete capture of the natural," even if, following Barthes, it cannot provide the "specter of absolute freedom" or a fully "unobstructed view" (Gorman 242, emphasis in original).

To understand environmental photography in this more nuanced way helps us understand the medium not only as rhetorical but also as always already intra-acting in material discursive practice; thus, such an understanding helps us conceptualize maps and images as not merely depicting the "reality" they set out to represent but also, more agentially, as participating intra-actively, as implicated in "matters of practices, doings, and actions" (Barad, *Meeting* 135). As Karen Barad also reminds us, "even when apparatuses are primarily reinforcing, agency is not foreclosed" (178). Thus, paradoxically, the albatross's inclusion in the *Atlas* at once marks its body as vulnerable, as the *Atlas* also attempts to advocate on behalf of this vulnerable species.

Moreover, for Barthes, Gorman says,

> there is room for and value in investigating the rhetoric of the message without a code, for delineating not how it functions as a simple vehicle for connotation, but rather how it can exist for spectators as a magic, and he determines that this is both the genius of photography and the locus of effects that determine which photographs matter to him. Certain photographs, he claims, exert an attraction based upon their ability to move a viewer. (245)

As Gorman notes, the "attraction of photography, then, is hinged upon an effect we could consider rhetorical" (246). Rhetorical artifacts such as photographs of the physical environment and the bodies that inhabit it, for example, help shape "the cultural meaning and categories" that subsequently allow humans "to take substantive, positive steps toward change. We can only act based upon our understanding of what nature is and how we might protect it," even if those understandings are based on culturally constructed representations of reality (Gorman 254).

Such ideas are not incompatible with the notion of the image as affectual, as haptic, and as a means of sharing or transmitting the elemental. In a manner quite different from the albatross photo discussed in chapter 2, this photo also configures an agential cut—one that posits an ontological configuration that bears a more affirmative recuperative power. This albatross thrives in its natural environment. The close-up image focuses on its facial features—its gaze fixed not on a camera but more so on its environment as it glides easily and seemingly calmly over a vast expanse of ocean. Clicking on the image to enlarge it, viewers get a sense, again, of this creature's impressive wingspan and its place in the world; the image transmits a seemingly peaceful, elemental oceanic atmosphere. Here again, nature photography participates in material discursive, embodied practice that manifests the agential intra-actments of matter. As discussed in chapter 2, this embodied practice, while not impervious to critiques of representationalism, also constitutes a rhetorical practice that enacts the elemental atmosphere of the Patagonian Sea and the bodies that inhabit it. The *Atlas* thus participates in and performs an "environmental meshworks," which, in the rhetorical configurations it helps enact, can also potentially help foster more dynamic and ethical relations with our worlds. As Cohen reminds us: "Narrative is the intermediary by virtue of which these environmental meshworks, mangles and networks are articulated, documented, vitalized" (54).

At the same time, there is no complete "capture of the natural"—humans, nonhuman animals, technologies, environments, all participate in the intra-actments that come to constitute visual-material rhetorical artifacts. Which configurations bear consequence and why also depends on the context in which they are immersed, picked up, carried along, and interpreted. Again, though, we see a perhaps common theme emerge with this configuration, this environmental meshwork—through its depiction of bodies and matter; through its depiction that *every body* matters. This is an agential performance aligned with compassionate conservation; as such, it can help make salient these rhetorical entanglements, and ultimately, prompt enactments that can help shape productive dialogue and policy making.

To the right of the photograph, viewers will then find the "Nesting Sites" map (see figure 2). (See chapter 2 for further discussion of the albatross as a vulnerable species.) The purpose of this map is to represent the populations of wandering albatross that nest and breed in the Patagonian Marine Ecosystem. Latitudes and longitudes are visible along the map's x and y axes, respectively, and a legend in the top left corner orients readers toward North and notes a scale of 1 centimeter to 340 kilometers. Landforms and surrounding ocean are shown in grayscale, presumably in order to emphasize the use of green and blue to communicate information about albatross populations studied and represented. Consistent with this reading and the information conveyed in the map's caption, the bright green dot and blue text represent the nesting colonies of wandering albatrosses on the Island of South Georgia[5] and the "percentage of the world population that each area represents relative to the total number" (Falabella et al., "The Maps"). Blue text also refers to "populations for which the *Atlas* provides distribution data"; thus, the blue text that reads "Is. Georgias del Sur: 18%," in combination with the green dot, means that the *Atlas* provides distribution data related to populations of wandering albatross residing on the Island of South Georgia. Further, the text to the right of the map notes that the "world breeding population" of wandering albatrosses is "estimated at only 8,050 pairs" and that the species was designated "vulnerable" in 2008 by the International Union for Conservation of Nature; thus, if the wandering albatross colonies on the Island of South Georgia represent 18 percent of the world population of wandering albatross, and the world breeding population is estimated at 8,050 pairs, the *Atlas* provides distribution data for approximately 1,149 pairs of wandering albatross, or the 18 percent of the world's population that nest on the Island of South Georgia. The blue circle around the green dot

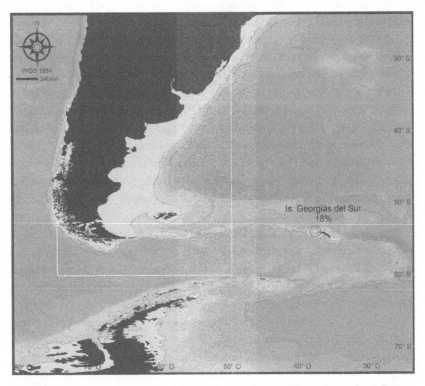

FIGURE 2. Regional nesting sites of the wandering albatross (Diomedea exulans). Datos: J. Croxall, P. Trathan y R. Phillips. En: Falabella, V., Campagna, C., y Croxall, J. (Eds). 2009. *Atlas del Mar Patagónico*. Especies y Espacios. Wildlife Conservation Society y BirdLife International. http://www.atlas-marpatagonico.org.

represents the "colonies of origin" of the wandering albatrosses studied "with remote tracking devices." In other words, the wandering albatrosses studied and represented in the *Atlas* originated in colonies in and around the Island of South Georgia (Falabella et al., "The Maps," "Wandering Albatross"; Croxall, Trathan, and Phillips, "Regional Nesting").

Following the "Nesting Sites" map are three maps that show the principal feeding areas and seasonal usage areas (spring-summer and autumn-winter) for the wandering albatross. The purpose of these maps is, ultimately, to demonstrate that the Continental Shelf and Continental Slope (areas of ocean closer to and farther from the coast, respectively) are important habitats for marine species throughout the year, regardless of seasonal variation or migration and nesting patterns. To demonstrate the albatrosses' reliance on the shelf and slope regions, researchers used the GIS data gleaned from tracking the migratory and foraging trips made by these birds to create what are called "density distributions and utilisation distribution contours" that "indicate the distribution range of the animals studied and the areas with similar probabilities of occurrence" (Falabella et al., "The Maps"). The researchers define geographical information systems, or GIS, as "a set of tools that allows geographically referenced information to be stored, edited, analysed, integrated, shared and displayed" (Falabella et al., "GIS"). Using GIS, researchers were able to take remote tracking data from the birds' migratory and foraging trips, and from that data make estimations about patterns of usage and where the birds are most and least likely to congregate. These estimations can be converted using what is called the "kernel density" feature in GIS, to create maps that show broader density distribution and usage patterns ("How Kernel Density"). In the case of the maps in the *Atlas,* utilization distribution contours are represented at intervals of 50 percent, 75 percent, and 95 percent density. As the researchers describe:

> The darkest areas (50%) identify the zones where individuals remained for the longest time. Therefore, the 50% contour reveals the areas of highest density or probability of occurrence (they do not necessarily indicate the zones where individuals feed, but do indicate areas of intense use). As we expand the area of the contour to the 75% or 95% zones, the distribution range where the probability of occurrence is lowest can be seen. Lines indicate the complete distribution range (100%). (Falabella et al., "The Maps")

In the "Principal Feeding Areas" map (see figure 3), it is clear that the Continental Slope and the Argentine Basin compose the primary feeding area, or the area of most "intense use," for the wandering albatross. These regions are highlighted in dark teal, or the 50 percent contour, as the legend indicates, and thus represent the area of highest density for the albatross. The text in the map's caption supports this reading, stating: "The slope and the Argentine Basin are the principal feeding areas for the Wandering Albatross from South Georgia year round. Unlike other albatrosses, there is little use of shallow waters on the continental shelf" (Croxall, Trathan, and Phillips, "Principal"). The caption also invokes the use of remote tracking technology to monitor marine species, noting that the data used to create this map are based on 105 trips made by both male and female wandering albatrosses residing on the Island of South Georgia.

The maps on the wandering albatross page provide evidence for this seabird's heavy reliance on the Continental Slope. The seasonal usage and distribution patterns in the Spring-Summer and Autumn-Winter maps continue to depict heavy usage of the Continental Slope by both sexes of wandering

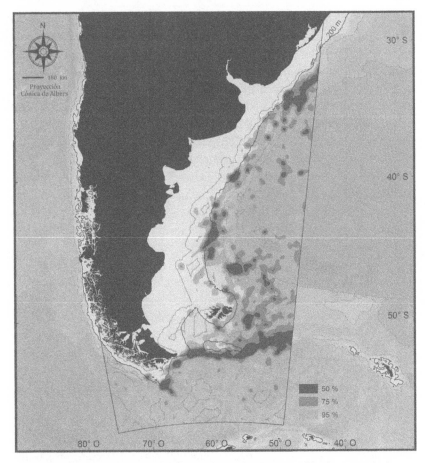

FIGURE 3. Wandering albatross (Diomedea exulans): Principal feeding areas in the Patagonian Sea. *Datos*: J. Croxall, P. Trathan y R. Phillips. *En*: Falabella, V., Campagna, C., y Croxall, J. (Eds). 2009. *Atlas del Mar Patagónico. Especies y Espacios.* Wildlife Conservation Society y BirdLife International. http://www.atlas-marpatagonico.org.

albatross. Combined with photographs of the albatross, data about its vulnerable status, and additional text that describes its primary diet of squid and fish, noting also, for example, that albatrosses will "follow vessels frequently, competing with other species to take advantage of fishing discards," the elements of the page together convey not only the aesthetic value of the wandering albatross and the importance of the ecosystem for this species, but also the precarious status of the species as well as its risky interactions with and reliance on the fishing industry (Falabella et al., "Wandering Albatross"). In other words, the wandering albatross page configures the Continental Slope as a heterotopic, contested space that this species must negotiate.

Moreover, researchers converted data about the albatrosses' trips into maps that show the areas of ocean most critical to these birds' ability to thrive. From a material feminist perspective, tracking devices participate in paradoxically embodied knowledge-making; that is, they allow the albatrosses' movements to be recorded and reproduced in the form of visual-material environmental accounts that make bodies visual and visible through the mobilization of power relations that leverage the body in the name of advocacy. In this way, as Teston argues, "wearable technologies, even as they afford access to certain kinds of body data, are nonhuman actors that intra-act with other structural conditions to determine whose bodies count" ("Rhetoric" 253). The tracking devices utilized in the production of the *Atlas* similarly participate in those paradoxical practices of visualization in which vulnerable bodies are simultaneously made more vulnerable through practices of revealing, and yet are perceived as more easily protected, and worthy of *advocating for,* through these very practices. That is, in making these species vulnerable through the practices of visualization, these practices also, paradoxically, seek to engage our curiosity about nonhuman animals through more relational modes of knowledge-making.

REMOTE TRACKING TECHNOLOGY, VISUAL-MATERIAL ENVIRONMENTAL RHETORICS, AND THE CONSERVATION OF MARINE SPECIES: TOWARD A POSTHUMAN, COMPASSIONATE CONSERVATION

Perhaps the most remarkable aspect of the *Atlas* thus pertains to the manner in which much of its cartographic data was collected. Again, the *Atlas* is the first of its kind to use remote tracking technologies to monitor and record the trips made by species of marine mammals, marine turtles, and seabirds in the region. While the maps in the "Spaces" and "Species" sections provide the organizational framework for the *Atlas* itself, the page describing the researchers' use of GIS technology contains some of the *Atlas*'s most rhetorically powerful imagery related to the remote tracking of marine species and the intra-activities that catalyze the emergence of the rhetorical configuration that is the *Atlas*.

As the researchers describe, the GIS database used to create the density maps houses "285,000 localisations, describing thousands of migratory and foraging trips of seabirds, marine mammals and sea turtles" (Falabella et al., "GIS"). Researchers used a variety of remote tracking technologies to record the trips of these marine species: "Most of these data were obtained by satellite transmitters (PTT), although geolocators (GLS) and recorders for global positioning systems (GPS) were also deployed" (Falabella et al., "GIS"). Jux-

FIGURE 4. Elephant seal with satellite tracking device. Photograph courtesy of Victoria Zavattieri. Falabella et al. *Atlas of the Patagonian Sea. Species and Spaces,* 2009.

taposed with this discussion of remote tracking technology is a photo of an elephant seal with a satellite tracking device placed on its head (see figure 4). The photo also includes a caption that describes the placement of the device from a technical perspective: "At sea, when elephant seals surface to breathe, only the head emerges above water. Thus, the instruments must be placed on it to allow a transmission to the satellites. In other species (such as birds), the back is the most suitable location to deploy transmitters" (Falabella et al., "GIS").

As I discuss more below, I suggest that the photo of the elephant seal in many ways constitutes a visual analog for how we might understand the work of the apparatus in the agential realist account. That is, in a manner theoretically similar to but topically different from Jordan's albatross photos, this image likewise, following Alaimo, "discloses trans-corporeality" (*Exposed* 130). In doing so, it helps us conceptualize tracking technologies neither as "mere instruments or devices that can be deployed as neutral probes of the natural world," nor as human manifestations or human/nonhuman assemblages (Barad, *Meeting* 142). Rather, for Barad, such apparatuses are material discursive phenomena; they are "open-ended practices" that are always-already reconfiguring our worlds

(170). Thus, as described also in chapter 2, we may understand images, imaging procedures, human bodies, animal bodies, and elemental space as bound up in *"material-discursive practices—causal intra-actions through which matter is iteratively and differentially articulated, reconfiguring the material-discursive field of possibilities and impossibilities in the ongoing dynamics of intra-activity that is agency"* (Barad 170, emphasis in original).

If apparatuses are open-ended practices that configure worlds in specific ways, we must also, following Teston, consider that apparatuses intra-act with the structural conditions of their possibility in ways that have corporeal, "on-the-ground" implications for whose bodies count and how they count. That is, material intra-action does not preclude ethical practice, as Alaimo also reminds us (*Exposed* 133). Thus, as I discuss next, the researchers' attention to the specific placement of remote sensing devices on the bodies of marine species speaks not only to the history and shifting approaches of using tracking technologies in wildlife research, but also to their own attention to ethical practice, and to the ways that humans, nonhuman animals, environments, and technology intra-act agentially in the configuring of posthuman knowledge-making related to the *Atlas*.

Wildlife Tracking and Compassionate Conservation as Embodied Practice

Discussions of tracking wildlife for conservation gained ground in the early 1970s, around which time legislation like the National Environmental Policy Act of 1969, the Marine Mammal Protection Act of 1972, and the Endangered Species Act of 1973 began emphasizing "science and technology as the most promising means of mitigating the effect on wild animals of growing human populations and levels of consumption" (Benson 2). Initial attempts in the 1960s to radio-tag dolphins explored "the relationship between vocalizations and behavior" in marine mammals, though the technology at that point made such efforts "barely feasible" (Benson 140). Early tracking technologies like acoustic tags were eventually ruled out "because of concerns about the animals' dependence on sound for communication and navigation" (Benson 142). Additionally, marine mammals often required capture in order to attach the devices. Later developments in the early 1990s made tagging more feasible and "non-intrusive," as newer tags could be "attached to free-swimming whales by suction cup" (Benson 174–75). This shift toward and interest in less intrusive practices in wildlife telemetry is consistent with the broader goals of compassionate conservation.[6]

The *Atlas* researchers likewise took measures to reduce as much as possible any intrusion into the lives of the marine species involved in their study. I argue here, following Bekoff, that while conservation efforts may never fully or entirely be outside the reach or purview of human intervention, humans can and ought to practice conservation with a critical awareness that reduces as much as, and whenever, possible, intrusion into the lives of the species involved. I argue that such awareness and efforts, using the *Atlas* as a case in point, can move us closer toward visualizing a posthuman conservation informed by the principles of compassionate conservation.

The researchers' protocol for attaching the satellite tracking device to the seals tracked for the *Atlas* project did require some mode of human intervention; however, the seals were not physically harmed during the protocol, and efforts were made to minimize their disturbance.[7] In brief, "the procedure involved approaching a sleeping or resting seal, injecting the drug and retreating quickly, requiring less than 1 min to perform. The behavior of the subject was then observed at a distance to decrease disturbance during induction. Immobilizations were done at low tide as a safety measure to prevent seals from moving to the ocean during the induction phase" (Campagna et al. 1795). The tracking devices were then "attached on the head with marine epoxy . . . to facilitate transmission of location as the animal surfaced between dives. Immobilizations were smooth and uneventful; all animals behaved normally within 2 h of the injection" (Campagna et al. 1795). On the one hand, again, this approach does involve some mode of human intervention into the lives of marine species; on the other hand, the researchers' approach to tagging is far less intrusive than earlier approaches chronicled by Benson, for instance, or other possible current approaches, and the researchers sought to reduce disturbance as much as possible.

As Bekoff argues, to engage in fieldwork, or to study animals in their natural habitats, "is far better than studying animals in cages and labs. Yet fieldwork can also be invasive, and the current regulations used to protect animals are not enough. In order to study wild animals and track their habits, scientists not only observe animals as unobtrusively as they can but also capture individuals, measure them, weigh them, evaluate their health, often tag them, and release them" (*Animal* 154–55). The *Atlas* researchers were indeed attentive to these issues, and their approach did not entail any capture/release, relocation, or surgical implantation. They also took measures to reduce as much as possible the actual duration of the encounter, approached these species in their own setting, and conducted observations from a distance whenever possible.

Moreover, by tracking these marine species remotely, and by using technologies that are as minimally intrusive as possible, the researchers aimed to gather knowledge that reflects the lives and behavior of these species in their natural environment. As Bekoff further acknowledges: "Admittedly, it's a difficult situation because we need to do research to learn more about the animals we want to understand and protect. But we can always do it more ethically and humanely—to make sure we don't harm animals in our pursuit of knowledge about them, and to be sure that the information we collect reflects their actual needs and behavior in the wild" (*Animal* 156–57). For example, recent research has also indicated a need to further examine "the behavioral effects of external devices on cetaceans with reference to pretagging behavior" (Jewell 504). One such study noted "changes in log-rolling behavior, roll duration, dive duration, daily food intake, and surfacing areas" of a single harbor porpoise, following the attachment of a radio transmitter to its dorsal fin (Jewell 504). As Zoe Jewell argues, while more invasive methods have clearly contributed to knowledge in conservation biology, researchers must still be attentive to the impacts of monitoring on "the quality of observations. However, it is often impractical, given the relative paucity of funding, and urgency of many conservation initiatives, to run control observations on unmarked and undisturbed populations alongside our test subjects" (505). Jewell thus suggests "increased testing and adoption of noninvasive techniques that do not rely on marking and cause no disturbance or minimal disturbance" to the individual or the population being studied (505).

Such noninvasive research methods also hold potential for involving local communities, and not unlike projects of citizen science, the "traditional ecological knowledge of indigenous peoples, honed over millennia, can inform more sustainable means of monitoring" (Jewell 506). Here, for instance, Jewell considers the ways that scientists might partner with or work alongside local communities who may report "sightings or signs of target species" (506). As Haraway also writes, "contemporary indigenous people and peoples, in conflict and collaboration with many sorts of partners, make a sensible difference" (*Staying* 5). Ultimately, Jewell argues that a critical awareness of an animal's well-being should be a central tenet of research projects that involve the tracking of species, and that "conservation science can move forward by recognizing that ethical treatment of animals improves the quality of data collected and the strength of monitoring and management decisions" (506).

While the notion of conducting research in order to "understand and protect" nonhuman animals still arguably puts humans in a position of privilege, an ethic of compassionate conservation complicates this idea by also advocating for a critical awareness for the care and consideration of the lives of individual animals, for a risk-benefit analysis that decenters human interests and puts the animal's best interests at the forefront, and for an ethic of do no harm (Bekoff, *Animal* 157). Nonetheless, as this book has argued, the ability to visualize the heretofore unvisualizable through the practices and products of technoscience is a complicated and paradoxical enactment of embodied communication in which vulnerable bodies are simultaneously made more vulnerable through practices of revealing, and yet perceived as more easily protected through those very practices—a paradox that materializes through an interest in understanding and communicating about our relationships with other species through the practices of seeing and tracking that often mark our witting or unwitting attempts to control the natural world. Such visualization practices are paradoxical in their normalization and mechanisms of control, on the one hand, and in their potential for enacting or performing a kind of "embodied communication," or "becoming with," on the other hand.

While even minimally intrusive research is not a panacea, projects like the *Atlas* do their best to engage species on their own terms, to minimize disturbance, and to decenter the human vantage point by visualizing the individual habits and routines of our marine kin. As Haraway reminds us, "situated technical projects and their people" can make important contributions to the building of productive worlds, which we may inhabit with our nonhuman kin (*Staying* 3).

The *Atlas,* for instance, also does important conservation work through its decentering of human exceptionalism by way of what Bekoff calls "rewilding" (*Rewilding*). That is, as described earlier, Bekoff's compassionate conservation advocates for a hands-off approach to intervening in the natural world; nonetheless, he also recognizes that at the end of the day, humans are likely still in a position to make decisions about the lives of nonhuman species. To this end, he advocates for what he calls "rewilding projects" (*Rewilding*). Such projects aim to upend human exceptionalism and embrace instead a more ecological approach: "Rewilding aims to undo two particularly damaging and self-destructive attitudes; one, that humans as a species are 'better' and 'more important' than other animals, and two, that humans are somehow immune from the incredible destruction that our activities are causing to the planet" (*Rewilding* 46).

Rewilding thus seeks to work against the domination of humans over nature: "It reflects the desire to (re)connect intimately with all animals and landscapes in ways that dissolve borders. Rewilding means appreciating, respecting, and accepting other beings and landscapes for who or what they are, not for who or what we want them to be" (Bekoff, *Rewilding* 13). A rewilding project might involve the creation of wildlife bridges or underpasses, such that animals "can move freely between fragmented areas," as opposed to the creation of cordoned-off parks or spaces that sequester animals in designated areas (12). Thus, while rewilding projects still involve some form of intervention or decision-making, their goal is quite different; rather than reinforcing hegemonic structures of domination, they are meant to foster "coexistence and compassion for animals and their homes," as well as a sense of compassion and awareness that softens and redefines the borders in our own interactions with animals (12).

While Bekoff describes rewilding projects as pertaining to the physical environment, I argue that the *Atlas* counts as a conservation project of digital rewilding. Moreover, with these ideas in mind, I argue that the *Atlas of the Patagonian Sea* not only represents a move in the direction of compassionate conservation research in an age of technoscience, it also speaks to a cultural and scientific configuration of knowledge-making in which humans, nonhuman animals, technology, and the elemental intra-act agentially in the co-construction of embodied, visual-material rhetoric.

AGENCY AND POSTHUMAN KNOWLEDGE-MAKING IN THE *ATLAS*

Recent advances in satellite telemetry have continued to shift understandings of the technology and its uses, and the *Atlas* in many ways exemplifies these shifting applications and their rhetorical implications. As Benson describes: "Instead of being seen as experts whose technologically mediated intimacy with wild animals gave them authority to speak on their behalf, scientists could now be seen as mediators of a kind of virtual intimacy between individual animals and mass audiences, or even as audiences themselves" (190). I would extend this argument to add that projects like the *Atlas* enact and reveal a trans-corporeality that is aligned with, or at least moves us closer to, a posthuman notion of conservation.

The *Atlas*'s photo of the seal with the tracking device, for example, undoubtedly engages the viewer and invites a curiosity about the life of this creature and its experience in the world. The seal is depicted as part of the natural world—seemingly at home in its physical environment and unaware of the device it carries. At the same time, from a conservation perspective, the device constitutes an intervention into the seal's existence, its everyday routine. The photo discloses trans-corporeality by making salient the entanglement of bodies, technologies, and environment in the rhetorical configuration that constitutes the *Atlas,* or the knowledge made possible through what Benson might describe as this marine creature's mediated body. I would further extend this notion of meditation to suggest an even more holistic, entangled agential assemblage—one in which the tracking device is not merely a prosthesis, nor is this creature necessarily deemed cyborg; rather, I understand humans and nonhuman animals as part of material discursive phenomena, in which the intra-actions of humans, nonhuman animals, and technologies participate in material discursive practices that configure specific rhetorical contexts and artifacts. In this sense, that is, bodies are trans-corporeal and "not objects with inherent boundaries and properties; they are material-discursive phenomena" (Barad, *Meeting* 153). Such an understanding, however, does not exempt further consideration of human and nonhuman agency in such accounting practices.

Moreover, not dissimilar to the longer analysis of the photo of the Laysan albatross in chapter 2, or the photo of the wandering albatross in this chapter, the photo of the elephant seal, as an artifact of visual-material rhetoric, provides a means of sharing elemental space. It reveals to the audience of the *Atlas* the trans-corporeal body in the world—the photo is a configuration of agential intra-actment that not only makes salient the embodied, posthuman animal body but, in doing so, also makes salient a posthuman knowledge borne out of the agential intra-actments of humans, marine species, environments, and technologies. This posthuman knowledge-making is complicated in its multilayered embrace, or in what Boyle might refer to as the characteristic "betweenness" that it performs ("Writing" 540). With this, I also feel compelled to note that the "betweenness" I describe, and the *Atlas*'s agential intra-actments, make salient a posthuman knowledge that embraces neither humanism nor antihumanism, and that neatly portrays neither individual agency nor a single group's vision, per se. That is, there is no tidy portrayal here. As an artifact of visual-material rhetoric that reveals the complex, trans-corporeal entanglements of the Anthropocene and the myriad actors, bodies, and intra-actions that perform this accounting, the *Atlas* arguably enacts a configuration of what ethical obligation to the Patagonian Sea and its marine inhabitants might entail or look like. Again, neither the agential realist, trans-corporeal account nor its companion understanding of posthumanism necessarily precludes consideration of ethical responsibility. Additionally, such understandings further inform how we might conceptualize a posthuman conservation.

On the one hand, for instance, the seal photo, taking it again as an example, may be seen as reflecting what Cary Wolfe describes as a "humanist posthumanism," as it "reinstalls a very familiar figure of the human at the very center of the universe of experience . . . or representation" ("From" 148). In this view, the photo foregrounds human technological intervention into the life of this marine mammal, thus placing the human, or a representation of human-attributed action—the ability to track—at the center of the image. On the other hand, the photo *also* posits what Wolfe refers to as a more posthumanist version of posthumanism—one that "take[s] seriously the ethical and even political challenges of the existence of nonhuman animals" by implicitly communicating the vulnerability of these species and the technoscientific, conservation-based measures being taken to help allay those threats ("From" 148).

That is, by situating the *Atlas* and its concomitant agential components as enacting an ethical obligation to help advocate for marine species, the photo may be understood as tapping into a trans-corporeality aligned with what might be akin to a posthuman environmentalism. At the same time, and not necessarily incompatibly, the *Atlas* implicitly participates in a posthumanist, performative, material discursive practice—one that does not understand ethical obligation as individually sourced, per se, but that does not preclude broader, more complex considerations of ethical obligation in material discursive practice, either.

Barad proposes a *"posthumanist performative* approach to understanding technoscientific and other naturalcultural practices that specifically acknowledges and takes account of matter's dynamism" (*Meeting* 135, emphasis in original). As described in earlier chapters, this approach moves away from questions of whether a representation such as a map accurately depicts the "reality" it sets out to depict, and closer toward "matters of practices, doings, and actions" (135). These active, or intra-active, posthuman practices circulate in ways that constitute multispecies entanglements and can help foster the sort of "becoming with" that Haraway argues is necessary for productive world-making; that Bekoff sees as necessary for compassionate conservation; and that is part of agential realism's purview, especially when aligned also with the concerns of trans-corporeality. Again, as Boyle not dissimilarly describes, in drawing also on Rickert's work: "The key for a posthumanist rhetoric . . . is an acknowledgment of a kind of betweenness among what was previously considered the human and nonhuman. Such a betweenness, it is important to note, is irreducible to supplement or prosthesis that had been emphasized in early cyborg-inflected critical theory. For rhetoric, a posthumanist orientation helps lead to an ecological or an 'ambient rhetoric'" ("Writing" 540). Thus, Boyle says, "posthumanism aids in rethinking practice as ecological, irreducible to an individual's agency" (540). I agree, and I would add that I nonetheless appreciate the notion that posthumanism, like trans-corporeality and agential realism, does not necessarily preclude related considerations of agency as they may pertain to ethical obligation, even though such considerations, in this configuration, are only ever one component of a broader agential puzzle in which multifaceted, agential intra-actions abound.

As Bennett reminds us, distributive agency does not attribute a subject "as the root cause of an effect"; rather, she writes, there are "always a swarm of vitalities at play" (*Vibrant* 31–32). Such an understanding does not preclude the function of intentionality but likewise does not view it as defining of an outcome (32). Nonetheless, Bennett does feel it is possible to consider the role that humans might play within the assemblage (38). Boyle, too, argues that an individual's agency is less important for a posthumanist account but that it is possible to consider how humans might engage politically or ethically within the assemblage ("Writing" 544). Rather, drawing also on Stormer and McGreavy, Boyle argues that we need to consider "how we account for practice as an exercise of an ecology's tendencies" in order to increase the capacities of those ecologies (544). And Barad also reminds us that technoscience does not position us as outside observers of the world; "rather, we are part *of* the world in its ongoing intra-activity" (*Meeting* 184, emphasis in original).

Given these ideas, the *Atlas* makes salient several important components of an environmental posthumanism. First, in the tradition of Hayles, humans have never really been separate from technology; we are bodies enmeshed with and who co-construct knowledge with and through technology. Additionally, the *Atlas* arguably enacts an "ethics of interaction," or what Braidotti calls "co-presence," or "the simultaneity of being in the world together" (169). Next, the *Atlas*, through the visualizations it configures, implicitly eschews human exceptionalism and advocates a more relational, entangled agency that decenters the human vantage point as it assumes, relies on, and leverages a curiosity about marine species.

Knowledge projects such as this have the potential, in drawing on Braidotti, to redefine "kinship and ethical accountability" in ways that enact ethical obligation for our nonhuman kin with whom we share the planet (Braidotti 103). Again, readers should not mistake my interest in decentering the human vantage point for a subsequent sliding into antihumanism or a privileging of the nonhuman animal, for as Davis has rightly argued, "flipping the privilege" serves to perpetuate structures of domination (137). Rather, I am interested in a more ecological coexistence that becomes possible when we momentarily tap into the aspects of ethical obligation that trans-corporeality allows for, and that agential realism does not preclude, and function instead from a place of compassion for and curiosity about the species with whom we share our worlds. As Barad also describes:

> There is an important sense in which practices of knowing cannot fully be claimed as human practices, not simply because we use nonhuman elements in our practices but because knowing is a matter of part of the world making itself intelligible to another part. Practices of knowing and being are not isolable; they are mutually implicated. We don't obtain knowledge by standing outside the world; we know because we are *of* the world. We are part of the world in its differential becoming. (*Meeting* 185, emphasis in original)

In these ways, the *Atlas* participates in the differential becoming of the world through an implicitly posthumanist, performative approach to technoscientific practice, albeit one that also presents an interesting paradox. That is, such an approach to technoscientific practice does not claim a "knower" external to the natural world or an exterior observational point; it does not necessarily or explicitly claim practices of knowing as human practices, largely because part of the world reveals itself or makes itself intelligible to another part. In this paradoxical agential realist account, the practices that help make worlds intelligible also configure nonhuman animals as participating in material discursive practices in ways that circle back to questions of nonhuman subjectivity and agency. That is, the tracking device, as enmeshed in posthumanist, technoscientific practice, also marks the vulnerable body, and in doing so, arguably intervenes in the seal's autonomy as an independent creature. This idea raises questions about how humans conceptualize the autonomy of nonhuman animals—a consideration central to compassionate conservation.

In the collection *Representing Animals,* Marcus Bullock considers that humans need nonhuman animals more than nonhuman animals need us; as he puts it, "while we may be only an inessential part of their habitat, they are an indispensable element of ours. . . . As long as we remain out of sight and sound and scent, they do not think about us. . . . We are simply a disturbance in their lives that would have no existence if it ceased to occur" (106–7). Bullock states that scientific observation has revealed many similarities between human and nonhuman animals, "and yet the very study that permits us to learn of this similarity also establishes it as a profound form of difference between them and us" (107). Thus, he says, we continue to understand "the world of an animal" as different from "the world that we construct for ourselves" (107). Moreover, he suggests, we require this understanding in order to justify our relationship with the excesses that make us human: "Our sensory apparatus burdens us, as reflexively conscious beings fully aware of time and change, with the inescapable demand that we bring that excess to order by all the conflicting means of language" (107).

Arguing against human exceptionalism and anthropocentrism, and implicitly for a sort of posthuman, multispecies entanglement, Bullock also contends that humans would be remiss in perpetuating "the rigidly assured vision that sees nothing but the operation of human knowledge anywhere in the universe. The steadfast refusal to see expressiveness anywhere merely becomes another species of anthropomorphism," one that insists on "hearing only silence and seeing only empty matter in the language of animal forms" (112). Bekoff similarly argues that

> our fellow animals not only think, but they feel—deeply. Animals live and move through the world with likes and dislikes and preferences just like we do. This is not being anthropomorphic. We're not inserting something human into them that they don't have. It doesn't matter whether their thoughts and emotions are exactly the same as our thoughts and emotions. Both their feelings and ours are essential for a meaningful life. (*Animal* 76)

Bekoff says that "what's truly anthropomorphic is to assume that animals don't think or feel"; this, he says, quoting from Terry Tempest Williams, is "the ultimate act of solipsism" (*Animal* 77).

Barad's agential realism helps diffuse some of the tensions inherent in questions about nonhuman animal agency through its broader understanding of humans, nonhumans, and matter as participating in larger material discursive practices in which we all intra-act, and as enacting specific configurations for which we are responsible: "We are responsible for the cuts that we help enact not because we do the choosing (neither do we escape responsibility because 'we' are 'chosen' by them), but because we are an agential part of the material becoming of the universe. Cuts are agentially enacted not by willful individuals but by the larger material arrangement of which 'we' are a 'part'" (*Meeting* 178–79). In this formulation, Willey reminds us, "objectivity and agency are bound up with responsibility and accountability—we, producers of knowledge, are thus bound to consider the possibilities, both enabling and violent—of interacting with the world by studying it. In this sense, we become responsible not only for the knowledge we seek but for what exists" (1008). Finally, Alaimo reminds us that from an ethical perspective, we are "always caught up in and responsible for material intra-actions" (*Exposed* 133). Haraway, however, helps us hold a lens to the question of nonhuman animal agency more specifically.

In her well-known critique of the National Geographic Channel's 2004 television series *Crittercam*, which followed the lives of marine creatures and other nonhuman animals by outfitting them with high-tech video cameras that allowed viewers to see from their perspective, Haraway moves through an increasingly complex set of critiques about the knowledge-making accomplished through such "world-making encounters"; these critiques ultimately culminate in questions of animals' hermeneutic agency around such projects of visualization (*When* 249). On the surface, Haraway notes, the nonhuman marine creatures are the show's "central protagonists" (250). The camera is presented as a high-tech video tool "worn by species on the edge," and the information gathered through such pursuits "come[s] from that sacred-secular place of endangerment, of threatened extinction, where beings are needy of both physical and epistemological rescue" (252). As Haraway aptly puts it: "Reports from such edges have special power" (252). On the surface, then, the appeal of *Crittercam*—both the television series and the technology itself, lies in its ability to provide an "immediate experience of otherness, inhabitation of the other as a new self, sensation and truth in one package without the pollution of interfering or interacting" (252).

Notable, too, is that the idea for *Crittercam* came from a graduate student who watched a remora (a small suckerfish that attaches itself to larger fish) attach itself to a shark; the graduate student, envious of the remora's "intimate knowledge of shark life," then built a device that could accomplish a similar task (Haraway, *When* 253). Thus, if we consider the remora as an analog for *Crittercam*, "then we have to think about just what the relationships of human beings are to the animals swimming about with sucker cameras on their hides" (253). It is at this point that Haraway feels we begin to move beyond the "cartoon ideology of immediacy and stolen selves" to ask more intriguing questions about our relationships to nonhuman animals and their hermeneutic agency in such technoscientific scenarios (253).

As Haraway points out: "Clearly, the swimming sharks and loggerhead turtles are not in a 'companion animal' relationship to the people, on the model of herding dogs or other critters with whom people have worked out elaborate and more-or-less acknowledged cohabitations. The camera and remora are more about accompanying than companioning" (*When* 253). So, then, if accompaniment is the theme, this raises the larger question that Haraway acknowledges is "simple to ask and the devil to answer: What is the semiotic agency of the animals in the hermeneutic labor of Crittercam?" (261). As Haraway rightly argues, "it shouldn't take recounting twenty-five years of feminist theory and science studies" to understand that these creatures are not just "objects" that collect data on behalf of human subjects, and neither are they "completely symmetrical actors whose agency and intentionality are just cosmetically morphed variants of the unmarked kind called human" (262). Rather, she acknowledges a kind of multispecies entanglement not incompatible with Barad's agential realism and an understanding of bodies as intra-acting in broader material discursive practices, replete with "the relentlessly fleshly entanglements of this particular techno-organic world" (262).

In questioning, for example, whether marine mammals have agency in the fact of their being tracked to learn more about their habits and habitats, Haraway argues that technologies and humans adapt to and "cohabit each other in relation to particular projects or lifeworlds. . . . I must adapt to the specific animals even as I work for years to learn to induce them to adapt to me and my artifacts in particular kinds of knowledge projects" (262). According to Don Ihde, she notes that technologies and humans often adapt to one another and subsequently contends that "surely the same insight applies to the animal-human-technology hermeneutic relation" (262). To conceptualize an animal-human-technology hermeneutic relation in such a way then means that we "are all enmeshed in hermeneutic labor (and play) by the material-semiotic requirements of getting on together in specific lifeworlds" (262–63).

Haraway implicitly provides an animal studies–oriented frame for Barad's, Willey's, and Alaimo's acknowledgments of our ethical obligation within agen-tial realist accounts when she argues that "situated human beings have epis-temological-ethical obligations to the animals. Specifically, we have to learn who they are in all their nonunitary otherness in order to have a conversation on the basis of carefully constructed, multisensory, compounded languages" (*When* 263). Moreover, Haraway's call for such "carefully constructed, multi-sensory, compounded languages" not only harkens back to the concerns of compassionate conservation in technoscience but also helps further acknowl-edge the consequences of visual-material rhetorics; how we make and present knowledge about nonhuman animals; and how we understand and conceptu-alize, implicitly and explicitly, our relationships with them.

Technoscience then participates in the construction of these compounded, corporeal, elemental languages and their emergent rhetorical, environmental accounts. That is, technologies are always already discursive and compound, always comprising multiple, active, interpretive agents at play with one other:

> They are composed of diverse agents of interpretation, agents of recording, and agents for directing and multiplying relational action. These agents can be human beings or parts of human beings . . . , machines of many kinds, or other sorts of entrained things made to work in the technological compound of conjoined forces. (Haraway, *When* 250)

Here I would add that we must also be mindful of the necessarily paradoxi-cal nature of the technological compound in the agential realist account. On the one hand, the projects of technoscience can productively shape knowledge through practices of visualization, and they can productively position science and the humanities as on equal footing in the necessarily interdisciplinary compassionate conservation account; at the same time, these practices of visualization also reveal vulnerable bodies through their striving to protect and advocate. Inherent in the paradox is the reminder that every rhetorical configuration, every visual-material artifact that participates in and performs material discursive practice, has consequences for world-making.

Environmental accounts such as those discussed in this book thus have the potential to enact an ethical obligation to animals that, while not the sole purview or aim of posthuman knowledge-making, is not precluded by it, either. Conservation mapping projects such as the *Atlas* speak to a cultural moment in which tracking technologies participate in material discursive practice in ways that intra-act with the bodies and lived experiences of non-human animals. In many ways, the *Atlas* constitutes a *posthumanist performative* approach to understanding technoscientific practice, and in doing so, also moves us incrementally closer to a posthuman conservation. The *Atlas,* and the visual-material rhetorical configuration that it constitutes, enacts a trans-corporeal, ethical obligation to world-making; in doing so, it invites or even instills a curiosity about the physical world around us—specifically, a curiosity about the bodies residing in that world, and a curiosity rooted in the desire to make that world a better place. That curiosity can help encourage the kind of "becoming with" that is compatible not only with Barad's agential realism and Braidotti's posthumanism but also with Bekoff's compassionate conservation.

CONCLUSION

As an artifact of visual-material, environmental rhetoric, the *Atlas* performs a posthuman, material discursive practice that configures a specific enactment of what counts as legitimate wildlife conservation in an age of technoscience. It is perhaps the quintessential technological compound: at once embodied, elemental, multisensory, discursive. The *Atlas* is a complex heterotopic artifact whose implicit and explicit arguments reflect an anthropocentric competition for resources within an ecosystem traditionally driven by humanistic concerns but shared by human and nonhuman animals. As a result, the *Atlas* draws on rationales for conservation that are rooted in combinations of ethical, utilitarian, ecological, and aesthetic attitudes. The *Atlas,* then, not only performs a contemporary understanding of what counts as culturally credible conservation mapping practice in an age of technoscience, but also reflects a curiosity about and a perceived need to better understand the lives of marine species and our coexistence with them in a threatened ecosystem. Harris and Hazen ask "what is at stake in defining and mapping protected areas for conservation" (50). Likewise, Blair questions the significance of the text's existence beyond its immediate role in the rhetorical situation. I argue that the *Atlas*, as a visual-material rhetorical artifact that participates in material discursive practice, not only discloses trans-corporeality, but in doing so, performs "rewilding" and thus helps move us incrementally closer to visualizing a posthuman conservation ethic.

That is, conservation in and of itself is not necessarily posthuman. As this chapter has endeavored to describe, to move closer to something akin to a posthuman conservation requires a letting go of human exceptionalism and a decentering of the human vantage point to then embrace the "betweenness" that rewilds, and thus opens the door to further curiosity about nonhuman animal life—that engages with an intersecting gaze, that is interested in communicating *with*, even more so than just seeing from the perspective *of*. A conservation anchored in an ecological approach that not only values interconnection but also understands humans, nonhumans, and matter as entangled and co-constitutive of world-making is then more akin to a material feminist, posthuman conservation that is also compatible with compassionate conservation and notions of intra-active agency.

Compassionate conservation acknowledges the interconnectedness of humans, nonhuman animals, and places; it acknowledges the need to set aside human exceptionalism and consider with curiosity the lives of our nonhuman kin. More than just seeing from the perspective of another, compassionate conservation is curious about what our fellow species might be thinking—how our gazes might intersect, and how we might communicate with one another in ways that also surrender the need to control and master nature. It also acknowledges the constantly shifting configurations of our worlds, stories in which we play a role but in which we hardly play the leading role, even when we think we might.

Moreover, a posthumanism aligned with trans-corporeality and agential realism is able to consider ethical responsibility to our worlds in an age of technoscience and the Anthropocene—it has the capacity to acknowledge human accountability while also decentering human exceptionalism and individual agency. Along similar lines, compassionate conservation is about more than seeing from another's perspective—it is about communication, engaging, intra-action, and becoming *with*. A posthuman conservation also informed by these ideas would then follow suit.

The notion of thinking and acting compassionately, however, *does* imply human intentionality and subjectivity, and so compassionate conservation does not necessarily set aside the implications of human knowledge-making. While Barad's agential realism is "not aligned with human intentionality or subjectivity" (*Meeting* 177), her notion of agency as intra-action does make room for consideration of our ethical responsibilities to the worlds in which we coexist with nonhuman animals: "Particular possibilities for (intra-)acting exist at every moment, and these changing possibilities entail an ethical obligation to intra-act responsibly in the world's becoming, to contest and rework what matters and what is excluded from mattering" (178). While Barad does not necessarily describe what exactly that ethical responsibility might entail, I have endeavored to provide some such possibilities here.

I argue, then, that the *Atlas* constitutes a move in the direction of posthuman conservation—it is a technoscience-imbued performance of what it means to be curious about the patterns, habits, and routines of our nonhuman kin. It is a visual-material, rhetorical consequence of the curiosities of scientists enmeshed in material discursive practice—in the curiosities that constitute productive world-making. The *Atlas* is about seeing, but it is also about listening and imagining; it catalyzes our curiosity in ways that help foster a posthuman environmental advocacy—one that, similar to the photos of the Midway, allows us to witness in ways that eschew voyeurism and enable a kind of "caring at a distance" (Silk 166) that can inspire transformative knowledge-making and more relational ways of understanding the lives of our nonhuman kin.

At the same time, we may never be able to *fully* call conservation efforts "posthuman" in the strictest of senses, for, at the end of the day, such knowledge projects do involve human decision-making to some extent, and they do, to varying extents, put humans in positions of power over nonhuman animals and nature. However, a compassionate conservation approach would work against the hegemonic power structures of human exceptionalism through knowledge projects that, like the *Atlas,* attempt to decenter privilege and work with nonhuman species in ways attentive to their lives and well-being. Thus, I have sought to demonstrate here some ways that conservation efforts may move even closer toward a posthumanist framework, through their willingness to acknowledge the operations of power and accountability within the agential assemblage; in their decentering the perceived needs of humans from the conservation equation; and in an understanding of visual-material rhetorical artifacts of conservation as mutually constitutive of the spaces and bodies they describe. A compassionate conservation approach is implicitly aligned with these ideas. A posthuman, compassionate conservation would thus be more attentive to ethical obligation but in a way that likewise eschews human exceptionalism and privilege, and understands conservation stories and knowledge projects as borne out of the ongoing agential intra-actions of human and nonhuman animal bodies, matter, technologies, and environments.

The *Atlas* takes us to a compound world where technoscience engages with the elemental and with bodies in ways that, while arguably constituting posthuman knowledge-making—while moving the needle steadily in what I argue is a more productive agential direction—still leave room to complicate the nature of our relationships with our nonhuman kin. In other words, there is always more to ponder and more to learn in the agential realist account. How might future confluences of material feminisms and animal communication further shift our practices of environmental accounting? Or rather, might we just leave the accounting practices, the storytelling, up to somebody else altogether?

In chapter 5, I begin to consider what it might look like, for instance, when animals engage even more fully in their own knowledge projects, unencumbered by the techno-curiosities or protective propensities of humans. This is not to suggest that the rhetorical consequences of such enactments are either fully negative or positive, per se, for this is not a book about the either/or, but rather that they constitute different versions, different stories of world-making, and that we need all of these accounts to create meaningful, contrasting, worldly configurations that can resonate with each other in productive ways. As a short prelude to the next chapter, then, I pose the question: If a cockatoo uses a stick to drum on a tree hollow in the forest, and no humans are around to hear his drumming, is he still a drummer? Perhaps we shall never know, as there will likely always be video footage that documents the lives of our feathered kin going about their daily lives among trees not yet felled. Nonetheless, as I attempt, next, to draw matters and things to a close, I have a sense, and in fact a hope, that we may instead keep the conversation ongoing.

CHAPTER 5

Conclusion

IN THIS CHAPTER, I revisit and expand upon some of the connections among the cases in this book and consider some of the implications of a visual-material, posthuman environmental rhetoric informed by an ideal of compassionate conservation. I also consider new conceptualizations of human/nonhuman animal relationships, particularly as they pertain to the intersections of posthuman rhetorics of compassionate conservation, material feminisms, rhetorics of animal communication, and ideas about multispecies ethnographies (van Dooren; Haraway, *Staying*). In looking ahead, I consider how the continued, ongoing confluence of these interdisciplinary ways of knowing can further shape and illuminate our various lived and embodied experiences.

Chapter 1 began by situating ethical responsibility as not constrained to human action alone, and yet here we are, at the conclusion, seemingly focused on what it means to enact ethical responsibility in the agential environmental account. This book has also been mindful of not swapping human exceptionalism for animal exceptionalism, but here we are, considering our own responsibilities to our vulnerable, nonhuman kin. However, closer inspection reveals that we are not tying ethical responsibility only to individual or human intentionality, and that we have not exchanged one form of privilege for another. Rather, a visual-material feminist, agential environmental accounting only adds nuance to how we conceptualize power, accountability, and enactments of ethical responsibility in these tales of visual-material Anthropocene technoscience.

Chapter 2 initially pointed us in the direction of what Alaimo has referred to as the "strange agencies of plastics" (*Exposed* 188). But Alaimo complicates the "nature" of these agencies with necessary nuance—with an understanding of, say, the plastic bottle cap not as a discrete object or fixed entity but rather as part of a larger intra-active network of toxic consumerism that has given way to vulnerable, toxic bodies. This is largely why, in chapter 2, I subscribe on the one hand to the "strange agencies" of plastic in the sense of their participation in the agential realist account, but like Bennett and Alaimo, I am less interested in imagining the proverbial "day in the life" of the plastic bottle cap, or as framing plastic as the central protagonist in this story, than I am in approaching the notion of plastic's "thing-power" largely through its toxic, corporeal contact with the bodies that it renders vulnerable. That is, I think it more valuable, meaningful, and responsible to consider plastic's agencies by way of the albeit more painful awareness of and empathy for the lives of the bodies affected by those agencies, and the ways of life that have precipitated those agencies in the first place. This is a much more emotionally difficult undertaking but, I believe, the more necessary one, if we are to simultaneously *stay with the trouble* of the present, to borrow again from Haraway, and think deliberately about the future in ways that can improve our worlds through relational rather than hierarchical means.

The photos of the Midway enact such a posthuman relational, deliberative response. By sharing the elemental, toxic space of the Midway and the bodies that have borne the consequences of its toxicity, the photos constitute affective, haptic, rhetorical inscriptions that make salient the vulnerable albatross and the at-once paradoxically beautiful and toxic world in which it resides, and of which we are all inseparably implicated. From the perspective of Spinoza's ethics, plastic comes into contact with albatross bodies in ways that are harmful and toxic—that are "decompositional" and thus unethical (Deleuze 19). The photos seek to enact a more compositional, recuperative ethics, as their narrator "grapple[s] with what it means to know, to be, and to act, when one is literally part of the emergent material world" (Alaimo, *Bodily* 111). In this way, visual-material rhetorics enable a grieving *with* that paradoxically opens the door to more productive knowledge-making and world-making, prompting an ineffable sort of becoming *with* that transcends a human-centered vantage point and potentially allows for more productive world-making (Haraway, *Staying* 39).

Chapter 3 prompted us to consider the discursive consequences of a risk society in which control appears missing in action and up for grabs; where the vibrational intensities of sonic, seismic testing technologies resonate nowhere near in sync with the vulnerable marine species who operate on quite different visceral and affective frequencies. Similar to the analysis in chapter 2, I situate the maps and emergent texts associated with the seismic testing debate as artifacts of visual-material rhetoric that participate in the larger intra-actments of material discursive practice. In doing so, I also consider how such rhetorical artifacts can help enact configurations of ethical obligation related to marine species and ecosystem protection by incorporating and making salient the marginalized voices of vulnerable marine species.

Ultimately, chapter 3 argued that these emergent texts signal an implicit interest in a posthuman conservation ethic. That is, because there is no escaping the fact of public debate surrounding the issue, this chapter necessarily considered the function of public debate in the agential assemblage, to subsequently reveal that the rhetorical artifacts associated with the debate paradoxically signal a move *away* from human exceptionalism and *toward* an interest in a more posthuman conservation ethic—toward an expressed interest in the becoming *with* that happens as participants in the assemblage intra-act in the emergent material world. Considering again the perspective of Spinoza's ethics, sonic testing emerges as potentially corporeally harmful and traumatic—as "decompositional" and not productive of thriving bodies (Deleuze 19). The emergent rhetorical accounts that describe such impending trauma seek to advocate—to enact a more compositional, recuperative ethic. In doing so, they help enact configurations of ethical obligation in a risk society. Issues of control emerge as paramount in this story: questions of and quests for control become paradoxical markers that may make vulnerable as they simultaneously seek to advocate on behalf of vulnerable bodies.

Chapter 4 tells a story with a bit more recuperative power, moving us incrementally closer toward a posthuman conservation ethic. That is, similar to the work of photography in chapter 2 and the emergent rhetorical artifacts in chapter 3, I understood the *Atlas* an artifact of visual-material rhetoric that participates in and performs the larger intra-actments of material discursive practice. In doing so, I also considered how cartographic practice, when understood as a rhetorical knowledge-making endeavor that is part of larger material discursive practices, can help enact configurations of ethical obligation and marine species and ecosystem protection by advocating for nonhuman animal bodies residing in the spaces represented through the map.

The *Atlas* also gains recuperative power through its relational approach to exploring the intra-actions of bodies and worlds. Tracking technologies, while not impervious to critiques of human intervention, emerge in this configuration as more productive of a posthuman conservation ethic. By leveraging technoscience in the name of multispecies knowledge-making, the *Atlas* seeks to build knowledge through interrelationship—arguably a more restorative and recuperative ethical enterprise. The *Atlas* is thus about seeing, but it is also about listening and imagining. It operates recuperatively, compositionally, at the intersections of curiosity and advocacy to engage a posthuman vantage point. It catalyzes curiosity and *rewilds*, to extend Bekoff (*Rewilding*), in productive ways that eschew voyeurism and inspire more relational and transformative knowledge-making.

Thus, we see in these cases an emergent pattern, whereby rhetorical artifacts have the potential to function as productive, ecological, relational, ethical enactments of material discursive practice. Rhetoric participates in productive enactments of world-making when it engages with the elemental to help facilitate our perceptions of places and bodies in ways that potentially transform relationships, when it helps reverberate the risks of technoscience for vulnerable bodies, or when it engages the embodied knowledge of vulnerable species in ways that can help recuperate marginalized voices.

Taken together, then, these cases illustrate why I favor a rhetorical approach to conceptualizing a posthuman conservation ethic. Rhetoric provides a potential means for channeling and catalyzing, potentially productively, a range of energies into configurations of ethical responsibility necessary for building worlds that do not flatten out but rather make multidimensional our relationalities with our nonhuman kin. A posthuman conservation rhetoric, working in the positive, can help recover marginalized voices by destabilizing human exceptionalism in ways that subsequently make salient the needs of otherwise less visible bodies. The paradox is that to illuminate is sometimes also to make vulnerable; this means, then, that we must act with additional care and discretion in our projects of technoscience.

A posthuman, compassionate conservation that draws on trans-corporeality and an intra-active notion of agency would then consider visual-material rhetoric from a vantage point that is also attuned to our ethical obligations for the species with whom our lives and worlds are entangled. As I have argued throughout this book, while I favor the intra-activity of agential realism, we must also be mindful not to lose sight of our ethical responsibilities to the vulnerable bodies with whom we share our worlds, and who often participate or are implicated in the enactments and configurations that constitute the emergent texts and knowledge projects of Anthropocene technoscience—vantage points that agential realism and trans-corporeality likewise accommodate. Discussions of agency are thus a critical part of theorizing a rhetoric of posthuman conservation, in which we necessarily shift our perspective from the perceived best interests and outcomes for humans and human needs, to the perceived best interests and outcomes for all the affected, vulnerable, nonhuman kin with whom we share our worlds.

To these ends, a posthuman conservation would be attentive to co-presence—mindful of the intra-actions of species, bodies, matter, spaces, institutions, in which there is no exterior authority impervious to the intra-actions that constitute world-making. It would be guided not by hierarchical mechanisms of control or transcendent systems of values but rather by a mode of thinking and acting steeped in compassion for and a sense of ethical responsibility to the worlds and bodies that are very much a part of us, and with whom we are inextricably interconnected.

Taken together, then, these cases also demonstrate that to be mindful of the lives of vulnerable others invites a more relational becoming *with*—one that has the potential to work against voyeurism and anthropocentrism to foster instead an ethic of transformation, care, and compassion.

Moreover, an aerial view of these cases depicts a trajectory that moves us incrementally closer to new directions for understanding rhetoric as pertaining not only to communication *about* animals but also to communication *with* and *from* animals. Chapter 4 perhaps moves us most explicitly in this direction, as the *Atlas* demonstrates one approach to engaging and catalyzing our curiosity about our nonhuman kin in ways that can produce new knowledge about environments and species. That said, scientific knowledge-making and environmental advocacy constitute specific contexts and exigencies for our interests in relating with other species, but they are not the only legitimate contexts and exigencies. That is, while large-scale conservation mapping projects such as the *Atlas* are invaluable to our understanding of how to engage and leverage the best interests of vulnerable marine species, we need not go big or go home in order to engage with and better understand the lives of our nonhuman kin.

What, then, might we ask, are the co- or multispecies, compassionate enactments of the mundane, of the everyday, in which rhetoric participates? Here, I return to our introductory peanut—to the curiosity it helps catalyze and to the communication it helps foster. That is, in the world of this writer, to engage with the scrub jays through the material rhetorical exchange of the peanut constitutes an enactment of care and fosters the kind of co-species communication that brings joy and meaning to otherwise precarious times. Such a realization is hardly news to scholars like Bekoff, however, who might understand such "reciprocal interactions" as part and parcel of an ethics of productive world-making:

> We owe it to all individual animals to make every attempt to come to a
> greater understanding and appreciation of who they are in their world and

in ours. We must make kind and humane choices. . . . There's nothing to fear
and much to gain by developing deep and reciprocal interactions with our
fellow animals. Animals can teach us a great deal about responsibility, compassion, caring, forgiveness, and love. (*Animal* 209)

Bekoff's comments here not only align with some of the larger arguments of
this book but also present some new considerations for understanding the role
of rhetoric in posthuman knowledge projects, and for those of us who study
rhetoric and communication and the environmental humanities. That is, we
would do well to further consider Bekoff's argument that "animals can teach
us a great deal about responsibility, compassion, caring, forgiveness, and love"
(*Animal* 209).

The scrub jays, for instance, in making known their presence each morning, communicate not only with me but with each other. They serve as look-
outs for each other, noting a safe environment or lack thereof. They let each
other know, through their consistent patterns of communication, that they
are *here*—available, interested, invested, present—and, perhaps, that their
strangely nonfeathered, human kin is available for them in these moments of
material, relational exchange. To be mindful of their patterns of communication is a worthy and necessary part of any posthuman, compassionate knowledge project—their communication about relationship is something we can
all learn from.

A recent article in *The New York Times*, "Drumming Cockatoos and the
Rhythms of Love," describes the palm cockatoo of northern Australia's use of
sticks and natural objects to "drum regular rhythms" (Yin). In doing so, they
are the only known nonhuman animal to combine the two skills of sound
production and tool use to create musical compositions (Yin). The birds presumably create these musical rhythms in order to impress potential mates, and
"even have their own signature cadences," or musical styles (Yin). The male
cockatoo typically begins its performance by fashioning a proper instrument,
either from a stick or a hard seedpod; next, he "taps a beat on his tree perch,"
sometimes adding in "a whistle or other sounds from an impressive repertoire
of around 20 syllables" (Yin). The performance includes a show of head-bob-
bing, wing-spreading, and the revealing of colorful patches of feathers, all in a
sustained attempt to impress and bond with the intended mate.

Researchers collected audio and video recordings of these cockatoos' performances over a period of seven years and analyzed 131 drumming sequences;
they found "that the birds produced regular, predictable rhythms, rather than
random thumps," and that "individual males differed significantly in percussive styles" (Yin). A rhetorically successful musical composition would then

result in courtship and breeding: "The birds sway together and gently preen each other's feathers, an act of pair-bonding that helps them prepare for breeding" (Yin).

As someone with both musical and ornithological interests, I find this example of animal communication endearing but also telling on a couple of levels, for what it both includes and excludes. First, somewhat interesting but perhaps not surprising are the study's seemingly anthropocentric underpinnings; that is, some of the study's findings are seen as providing insight into or raising questions about "whether human rhythm also originated as courtship display," and the "origin of human rhythm" more generally (Yin). The article closes by noting that if scientists can identify other nonhuman species who drum, we may come closer to uncovering answers about the origins of human rhythm. Here, we cycle back to some of chapter 3's focus on the range of potential rationales for valuing our relationships with nonhuman animals. The expressed significance of the palm cockatoo study seems to focus more on its anthropocentric implications; however, I argue that the ability of these birds to combine sound production and tool use to create unique musical composition has interest value and implications beyond that of revealing something about the origins of human rhythm and the implicitly heteronormative assumptions surrounding its potential connections to human courtship display.

That is, sticks and seedpods are not the tools of technoscience in the ways we have come to understand; they are truly the tools of the earth—elemental devices leveraged in the service of embodied knowledge-making through the agential enactments of vulnerable species. Thus, in this way, our agential accounting has shifted subtly; we may even posit that this is animal technoscience of a different agential order. However, in doing so, I also want to be cautious not to discredit the broader spectrum of the knowledge projects of technoscience, or the technologies and bodies and exigencies that enable or constrain them, for that is not at all my intention. Rather, it is through contrasting narratives that we may get a clearer sense of the range of possibilities for productive world-making that are dependent on ongoing, ever-changing configurations of contexts, exigencies, matter, and actors. This is also not to deny the presence of or possibility for ethical enactments carried out by other actors in the agential assemblage. Surely there are environmentalists working to oppose the mining industry that threatens these birds' habitats, and we may consider the fact that, if not for those biologists and other researchers who filmed the video footage of these cockatoos drumming on their tree hollows, we might not be discussing these cockatoo drummers in the first place. But given the broader context of the unique work carried out by these birds, it makes sense to cast the narrative light in such a way that decenters the human and illuminates with greater intensity the embodied knowledge-making of our ingenious, feathered kin. Such a rhetorical move seems potentially more rewarding than a framework that cycles back to questions of human exceptionalism. To attempt this more sustained focus on vulnerable nonhuman bodies then performs a variation on the theme of the broader work that this book seeks to accomplish.

That is, while insights about the palm cockatoo's musical compositions may provide insights into the origins of human rhythm, and while the study of music history and ethnomusicology are certainly worthy areas of study (it is not at all my intention to marginalize such endeavors; they are, in fact, interests of mine as well), my point is that we might think even more relationally and vibrantly about the musical, compositional talents of our feathered kin. For example, upon first reading this piece in *The New York Times,* I found myself imagining an arrangement that combines the percussive style of the palm cockatoo with, say, a piano accompaniment in the atonal tradition of Arnold Schoenberg or in the minimalist style of composer John Adams; such a project would understand knowledge about nonhuman animal lives as entangled, relational, and aesthetic rather than utilitarian or anthropocentrically informed. But we can travel further yet.

In *Flight Ways,* also referenced in chapter 2, philosopher and anthropologist Thom van Dooren draws on an ethnographic approach to compose what he calls a set of "extinction stories," a genre now characteristic of our Anthropocene times; however, he tells these stories uniquely from the perspective of "avian entanglements," or the struggles of threatened species of birds, such as the albatrosses of the Midway Atoll, the little penguins of Sydney Harbour in Australia, and the Hawaiian crow, and how these birds' lives "are woven into relationships with a diverse array of other species, including humans" (4). In his poignant chapter about the struggles of the Midway albatrosses, also set against the backdrop of the slow violence that has come to characterize the lives of these vulnerable species, van Dooren posits an ethnographically informed understanding of "species as 'flight ways'" (22). To understand species as flight ways "emphasizes the 'embodied temporality' of species . . . [and] ask[s] us to pay attention to species as evolving 'ways of life' that are shared, produced, and nurtured in the world through the work of successive generations of living beings" (22). Such an understanding is also compatible with compassionate conservation, as it "requires us to work across entirely different temporal horizons," acknowledging both the "vast evolutionary lineages stretched across millions of years" and the fragility of individual animal lives (22).

Moreover, through his focus on avian entanglements, van Dooren seeks to destabilize "human exceptionalist frameworks, prompting new kinds of questions about what extinction teaches us, how it remakes us, and what it requires of us" (5). As Haraway describes, van Dooren's narrative approach, which may also be described as a kind of multispecies ethnography, "succeeds in crafting a nonanthropomorphic, nonanthropocentric sense of storied place" (*Staying* 39). Van Dooren argues that the penguins of Sydney Harbour, for instance, have a specific relationship to place that transcends a more clinical understanding of "the ecological requirements of appropriate nesting 'habitat'" (68). This small colony of penguins returns each year to Sydney Harbour to breed and molt; however, these colonies have all but disappeared in recent years, due largely to development along this region of shoreline (64–65). Van Dooren is taken with the "image of a penguin returning to a burrow, to a breeding place, that is no longer there or has been transformed so dramatically that it is no longer habitable" (van Dooren 66). Like many such species, these birds are often at their most vulnerable when they return to their nesting sites to breed, and van Dooren is moved by the sad paradox of humans' development in littoral zones, or shoreline regions where water and land intersect, in order "to be closer to 'nature,' but in a way that makes life for penguins and other harbor dwellers impossible" (66).

Van Dooren is subsequently interested in how penguins "story" their places, or "how breeding places are rendered historical and meaningful to penguins" (68). His hope is that such accounts can help more explicitly connect the plight of vulnerable species with the plight of places likewise made vulnerable by the anthropogenic effects of climate change and overdevelopment. Such an approach reshapes human geography and anthropology's notions of sense of place and the elemental, relative to the lived, embodied experiences of nonhuman animals. Moreover, an anthropological, ethnographic approach that considers how such species "story" their places arguably intersects with new materialisms in the sense that it similarly understands materials, things, and places as the stuff of embodied communication. As van Dooren and other feminist geographers describe, place is not an abstract entity but rather is "nested and interwoven with layers of attention and meaning" (66).[1] Van Dooren likewise considers place "as a material-discursive phenomenon" (67).

The palm cockatoo, also known as the black palm cockatoo, has likewise been threatened by human development; in Australia's Cape York Peninsula, where the above-referenced study was carried out, these birds have been made vulnerable from the practices of aluminum ore mining, which poses threats to their habitat (Yin). Palm cockatoos mate for life; they can survive between forty and sixty years in the wild, and up to ninety years in captivity ("Black Palm"). The male's drumming ritual is thus not only a vital part of this species' ability to thrive but also an embodied practice that is intimately connected with place-making and relationship.

The cockatoo's selection of material from which to fashion a drumstick, the crafting of the drumstick itself from a carefully selected branch, and the actual act of drumming on the hollowed-out portion of what is often a eucalyptus tree, all have embodied consequences for embodied, relational worldmaking.[2] That is, when the male cockatoo chooses a branch from which to fashion a drumstick, he is often quite selective. As those with musical interests are aware, the type of wood used to make any instrument will greatly affect sound quality, timbre, and resonance; the cockatoo's choice of branch is no different. The male will then spend a good bit of time whittling and shaping its chosen branch into an instrument that will produce a successful tone and resonance when he drums on his carefully chosen, hollowed-out tree. The female also recognizes this exigency and will listen with interest to the male's percussion piece, in order to gauge not only the talent of her potential mate but likewise the quality of the tree itself as a potential nesting site. But this hollow is more than just a potential nesting site in the clinical, utilitarian sense; it is a venue for musical performance and the site of material, embodied place-making. In this way, the nesting site is more than a structure, more than a built form—it performs *dwelling*.

Tim Ingold's notion of dwelling, or the "dwelling perspective," draws upon and extends Heidegger's juxtaposition of building and dwelling in "Building, Dwelling, Thinking."[3] As Ingold describes, to understand a building, for instance, as architecture, is to presume more simply that "built form is the manifest outcome of prior design" (9). The notion of dwelling, on the other hand, "is intransitive: it is about the way inhabitants, singly and together, produce their own lives, and like life, it carries on. Critically, then, dwelling is not merely the occupation of structures already built: it does not stand to building as consumption to production" (10). Rather, "the forms humans build" (and here, we may easily extend the concept to forms built by nonhuman animals), "whether in the imagination or on the ground, arise within the currents of their involved activity, in the specific relational contexts of their practical engagement with their surroundings" (10). The palm cockatoo's intended dwelling, then, and the musical performance that sets the stage for that future dwelling, emerge through the embodied intra-actions of material discursive practice.[4] Moreover, I would add that to gauge suitability as a dwelling based on something as subjective and seemingly ineffable as the tonal quality that results from the application of a carefully crafted stick to the bark of a tree hollow is a fascinatingly, elementally beautiful enactment of world-making.[5] It perhaps constitutes the quintessential intra-action of bodies, material worlds, the elemental, and the affectual, ephemeral shimmers of tonality. Such an enactment, I would imagine, requires sustained, focused attention to bodies, matter, and resonance—truly the kind of attention to world-making and relationship that we can all learn from.

Finally, we may wonder, what then becomes of the drumstick, following this musical performance? In this performance of embodied world-making, no materials go to waste; as one video clip describes, when the male completes the drumming performance, he will often perch at the edge of the hollowed-out portion of the tree, "splinter up the stick, and add it to the nesting platform that's inside the hollow" ("Parrots"). Thus, the musical arrangement *is* dwelling—or conversely, dwelling *is* music. I cannot think of a more apt and beautiful approach to building a vibrant world in the face of continued threats to habitat. This is, perhaps, the ultimate enactment of unwitting, peaceful resistance; although, as I am on the edge of anthropomorphizing, I will catch myself and contend perhaps more subtly that the lively practices of these palm cockatoos illuminate, paradoxically, a truly sustainable account of nuanced, embodied practice that takes shape in the face of continued threats to their habitats and material selves. These embodied practices of world-making are something we can all learn from in our hopeful quest to become *with* our nonhuman kin as we cohabit worlds with the many species whom we ought to hold dear.

NOTES

NOTES TO THE PREFACE

1. I will acknowledge, however, following Leigh A. Bernacchi, that this narrative, while engaging with curiosity about the lived experience of the jays, is nonetheless authored by me, as human participant in this relationship, and so there perhaps enters an element of anthropomorphism, mindful as I may be of its presence as I write. That said, as chapter 2 describes in more depth, anthropomorphism is not necessarily a wholly negative enterprise, as it can often help provide a familiar frame for understanding perspectives other than our own.

Additionally, and perhaps more importantly, I recognize that to offer these jays peanuts does, on the one hand, constitute a mode of intervention into their lives, which may be perceived by some as an unbalancing of nature. On the other hand, however, as ecologist, animal behaviorist, and scholar of compassionate conservation Marc Bekoff argues: "Personal experiences with animals are essential for coming to terms with who they are" (*Animal* 68). I have given much thought over the years to the practice of feeding "backyard birds" (a term I'm also a bit uncomfortable with for its anthropocentric leanings), and those who know me would likely attest that I do not engage uncritically in any such relational practices. One of my main concerns has been that I do not want these feathered kin to become dependent on me as a food source; in this way, I subscribe to a philosophy of moderation, anchored also in the reassurance I have received from several organizations, that birds will indeed find food in our absence. (Of course, there are other places and contexts, such as at public parks, local beaches, and so on, where feeding species like ducks and pigeons presents somewhat different issues and concerns, and I am speaking here about the practice of feeding "backyard" songbirds more specifically.)

Thus, based on my reading, research, and thinking on the issue, I have come to understand my own position on feeding my songbird neighbors as aligned largely with the position articulated by the Humane Society of the United States, which, interestingly, is also aligned with one of the main tenets of compassionate conservation discussed in this book. In their helpful online article and statement, "Feeding Your Backyard Birds," the Humane Society acknowledges that "experts disagree about whether backyard bird feeding will significantly help bird populations. But feeding certainly can help individual birds in your neighborhood." The Humane Society goes on to state: "The general rule for feeding of any wild animal is: do not feed when it might cause harm." As this book will further discuss, one of the main principles underpinning compassionate conservation is likewise the principle of "do no harm" (Bekoff, *Animal*). In affirming and condoning the practice, the Humane Society subsequently provides answers to questions they commonly receive regarding best practices for how, when, and what to feed birds. Here, they note, for instance, that it is not necessary to feed birds year-round; rather, "bird feeding is most helpful at times of [year] when birds need the most energy, such as during temperature extremes, migration, and in late winter or early spring, when natural seed sources are depleted." This last point would support my observation that the jays seemed to want even more peanuts after the February 2017 storm that so impacted their hillside home, likely depleting any stashed food sources. Additionally, the California Department of Fish and Wildlife has a similar statement available online that describes best practices for feeding backyard birds. Finally, Bekoff writes, in the somewhat different but relevant context of conducting research about animals: "Perhaps researchers and others who deny animals their intelligence and rich emotional lives do so because they haven't taken the time to watch animals in situations where they can display their full repertoire of behavior" (*Animal* 69). I argue here and throughout this book that engaging with critical thought and compassion in this sort of emotional and communicative relationship not only allows for such an understanding of the jays' lived experiences, but more importantly, also allows us to live with and learn about each other in ways productive of multispecies relationships and embodied knowledge.

2. In an essay with which many of us in rhetoric and animal studies are familiar, Jacques Derrida, in "The Animal That Therefore I Am (More to Follow)," considers that moment when, emerging naked from the shower, he notices his small, domesticated house cat sitting, looking at him—watching him. Derrida recognizes in that moment that he feels shame, not only at the thought of his cat gazing upon his naked body but also, perhaps more so, he feels "ashamed for being ashamed" of his response to such a scenario (4). This realization prompts Derrida to ask the central question: "Ashamed of what and before whom?" Or, more pointedly, "Who am I, therefore?" (4–5). Here, however, Derrida's task is not so much "to answer this question as to be free of it" (Bruns 404).

Derrida questions the nature of the relationship between him and his cat, or between the human and the animal; however, as Gerald L. Bruns describes, "Derrida does not want to erase this difference but wants to multiply it in order (among other things) to affirm the absolute alterity or singularity of his cat, which cannot be subsumed by any category (such as *the* animal). His cat is an Other in a way that no human being . . . could ever be" (404). Moreover, as Donna Haraway describes in a brilliant critique of this essay that is worth reading in full, Derrida "identified the key question as being not whether the cat could 'speak' but whether it is possible to know what *respond* means and how to distinguish a response from a reaction, for human beings as well as for anyone else" (*When* 20). In doing so, on the one hand, Derrida "did not fall into the trap of making the subaltern speak"; on the other hand, however, "he did not seriously consider an alternative form of engagement either, one that risked knowing something more about cats and *how to look back,* perhaps even scientifically, biologically, and *therefore* also philosophically and intimately" (20, emphasis in original). In other words, within Derrida's more inwardly focused self-reflection was a missed opportunity. As Haraway argues, "with his cat, Derrida failed a simple obligation of companion species; he did not become curious about what the cat might actually be doing, feeling, thinking, or perhaps making available to him in looking back at him that morning. . . . Incurious, he missed a possible invitation, a possible introduction to other-worlding" (20).

On the one hand, Derrida aptly critiqued two predominant modes of representation: one that tends toward observing and writing about animals without ever meeting their gaze, and another that engages "animals only as literary and mythological figures" (21). However, Haraway argues that we ought not to stop there: "Positive knowledge of and with animals might just be possible . . . if it is not built on the Great Divides. Why did Derrida not ask, even in principle, if a Gregory Bateson or Jane Goodall or Marc Bekoff or Barbara Smuts or many others have met the gaze of living, diverse animals and in response undone themselves and their sciences?" (21). Here, Haraway argues for a more embodied communication that transcends the "writing technologies" and discursive practices with which Derrida and we are more familiar (21). With these ideas in mind, this book considers the ways that material discursive practice can help reconceptualize our relationships with our nonhuman kin in ways that can potentially enact configurations of ethical responsibility and relational, embodied knowledge that can lead to more productive world-making.

3. In many ways, the exchange of the peanut may be considered a variation on the theme of "bird-human ritual communication" that Leigh A. Bernacchi explores in "Flocking." While Bernacchi discusses more so the practice of bird watching and what it tells us "about our relationships with the more-than-human world" (158), I might add, via Bekoff (*Animal*) and Haraway (*When*), that such an exchange affords another means of embodied communicative practice in which we may learn about and with our feathered kin.

4. From the perspective of capitalist technoscience and the environmental footprint, the peanut is admittedly imperfect. A typical bag of store-bought, roasted, unsalted peanuts costs approximately $3.50 and makes its way to California from North Carolina. That said, bulk produce and more local food collectives provide additional resources that, while not a panacea, help offset such costs in other ways. To consider the intra-actions of the peanut then provides the stuff of another agential realist account—one that is beyond the scope of the current narrative but perhaps within that of future research. Here, I am reminded also of Deborah Barndt's *Tangled Routes*.

5. This book in many ways represents an extension of my earlier conceptualizations of a visual-material, posthuman environmental rhetoric. That is, writing in 2012, toward the close of *Locating Visual-Material Rhetorics,* I had considered the capabilities and the limitations of the map as text to help advocate for marine mammal species who were unable to be literally present in the setting of a federal court case about the deployment and impacts of low-frequency active sonar but who would be impacted by the outcome nonetheless. I argued that

> affected bodies need not be physically present in the setting of the debate and that visual-material rhetorical artifacts can work to advocate for bodies that might not otherwise be able to advocate for themselves. In other words, the map can function as an advocacy tool that helps protect those who cannot convey firsthand the impact of the debate on their [lives and] bodies, but who shoulder the consequences of the debate nonetheless. (183)

At the same time, I argued then that the visual-material rhetoric of the map, for instance, may also inadvertently continue to perpetuate dichotomized ways of knowing, or human/nonhuman binaries, and as such, may "foreclose possibilities of more embodied ways of knowing" (184). I speculated then, and I argue here, now, that what we need moving forward is a visual-material rhetoric that is also explicitly aligned with posthuman rhetorics in a way that, as Brooke has put it, would allow us to turn our backs on omniscience and the humanist values of mastery and control (791). When considered also in light of conservation and environmental policy, it would consider a posthuman understanding of such practices in ways that likewise eschew human control of the environment and operate in ways more attuned to a compassionate, posthuman conservation ethic.

NOTES TO CHAPTER 1

1. When I refer throughout this book to "world-making," I am drawing broadly on and extending the Heideggerian notion of "worlding" described in *Being and Time* (2008). Here, Heidegger takes the noun "world" and uses it as an active verb, to describe the idea of our "being in the world" in a way that also speaks to our sense of belonging, and even, as I take it, to our potential sense of responsibility to the world and to place-making: "Being in a world is something that belongs essentially. Thus Dasein's understanding of Being pertains with equal primordiality both to an understanding of something like a 'world,' and to the understanding of the Being of those entities which become accessible within the world" (33). I appreciate this definition for its flexibility and its responsiveness to the always ongoing, shifting contexts that constitute and characterize our potential for being in and becoming *with* the world, and the opportunities for participating in world-making that such being in and becoming *with* afford. World-making also aligns with new and vital materialisms in its understanding of things as implicated in the world's becoming—in its relating of "worlding" to things, or to "thinging." Thus, "worlding and thinging are inextricably intertwined, for without things that thing, there is no worlding—the thinging of the thing is the worlding of the world" ("Worlding").

Moreover, not dissimilar from the workings of Bennett's agential assemblage, Heidegger emphasizes that "worlding is not of our own making, but rather a matter of responsiveness to particular things" ("Worlding"). When we consider these ideas in the context of new materialist thought, we may understand world-making as bound up in and performing the intra-actions of worlds, bodies, matter, and ecosystems, such that world-making and the potential for ethical responsibility that it may configure does not fall solely within the purview of human action but is rather part of the broader, ongoing intra-actions that constitute material discursive practice. In this way, I understand world-making as knowledge-making, and knowledge-making as world-making.

2. Davis critiques gynocentrism, which argues for the privileging of feminist ideology over the logocentric frameworks that privilege and perpetuate masculinist, hegemonic binaries. On the one hand, gynocentrism is "successful as a negative deconstruction—a strategy that sets the privilege in motion, that keeps it shuffling back and forth," but on the other hand, "flipping the privilege only perpetuates the logocentric structure itself. . . . It's the either/or structure itself that promotes phallocracy" (137).

3. Stormer and McGreavy interestingly and clearly organize their article around "three interrelated transitions from agency to capacity, violence to vulnerability, and recalcitrance to resilience" (3). While this book does not follow their precise framework, per se, it aligns with their broader arguments about the value of "emphasizing the ecology of entanglements between entities over the abilities that are inherent to humans" (5). The organizational and rhetorical moves they make, such as the more explicit separation of "capacity from agency," work well to help interrogate the assumption, for instance, that "human limits define rhetorical limits" (5). Thus, their article has been instrumental in my own thinking about agency in conceptualizing this book.

4. See chapter 3, note 8 for further discussion of Alaimo's notion of the material memoir and its relevance for visual-material rhetorics.

5. For a more detailed exposition of some individual, earlier studies in material rhetoric, see chapter 2 of my *Locating Visual-Material Rhetorics*.

6. In this understanding, compassionate conservation's tenet of "first, do no harm," not wholly unlike its usage in medical ethics frameworks, is not necessarily about blame so much as it is about advocating for vulnerable bodies. The organization Compassionate Conservation also cites some additional principles, which arose out of the 2010 Oxford symposium of the same name. These principles are as follows:

> Recognis[e] that wild animals, whether free-ranging or in captivity, may be affected by the intentional or unintentional actions of humans as well as the natural processes within ecosystems and the wider environment. . . . Recognis[e] that both conservation and wild animal welfare should implicitly respect the inherent value of wild animals and the natural world, and that both disciplines should try to mitigate harms caused by humans to other species. . . . Believ[e] that all harms to wild animals should be minimised wherever and to the extent possible, regardless of the human intention and purpose behind them. . . . Propos[e] that the principles and actions that underpin Compassionate Conservation, by combining consideration of animal welfare and conservation, will lead to a reduction in harm and in the suffering of individual wild animals, and will improve conservation outcomes. ("Compassionate Conservation Guiding Principles")

7. I would be remiss not to note that the writing of this book has also prompted me to consider my own assumptions about what it means to protect species or intervene in ways that I would typically understand as helpful or innocuous. This is not to say that I no longer consider such interventions into or engagements with the lives of nonhuman animals as potentially purposeful or at times helpful (such as the practice of putting out backyard bird feeders, or assisting injured wildlife—two different but generally well-intended human interventions), but rather that I proceed from an even more critical awareness about how my actions participate in the broader configuration of worldly experiences from multiple perspectives.

8. Some thoughts about mediation: Drawing on the work of Don Idhe and Merleau-Ponty, Haraway suggests that technologies are not necessarily mediations or interfaces but rather "infoldings," and instead refers to the notion of *infolding* "to suggest the dance of world-making encounters. What happens in the folds is what is important. Infoldings of the flesh are worldly embodiment" (*When* 250). While I certainly appreciate the term "infolding" to help get at the entanglement of bodies in and with technologies, I do not explicitly employ it here, as I feel that Braidotti's understanding of a posthuman "co-presence," as well as Barad's agential realism, coupled with her notion of posthuman performativity (*Meeting*), allow us to thoughtfully interrogate the linkages between human, nonhuman animal, and technologies in creative and nonreductive ways.

    More specifically, it is also interesting to note that Haraway and Barad move away from using the term "mediation." Both seem to view mediation as on par with the idea of discrete borders, or interfaces that imply a kind of divide that may prevent or provide access to worlds. I certainly understand these points. However, I think of mediation subtly differently, as an ongoing process that can open the door to the posthuman "betweenness" that Boyle ("Writing") describes—as inviting what Latour (*We Have*) describes as more integrated hybrids or composites—as participating in the practices of embodiment, as blurring and making malleable the borders that perhaps once made salient the contours of subject and object but, as with posthumanism, now make them indistinguishable. Likewise, I do not necessarily think of mediation as *only* complicating the shared spaces of the technological interface, but also, more fluidly and broadly, as participating in a range of trans-corporeal, material encounters (Alaimo, *Bodily*) and as bearing the potential to shape and co-construct embodied knowledge across a range of spaces, contexts, species, bodies, and worlds. I see mediation as aligned with embodiment, as a colleague of posthumanism, and as participating in the sort of knowledge-making whereby humans, nonhuman animals, and their environments mutually constitute each other. Such an understanding can then help shape more productive dialogues and participate in the ongoing building of worlds. Thus, I see mediation as helping to blur divides and as further allowing for an understanding of bodies and worlds not as boundaried objects but as material discursive phenomena. In other words, such an entangled mediation, when understood as blended into posthuman, material discursive practice, can function in this more holistic sense.

NOTES TO CHAPTER 2

1. Statistics about the amount of plastic consumed annually versus the amount recycled are staggering: "Americans discard about 33.6 million tons of plastic each year, but only 6.5 percent of it is recycled and 7.7 percent is combusted in waste-to-energy facilities, which create electricity or heat from garbage" (Cho). Nonrecycled plastic winds up in landfills, "where it may take up to 1,000 years to decompose, and potentially leak pollutants into the soil and water. It's estimated that there are also 100 million tons of plastic debris floating around in the oceans threatening the health and safety of marine life." Moreover, it is difficult and labor-intensive to separate plastics from nonplastics during processes of recycling, "and so far, there has been no easy solution" (Cho).

2. To view the series *Midway: Message from the Gyre,* and to learn more about Jordan's work, see www.chrisjordan.com.

3. One CNN article, for example, featured a short video segment from a longer CNN documentary, in which a journalist walked with a park ranger on Midway Island. The video begins with the park ranger stating to the journalist: "Every single albatross that you see across this landscape has been fed plastic" (Paton Walsh). The ranger then proceeds to cut open the corpse of a dead albatross, revealing a body riddled with plastic bottle caps and other small plastic objects. The video clip eventually shows President Obama giving an address about his designation of the MPA, in which he states: "Tomorrow I'm going to go to Midway, to visit the vast marine area that we just created" (Paton Walsh). In touring Midway Island, "Obama pledged to ensure 'not only that Midway itself is protected, that the entire ecosystem will be able to generate the kind of biodiversity that allows us to study it, research and understand our oceans better than we ever have before'" (Thompson).

4. On the one hand, I believe that the setting aside of land for marine protected areas and other parks-related projects is not to be undervalued in an age where human intervention can adversely impact the physical environment; however, cordoning off or creating boundaried spaces is not the only solution to our environmental crises, nor is such provisioning impervious to neoliberalist critique. That said, this analysis does not in any way seek to disparage the creation of MPAs and its related environmental policy work; rather, it argues that any provisioning of MPAs or similar policy should, whenever possible, take into account the cultures, perspectives, and livelihoods of indigenous cultures and other less mainstream knowledge-making practices and traditions.

I would also add that it is important to consider the subtle distinctions between the notions of "advocacy" and "rescue," or the potentially problematic neoliberalist notion that environmental policy can "rescue" places and species. Here, I am grateful to my colleague Linda Adler-Kassner, who, in a related conversation about environmental rhetoric and writing studies, suggested, and here I paraphrase, that *advocacy is about an interest in the insides of things,* that advocacy happens *from principle,* that advocacy is rightly about points of connection—about *kinship.* For a more formal discussion of these ideas, please see the "CCCC Chair's Address: Because Writing is Never Just Writing" (Adler-Kassner).

5. In its early iterations, this documentary film was called *Midway: Message from the Gyre.* Interestingly, early descriptions of the film similarly described "the albatross as a mirror of our humanity" (CDS Porch; see also Green Planet Films Blog).

6. In *Plastic Ocean,* Captain John Moore describes what is credited as his discovery of the "Great Pacific Garbage Patch" (Moore and Phillips). In this region of the Pacific Ocean, bits of microscopic plastic and larger plastic debris collect and circulate within a large system of rotating ocean currents called the North Pacific gyre (Smithsonian).

7. For additional scholarship that theorizes the discursive work of representing deceased animals and animal deaths in more everyday contexts, settings, and images, see Michael; Zertuche.

8. For a brief but thorough history of the feather trade, see Weeks.

9. Van Dooren's *Flight Ways* is worth reading in full for its beautiful and nuanced example of what Haraway refers to as multispecies ethnography. Van Dooren's work comprises a set of "extinction stories" told from the vantage point of the slow violence of "avian entanglements" (4). I further discuss his work in chapter 5.

10. Incidentally, with this statement Barad also encapsulates decades of debate within the field of cartography about whether cartographic practice reveals objective "truths" about the "real" world, versus whether mapping posits culturally constructed representations of the environment. Thus, the idea that scientific knowledge and visual representation reflect accurate models of "reality" has been critiqued for decades by scholars of feminist science studies, feminist geography, critical cartography, and the like. Critical cartographers and feminist geographers have long cautioned against understanding geographic information science (GIS) as merely a positivist endeavor or value-neutral tool with which we may produce "real" models of the environment (see especially Cosgrove, *Apollo* and "Introduction"; Crampton; Harley; Propen, "Cartographic" and "Critical"; and Schuurman). For further discussion of cartographic practice as embodied knowledge, see my "Cartographic."

11. Haraway makes these comments about grief in the context of van Dooren's chapter, "Mourning Crows: Grief in a Shared World," which uses a multispecies ethnographic approach to explore the ways that Hawaiian crows "mourn for the deaths of others of their kind" (van Dooren 125). Van Dooren argues that paying attention to how crows mourn "enables us to understand a little better the experiential world that Hawaii's crows inhabit. In doing so, we gain a 'thicker' sense of who these creatures might be, but also of what is being lost in their disappearance" (137). As Haraway adds, for van Dooren, "mourning is intrinsic to cultivating response-ability. . . . Outside the dubious privileges of human exceptionalism, thinking people must learn to grieve-with" (*Staying* 38).

12. For additional scholarship that considers animal representations as "hauntings," especially in popular culture-oriented images, see Zertuche. I should note that my primary interest in Ballif's analysis of mourning "the other—as *other*" and the paradox of the specter (462, emphasis in original) is not necessarily in the notion of the image as haunted, per se, but even more so in its related exposition of Derrida's notion of the "haptic eye," which I invoke and extend not only in ways that apply it to Marks's "haptic image" but also, ultimately, in terms of its ability to enable the sort of grieving *with,* via Haraway (*Staying*), that can potentially open the door to more productive knowledge-making and world-making.

NOTES TO CHAPTER 3

1. This chapter will focus on the debates about marine species protection primarily as they pertain to the California sea otter; my decision here is reflective of media articles about the debate as well as the generally long-standing view of the sea otter as a keystone species within California. Additionally, the California sea otter is sometimes referred to as

the southern sea otter, although, for the sake of clarity, I refer to the species only as the "California sea otter" within this book. Moreover, it may be of interest to some that within the United States, there are two subspecies of sea otter: "the Northern sea otter (Enhydra lutris kenyoni) and the Southern sea otter (Enhydra lutris nereis). Northern sea otters are found in the Aleutian Islands, Southern Alaska, British Columbia, and Washington. Southern sea otters, also known as California sea otters, live in the waters along the California coastline and range from San Mateo County in the north to Santa Barbara County in the south" (Defenders of Wildlife).

2. PG&E did eventually complete their seismic study in 2014, after adjusting its testing methods to forego the controversial high-energy offshore surveys, and ultimately concluded that the Diablo Canyon plant was seismically safe (see Sneed, "Diablo Canyon"; D. Baker). PG&E did not conduct the high-energy offshore surveys that were considered controversial and for which the California Coastal Commission had earlier denied permits on the grounds that they "had not done enough to protect marine wildlife from the extremely loud blasts of sound" (Sneed, "Diablo Canyon"). However, as one PG&E official described in a *San Luis Obispo Tribune* article, "The fact that the high-energy surveys were not conducted did not diminish the overall conclusions of the study. . . . Seismologists were able to fill in the gaps from the missing high-energy data using data from the low-energy surveys was well as data from the U.S. Geological Survey and other sources" (Sneed, "Diablo Canyon"). The NRC determined in late 2015 after reviewing PG&E's study that it could "be used to perform the next phase of the agency's regulatory process," which they anticipated to be completed by September 2016. (Charlton).

3. I am understanding the practices of "tracking" and "monitoring" differently here. When I refer to tracking, I am referring to the practice of using a GPS-type device to literally track the physical movements and possibly the biological changes of species like the California sea otter. When I refer to the practice of monitoring species, I am referring more broadly to a range of possible practices whose goal is to watch for changes in species behavior, but that might not necessarily involve the more intrusive physical implantation or attachment of GPS-like devices. Such monitoring practices, as they were described in PG&E's mitigation plans, may involve human spotters or observers on board research vessels to alert researchers if marine mammals are in the vicinity during seismic tests. Or, they may involve aerial observations, or acoustic or beach monitoring, also to discern the location of marine mammals to watch for any behavioral changes or signs of stress during seismic testing.

4. My goal in this chapter is to describe the tests and mitigation measures such that readers have details sufficient enough to understand the main tenets of the debate as they pertain to larger arguments and questions about the connections between visual-material environmental rhetorics and compassionate conservation and human/nonhuman animal relationships; however, myriad information exists regarding the specifics of the proposed tests and mitigation measures. While it is beyond the scope and need of this chapter to review or analyze all of those documents, readers interested in obtaining additional information on the issue should visit in particular PG&E's Web pages "Seismic Safety and Advanced Seismic Testing," at https://pge.com/myhome/edusafety/systemworks/dcpp/seismic/3D.shtml, and "Seismic and Tsunami Safety at Diablo Canyon," at https://www.pge.com/en_US/safety/how-the-system-works/diablo-canyon-power-plant/seismic-safety-at-diablo-canyon/seismic-safety-at-diablo-canyon.page.

5. More recently, on June 21, 2016, PG& E announced in a press release that Diablo Canyon will be shut down by 2025, that it will not pursue relicensing with the NRC (Sneed, "PG&E Agrees"), and that the plant's energy-generating capacity will be replaced with more cost-efficient and sustainable energy sources (see PG&E, "In Step").

6. Federal protections for sea otters are handled by the U.S. Fish and Wildlife Service, which works with the U.S. Geological Survey (USGS); both are bureaus of the U.S. Department of the Interior. Protections for harbor porpoises are overseen by the National Marine Fisheries Service (NMFS) (Sneed, "Nearly"). The NMFS is an office of the National Oceanic and Atmospheric Administration (NOAA); thus, the NMFS is sometimes referred to as NOAA Fisheries (NOAA Fisheries).

7. It is interesting to note that Surfrider employs the term "ocean users" to refer here to human users of the ocean ("Opposition" 2). We might speculate that this usage reflects the main focus of their mission on "the protection and enjoyment of the world's ocean, waves and beaches," which, while attentive to the welfare of marine species, is also concerned with human use of the ocean (Surfrider Foundation, "Our Mission").

8. For a wonderful conceptualization and analysis of material memoirs, see especially chapter 4 of Alaimo's *Bodily Natures*. Inspired by Audre Lorde's *Cancer Journals*, Alaimo develops the idea of the "material memoir" to describe the body's enmeshment in "power structures that have real material effects" (*Bodily* 86). She understands material memoirs as implicitly aligned with constructs of risk, as emphasizing that "personal experience cannot be directly reckoned with, not only because discourse shapes experience, but also because an understanding of the self as a material, trans-corporeal, and always emergent entity often demands the specialized knowledges of science" (86). Material memoirs thus provide "new ways of knowing our bodies and our selves," and the concept arguably has productive implications for rhetorics of health and medicine (86).

   In this book, I do not use the concept of material memoir in quite the same way that Alaimo might intend; however, I do see some interesting analogues for how we might understand, say, photography as a variation on the theme, as well as the emergent texts associated with the seismic testing debate as described in this chapter. That is, I think Alaimo's concept allows for an acknowledgment of how visual-material artifacts allow us to consider not only our role in the agential assemblage but also what ethical obligation might entail and look like, as well as questions of what it means to act ethically in worlds that are always already emerging, and in which we are always already immersed.

9. The local commercial fishing industry seems to have had the most extrinsically focused concerns about the seismic testing, and understandably so, given the potential impacts of the testing on the economy and their livelihood. The San Luis Obispo County Board of Supervisors, in response, wanted "its commercial fishing industry compensated for economic hardships created by the testing" (Cuddy). A representative from PG&E's external communications office had stated at the time "that the utility is in discussions with local commercial fishing interests to find a 'fair and equitable compensation' for economic disruptions during the time the seismic testing takes place" (Cuddy). A mediator was eventually brought in to help work out a compromise between local fishing industries and PG&E (Lambert). For more information related to that sub-debate, see Sneed, "Offshore."

10. Environment in the Public Interest (EPI) is known in San Luis Obispo as "the San Luis Obispo Coastkeeper." As their website describes, they are "a 501(c)(3) organization providing educational, scientific and technical support services with a primary mission to advocate the public interest in preserving habitat and biodiversity" (Hensley, "San Luis"). Finally, please note that the website containing material from Coastkeeper's position statement, as quoted in this chapter, is no longer active; however, readers may get a sense of Coastkeeper's mission by visiting their website at http://www.epicenteronline.org/.

11. Again, please note that the website that originally contained the position statements from the organizations Mothers for Peace, The Sierra Club, and Coastkeeper, called *The Rock: Celebrating Ten Years of Guarding the Central Coast*, is no longer active. However, readers may still get a sense of these organizations' stances on seismic testing more generally by visiting each of their respective websites.

12. The concept of a "keystone species" has nuanced definitions within ecology and biology. For the purposes of this discussion and this chapter, I understand the concept as it is generally currently understood, as referring to any "influential species" that have "great influence over their environment." As a result, keystone species are "sometimes singled out for protection," with the rationale that protecting a keystone species also serves the larger purpose of maintaining the ecosystem" (MacDonald). Sea otters specifically help protect kelp forest habitats by feeding heavily on sea urchins that would otherwise take over and reduce kelp forest ecosystems. Moreover, sea otters serve as sentinel or indicator species because of their tendency to come within close contact to pollutants like petroleum, which they are highly susceptible to, given its potential for compromising their fur's ability to maintain proper insulation. They also consume "approximately 25% of their body weight per day in shellfish and other invertebrates, and can concentrate and integrate chemical contaminants which may be directly toxic and/or alter their fur's insulating properties" (Jessup et al. 239).

13. In October 2012, according to a veterinarian and sea otter specialist at the Monterey Bay Aquarium, "47 otters in the Morro Bay area were outfitted with VHF [very high frequency] tags for daily monitoring" (Devitt). Tagging otters is a more invasive process that involves the capture, anesthetizing, and surgical implantation of locator devices. With porpoises, whales, and other pinnipeds, the process can be less intrusive, as discussed more in chapter 4. For an in-depth, interdisciplinary history of tracking and telemetry in wildlife management, see Benson.

NOTES TO CHAPTER 4

1. The field of animal studies may be defined as "the interdisciplinary study of the relationship between humans and other animals" ("Animal Studies"). Broadly construed, such explorations may focus on questions of animal rights, the function of anthropocentrism in humans' conceptualizations of the use or value of nonhuman species in society, or the ways in which anthropomorphism shapes our understandings of human/nonhuman animal relationships, among, of course, many other possibilities. For a highly comprehensive reading list, see Kalof, Bryant, and Fitzgerald.

2. Critical cartography, often considered a contemporary subdiscipline of cartographic studies, understands geographic knowledge as reflective of cultural contexts and power relations (Crampton and Krygier 11). Many scholars who study critical cartography also explicitly understand mapping as a rhetorical practice that emphasizes the "discursive power of the medium, stressing deconstruction, and the social and cultural work that cartography achieves" (Kitchin, Perkins, and Dodge 3–4).

3. For a more detailed discussion and analysis of Foucault's six principles of heterotopology, see chapter 2 of *Locating Visual-Material Rhetorics*.

4. Readers may view this photo by visiting http://atlas-marpatagonico.org/species/8/wandering-albatross.htm.

5. It is important to provide a brief clarification about place names. The *Atlas* uses a South American, Argentinean perspective when referring to locations in the Patagonian Sea region. The Island of South Georgia, for example, from a North American perspective, is more commonly known as the British Overseas Territory of South Georgia and the Sandwich Islands. Moreover, the *Atlas* is available in both English and Spanish (the site's home page allows viewers to choose between English and Spanish versions), and many of the downloadable maps in the *Atlas* include captions with both English and Spanish translations, and often refer to place names in Spanish (e.g., Is. Georgias del Sur). In this chapter, I use the South American, English-language version of the place name (Island of South

Georgia), except when quoting directly from a map that notes the place name in Spanish (Is. Georgias del Sur).

6. For more detailed discussion of the history of wildlife telemetry, see Benson's important work, *Wired Wilderness,* which chronicles the history of wildlife radio telemetry over the past several decades and its implications for knowledge-making across disciplines such as wildlife biology, environmental studies, and the history of science and technology. Of specific interest to this chapter is his discussion of the evolution of radio-tagging practices and their relevance for the tracking of marine species—an endeavor made more difficult by the often "harsh and inaccessible" environments in which many such species live (139).

   Throughout the 1970s and 1980s, research in this area proceeded, due largely to perspectives among biologists and government agencies that tracking technologies had "'special merit' for understanding the migrations of whales and the relationships between different populations of the same species" (144). At the same time, animal protectionist groups voiced concern over the philosophical implications of wildlife management and the levels of human intervention required by monitoring wildlife and marine species specifically. In 1972, President Nixon signed the Marine Mammal Protection Act (MMPA) into law, which established "a blanket moratorium on the take of marine mammals, where 'take' was defined as harassment, injury, or killing" (147). The MMPA also put in place a "system of permits and waivers that would allow such take to continue for a variety of reasons, including scientific research" (148). As Benson describes, the passage of the MMPA "was only the beginning of a longrunning struggle over its implementation," one that continues today (148). Questions over what counts as "benign" research related to marine mammal populations continued, and at the 1983 Global Conference on the Non-Consumptive Utilization of Cetacean Resources, "benign research" came to be defined by conference participants as "research that does not depend on the human-caused death of wild animals nor involve significant stress or injury to them"; this definition was understood as allowing for the use of "aerial photography, radio tracking, visual camera scanning, listening to whale sounds, and satellite telemetry" (162). Some conference attendees challenged these definitions, arguing that framing "the relationship between humans and cetaceans" as one involving "use" was problematic to begin with (162). Of course, questions about the attitudes constituting humans' relationships with and valuing of nonhuman animals remain in the foreground of many conservationist research programs today.

7. I learned of some of these details from the researchers, when they guided me toward the helpful article by Campagna et al. I am very grateful for these clarifications.

NOTES TO CHAPTER 5

1. Feminist and human geography have long been concerned with "sense of place," which would understand place as constituted by contextual relations and embodied knowledge as opposed to the enactments of boundaries or exclusionary practices (McDowell and Sharp 201; see also Massey).

2. Palm cockatoos may be referred to as "hollow nesters," meaning they prefer to nest in hollow-bearing trees. They prefer living trees and often take up residence in "Darwin stringybark *Eucalyptus tetrodonta*" (Rowland 2; for more information on their habitat preferences and nesting practices, also see Rowland).

3. Ingold draws on Heidegger's essay "Building, Dwelling, Thinking" (in *Poetry, Language, Thought*), in which Heidegger likewise opposes buildings and structures to the notion of "dwelling," in order to recover what he feels is the more fundamental meaning of dwelling, as referring to "being, encompassing the entire way in which one lives one's life on earth" (Ingold 10). As Heidegger writes, which Ingold also recounts, the German verb *bauen,* "to build, is really to dwell; it also gives us a clue as to how we think about the dwelling it sig-

nifies. . . . I dwell, you dwell. The way in which you *are* and I am, the manner in which we humans *are* on the earth, is *Buan,* dwelling. To be a human being means to be on the earth as a mortal. It means to dwell" (Heidegger, *Poetry* 145, emphasis in original). Thus, building is not logically prior to dwelling, nor does dwelling determine the designs implemented through building (Ingold 10). Rather, they are somewhat co-constituted, or, as Heidegger writes, "dwelling and building are related as end and means" (*Poetry* 144). These ideas then inform what Ingold calls the "dwelling perspective" (10), which I invoke and extend in this chapter, also following van Dooren, to understand the ways that nonhuman animals also dwell.

4. The concept of "dwelling" has clear implications for medical rhetorics as well. As Teston describes, for instance, to "dwell with disease is to be radically present and attuned to spatial and temporal contingencies of constantly changing phenomena" (*Bodies* 175).

5. While I do not claim expertise about the specific resonances of tree bark (although this analysis has further piqued my interest), initial reading suggests, not surprisingly, that the female can intuit something about the quality of the potential nest site based on the quality of the sonic reverberations of the percussive performance, if you will. For further research, see "Palm Cockatoos"; "Black Palm Cockatoo"; Rowland; Zingsheim.

WORKS CITED

Adler-Kassner, Linda. "CCCC Chair's Address: Because Writing is Never Just Writing." *College Composition and Communication* 69.2 (2017): 317–40. Print.

Alaimo, Stacy. *Bodily Natures: Science, Environment, and the Material Self.* Bloomington: Indiana UP, 2010. Print.

———. *Exposed: Environmental Politics and Pleasures in Posthuman Times.* Minneapolis: U of Minnesota P, 2016. Print.

Anderson, Jennifer. "Audubon to File Suit over Bird 'Slaughter.'" *Portland Tribune* 31 Mar. 2015. Web. 18 June 2016.

"Animal Studies at Michigan State University." Michigan State University, 2011. Web. May 2011. <http://www.animalstudies.msu.edu/>.

Baker, David R. "PG&E: Diablo Canyon Nuclear Plant Can Withstand 10,000-Year Quake." *SFGate.com* 12 Mar. 2015. Web. 29 Oct. 2017. <http://www.sfgate.com/news/article/PG-E-Diablo-Canyon-nuclear-plant-can-withstand-6131396.php>.

Baker, Steve. "'They're There, and That's How We're Seeing It': Olly and Suzi in the Antarctic." *Ecosee: Image, Rhetoric, Nature.* Ed. Sidney I. Dobrin and Sean Morey. Albany: State U of New York P, 2009. 153–68. Print.

Ballif, Michelle. "Regarding the Dead." *Philosophy and Rhetoric.* 47.4 (2014): 455–71. Print.

Barad, Karen. "Invertebrate Visions: Diffractions of the Brittlestar." *The Multispecies Salon.* Ed. Eben Kirksey. Durham: Duke UP, 2014. 221–41. Print.

———. *Meeting the Universe Halfway: Quantum Physics and the Entanglement of Matter and Meaning.* Durham: Duke UP, 2007. Print.

Barndt, Deborah. *Tangled Routes: Women, Work, and Globalization on the Tomato Trail.* Lanham: Rowman & Littlefield, 2007. Print.

Barnett, Cynthia. "Hawaii Is Now Home to an Ocean Reserve Twice the Size of Texas." *National Geographic* 26 Aug. 2016. Web. 31 Mar. 2017. <http://news.nationalgeographic.com/2016/08/obama-creates-world-s-largest-park-off-hawaii/>.

Barnett, Scot, and Casey Boyle. "Introduction: Rhetorical Ontology, or, How to Do Things with Things." *Rhetoric, Through Everyday Things.* Ed. Scot Barnett and Casey Boyle. Tuscaloosa: U of Alabama P, 2016. 1–14. Print.

Barthes, Roland. *Camera Lucida: Reflections on Photography.* Trans. Richard Howard. New York: Hill and Wang, 1981. Print.

Beck, Ulrich. "Risk Society Revisited: Theory, Politics and Research Programs." *The Risk Society and Beyond: Critical Issues for Social Theory.* Ed. Barbara Adam, Ulrich Beck, and Joost Van Loon. London: Sage, 2000. 211–29. Print.

———. "The Terrorist Threat: World Risk Society Revisited." *Theory, Culture & Society* 19 (2002): 39–55. Print.

Bekoff, Marc. *The Animal Manifesto: Six Reasons for Expanding Our Compassion Footprint.* Novato: New World Library, 2010. Print.

———. *Rewilding Our Hearts: Building Pathways of Compassion and Coexistence.* Novato: New World Library, 2014. Print.

Bennett, Jane. "The Force of Things: Steps toward an Ecology of Matter." *Political Theory* 32.3 (2004): 347–72. Print.

———. "Systems and Things: On Vital Materialism and Object-Oriented Philosophy." *The Nonhuman Turn.* Ed. Richard Grusin. Minneapolis: U of Minnesota P, 2015. 223–39. Print.

———. *Vibrant Matter: A Political Ecology of Things.* Durham: Duke UP, 2010. Print.

Benson, Etienne. *Wired Wilderness: Technologies of Tracking and the Making of Modern Wildlife.* Baltimore: Johns Hopkins UP, 2010. Print.

Bernacchi, Leigh A. "Flocking: Bird-Human Ritual Communication." *Perspectives on Human-Animal Communication: Internatural Communication.* Ed. Emily Plec. New York: Routledge, 2013. 142–61. Print.

Biesecker, Barbara A. "Remembering World War II: The Rhetoric and Politics of National Commemoration at the Turn of the 21st Century." *Visual Rhetoric: A Reader in Communication and American Culture.* Ed. Lester C. Olson, Cara A. Finnegan, and Diane S. Hope. Newbury Park: Sage, 2008. 157–74. Print.

"Black Palm Cockatoo." *Singing Wings Aviary* 2017. Web. 5 July 2017. <http://www.singing-wings-aviary.com/black-palm-cockatoo.htm>.

Blair, Carole. "Contemporary U.S. Memorial Sites as Exemplars of Rhetoric's Materiality." *Rhetorical Bodies.* Ed. Jack Selzer and Sharon Crowley. Madison: U of Wisconsin P, 1999. 16–57. Print.

Boyle, Casey. "Pervasive Citizenship through #SenseCommons." *Rhetoric Society Quarterly* 46.3 (2016): 269–83. Print.

———. "Writing and Rhetoric and/as Posthuman Practice." *College English* 78.6 (2016): 532–54. Print.

Braidotti, Rosi. *The Posthuman.* Malden: Polity, 2013. Print.

Brooke, Collin Gifford. "Forgetting to be (Post)Human: Media and Memory in a Kairotic Age." *JAC* 20.4 (2000): 775–95. Print.

Brouwer, Dan. "The Precarious Visibility Politics of Self-Stigmatization: The Case of HIV/AIDS Tattoos." *Visual Rhetoric: A Reader in Communication and American Culture.* Ed. Lester C. Olson, Cara A. Finnegan, and Diane S. Hope. Newbury Park: Sage, 2008. 205–26. Print.

Bruns, Gerald L. "Derrida's Cat (Who Am I)?" *Research in Phenomenology* 38 (2008): 404–23. Print.

Bullock, Marcus. "Watching Eyes, Seeing Dreams, Knowing Lives." *Representing Animals.* Ed. Nigel Rothfels. Bloomington: Indiana UP, 2002: 99–118. Print.

Butler, Judith. *Precarious Life: The Powers of Mourning and Violence.* New York: Verso, 2004. Print.

CalCoast News. "Diablo Canyon Nuclear Power Plant Temporary Shut Down." *CalCoast News* 26 Apr. 2012. Web. 21 June 2014.

California Coastal Commission. "Offshore Seismic Survey Project Background Materials." 2012. Web. 29 Oct. 2017. <https://www.coastal.ca.gov/energy/seismic/seismic-survey.html>.

California Department of Fish and Wildlife. "Keep Wild Birds Safe: Tips for Backyard Wild Bird Feeders." Cordova: Wildlife Investigations Lab, California Department of Fish and Wildlife, 2017. Web. 10 July 2017. <https://www.wildlife.ca.gov/Conservation/Laboratories/Wildlife-Investigations/Monitoring/Avian-Influenza/Wild-Bird>.

Campagna, Claudio, et al. "Deep Divers in Shallow Seas: Southern Elephant Seals on the Patagonian Shelf." *Deep Sea Research Part I: Oceanographic Research Papers* 54 (2007): 1792–814. Print.

CDS Porch. "Environmental Artist Chris Jordan a Featured Guest at This Year's Duke Arts Festival, October 30 & 31." Ctr. for Documentary Studies at Duke U, 16 Oct. 2013. Web. 14 Nov. 2017. <http://www.cdsporch.org/archives/20443>.

Chappell, Bill. "Signs of Hope at Oroville Dam, After Overflow Sparked Large Evacuation Sunday." *National Public Radio.* Natl. Public Radio, 13 Feb. 2017. Web. 28 June 2017. <http://www.npr.org/sections/thetwo-way/2017/02/13/514955209/signs-of-hope-at-oroville-dam-after-water-overflowed-emergency-spillway>.

Charlton, April. "NRC Completes Prelim Review of Seismic Study for Diablo Canyon." *Santa Maria Times* 1 Feb. 2016. Web. 23 June 2016. <http://santamariatimes.com/news/local/nrc-completes-prelim-review-of-seismic-study-for-diablo-canyon/article_bf5408ff-1384–538b-96e5–4391cd1763df.html>.

Cho, Renee. "What Happens to All That Plastic?" *State of the Planet.* Earth Institute: Columbia University, 31 Jan. 2012. Web. 25 Apr. 2017. <http://blogs.ei.columbia.edu/2012/01/31/what-happens-to-all-that-plastic/>.

Christie, Andrew. "Position Statement." From "Environmental Groups Line Up to Oppose PG&E's Seismic Testing." *The Rock: Celebrating Ten Years of Guarding the Central Coast.* 20 Sept. 2012. Web. 7 July 2016. <http://www.rockofthecoast.com/2012/09/20/environmental-groups-line-up-to-oppose-pges-seismic-testing/>.

Cohen, Jeffrey Jerome. "Elemental Relations." *O-Zone: A Journal of Object-Oriented Studies.* 1 (2014): 54–61. Print.

Collins, Vicki Tolar. "The Speaker Respoken: Material Rhetoric as Feminist Methodology." *College English* 61.5 (1999): 545–73. Print.

Compassionate Conservation. "Compassionate Conservation Guiding Principles." Compassionate Conservation, 2015. Web. 16 June 2016. <http://compassionateconservation.net/about/principles/>.

Corbett, Julia B. *Communicating Nature: How We Create and Understand Environmental Messages.* Washington, DC: Island, 2006. Print.

Cornell Lab of Ornithology. "California Scrub-Jay." *All About Birds.* Web. Mar. 23, 2017.

———. "Laysan Albatross." *All About Birds.* Web. May 21, 2015.

Cosgrove, Denis. *Apollo's Eye: A Cartographic Genealogy of the Earth in the Western Imagination.* Baltimore: Johns Hopkins UP, 2001. Print.

———. "Introduction: Mapping Meaning." *Mappings.* Ed. Denis Cosgrove. London: Reaktion Books, 1999. 1–23. Print.

Crampton, Jeremy W. *The Political Mapping of Cyberspace.* Chicago: U of Chicago P, 2003. Print.

Crampton, Jeremy W., and John Krygier. "An Introduction to Critical Cartography." *ACME: An International E-Journal for Critical Geographies* 4.1 (2006): 11–33. Web. June 2009.

Croxall, John, P. Trathan, and R. Phillips, Dataholders. "Principal Feeding Areas." *Atlas of the Patagonian Sea. Species and Spaces.* Ed. Valeria Falabella, Claudio Campagna, and John Croxall. Buenos Aires: Wildlife Conservation Society and BirdLife International, 2009. Web. Nov. 2011. <http://atlas-marpatagonico.org/species/8/wandering-albatross.htm>.

———. "Regional Nesting Sites of the Wandering Albatross (*Diomedea exulans*)." *Atlas of the Patagonian Sea. Species and Spaces.* Ed. Valeria Falabella, Claudio Campagna, and John Croxall. Buenos Aires: Wildlife Conservation Society and BirdLife International, 2009. Web. Nov. 2011. <http://atlas-marpatagonico.org/species/8/wandering-albatross.htm>.

Cuddy, Bob. "Planned Seismic Tests Near Diablo Canyon on the Agenda for Tuesday's Board of Supervisors Meeting." *San Luis Obispo Tribune* 25 Oct. 2012. Web. 30 May 2013.

Davies, Jeremy. *The Birth of the Anthropocene.* Oakland: U of California P, 2016. Print.

Davis, Diane. *Breaking Up (at) Totality: A Rhetoric of Laughter.* Carbondale: Southern Illinois UP, 2000. Print.

Defenders of Wildlife. "Basic Facts about Sea Otters." Defenders of Wildlife, 2016. Web. 24 June 2016. <http://www.defenders.org/sea-otter/basic-facts>.

Deleuze, Gilles. *Spinoza: Practical Philosophy.* Trans. Robert Hurley. San Francisco: City Lights, 1988. Print.

Derrida, Jacques. *The Animal That Therefore I Am.* Ed. Marie-Louise Mallet. Trans. David Wills. New York: Fordham UP, 2008. Print.

Devitt, Elizabeth. "PG&E-funded Otter Study to Go on Despite Setback from California Coastal Commission." *Monterey Herald* 14 Nov. 2012. Web. 23 June 2016. <http://www.montereyherald.com/20121114/pge-funded-otter-study-to-go-on-despite-setback-from-california-coastal-commission>.

Dickinson, Emily. "Forever—is composed of Nows." *The Poems of Emily Dickinson: Reading Edition.* Ed. Ralph W. Franklin. Cambridge: Belknap, 1999. Print.

Dickson, Barbara. "Reading Maternity Materially: The Case of Demi Moore." *Rhetorical Bodies.* Ed. Jack Selzer and Sharon Crowley. Madison: U of Wisconsin P, 1999. 297–313. Print.

"Disclose." *Merriam-Webster Unabridged Dictionary.* 2017. Web. 4 May 2017.

Engås, A., S. Løkkeborg, E. Ona, and A. V. Soldal. "Effects of Seismic Shooting on Local Abundance and Catch Rates of Cod (Gadus morhua) and Haddock (Melanogrammus aeglefinus)." *Canadian Journal of Fisheries and Aquatic Sciences* 53.10 (1996): 2238–49.

Etling, Bert. "More Critics Decry Seismic Testing Off the Central Coast." *San Luis Obispo Tribune* 18 Oct. 2012. Web. 30 May 2013. <http://www.sanluisobispo.com/news/local/community/cambrian/article39426558.html>.

Falabella, Valeria, Claudio Campagna, and John Croxall, eds. *Atlas of the Patagonian Sea. Species and Spaces.* Buenos Aires: Wildlife Conservation Society and BirdLife International, 2009. Web. Nov. 2011. <http://www.atlas-marpatagonico.org>.

———. "The *Atlas.*" *Atlas of the Patagonian Sea. Species and Spaces.* Buenos Aires: Wildlife Conservation Society and BirdLife International, 2009. Web. Nov. 2011. <http://atlas-marpatagonico.org/the-atlas.html>.

———. "GIS." *Atlas of the Patagonian Sea. Species and Spaces.* Buenos Aires: Wildlife Conservation Society and BirdLife International, 2009. Web. Nov. 2011. <http://atlas-marpatagonico.org/gis-database.html>.

———. "Home." *Atlas of the Patagonian Sea. Species and Spaces.* Buenos Aires: Wildlife Conservation Society and BirdLife International, 2009. Web. Nov. 2011. <http://atlas-marpatagonico.org/home-spaces-species.html>.

———. "The Maps: Interpreting the Maps in the *Atlas.*" *Atlas of the Patagonian Sea. Species and Spaces.* Buenos Aires: Wildlife Conservation Society and BirdLife International, 2009. Web. Nov. 2011. <http://atlas-marpatagonico.org/the-maps.html>.

———. "Wandering Albatross: *Diomedea exulans.*" *Atlas of the Patagonian Sea. Species and Spaces.* Buenos Aires: Wildlife Conservation Society and BirdLife International, 2009. Web. Nov. 2011. <http://atlas-marpatagonico.org/species/8/wandering-albatross.htm>.

Fausch, Deborah. "The Knowledge of the Body and the Presence of History—Toward a Feminist Architecture." *Architecture and Feminism: Yale Publications on Architecture.* Ed. Debra Coleman, Elizabeth Danze, and Carol Henderson. New York: Princeton Architectural P, 1996. 38–59. Print.

Ferlinghetti, Lawrence. "Seascape with Sun & Eagle." *Wild Dreams of a New Beginning.* New York: New Directions, 1988. Print.

Foucault, Michel. "Of Other Spaces." Trans. Jay Miskowiec. *Diacritics* 16 (1986): 22–27. Print.

Gillespie, Kathryn. "Witnessing the Afterlives of Plastic: The Emotional Geographies of Chris Jordan's Midway." *The Lives and Afterlives of Plastic.* Online conference sponsored by Massey University, Political Ecology Research Centre. 26 June–14 July 2017. Web. July 2017. <http://perc.ac.nz/wordpress/the-lives-and-afterlives-of-plastic/>.

Gordon, Jonathan, et al. "A Review of the Effects of Seismic Surveys on Marine Mammals." *Marine Technology Society Journal* 37.4 (2003): 14–32. Print.

Gordon, Jeremy G., Katherine D. Lind, and Saul Kutnicki. "Introduction: A Rhetorical Bestiary." *Rhetoric Society Quarterly.* 47.3 (2017): 222–28. Print.

Gorman, Quinn R. "Evading Capture: The Productive Resistance of Photography in Environmental Representation." *Ecosee: Image, Rhetoric, Nature.* Ed. Sidney I. Dobrin and Sean Morey. Albany: State U of New York P, 2009: 239–56. Print.

Grabill, Jeffrey T., and Michelle Simmons. "Toward a Critical Rhetoric of Risk Communication: Producing Citizens and the Role of Technical Communicators." *Technical Communication Quarterly* 7 (1998): 415–41. Print.

Green, Marsha L. "The U.S. Navy's Low Frequency Active Sonar: Cause for Concern." Ocean Mammal Institute, n.d. Web. 28 July 2016.

Green Planet Films Blog. "Midway." Green Planet Films, n.d. Web. 14 Nov. 2017. <http://green-planetfilms.org/blog/midway/>.

Gries, Laurie E. *Still Life with Rhetoric: A New Materialist Approach for Visual Rhetorics*. Boulder: Utah State UP, 2015. Print.

Haas, Christina. "Materializing Public and Private: The Spatialization of Conceptual Categories in Discourses of Abortion." *Rhetorical Bodies*. Ed. Jack Selzer and Sharon Crowley. Madison: U of Wisconsin P, 1999. 218–38. Print.

Hancock, Travis. "How Albatrosses Taught Photographer Chris Jordan How to Grieve." *Honolulu Magazine* 22 July 2016. Web. 7 May 2017. <http://www.honolulumagazine.com/Honolulu-Magazine/July-2016/How-Albatrosses-Taught-Photographer-Chris-Jordan-How-to-Grieve/>.

Haraway, Donna J. *The Companion Species Manifesto*. Chicago: Prickly Paradigm, 2003. Print.

———. *ModestWitness@Second_Millenium.FemaleMan_Meets_OncoMouse: Feminism and Technoscience*. New York: Routledge, 1997. Print.

———. *Simians, Cyborgs, and Women: The Reinvention of Nature*. New York: Routledge, 1991. Print.

———. *Staying with the Trouble: Making Kin in the Chthulucene*. Durham: Duke UP, 2016. Print.

———. *When Species Meet*. Minneapolis: U of Minnesota P, 2008. Print.

Harding, Sandra. "Science Is 'Good to Think With.'" *Science Wars*. Ed. Andrew Ross. Durham: Duke UP, 1996. 16–28. Print.

Harley, J. B. "Deconstructing the Map." *Writing Worlds: Discourse, Text, and Metaphor in the Representation of Landscape*. Ed. Trevor J. Barnes and James S. Duncan. New York: Routledge, 1992. Print.

Harris, Leila, and Helen Hazen. "Rethinking Maps from a More-Than-Human Perspective: Nature-Society, Mapping and Conservation Territories." *Rethinking Maps: New Frontiers in Cartographic Theory*. Ed. Martin Dodge, Rob Kitchin, and Chris Perkins. New York: Routledge, 2009. 50–67. Print.

Hawhee, Debra. *Rhetoric in Tooth and Claw: Animals, Language, Sensation*. Chicago: U of Chicago P, 2017. Print.

Hayles, Katherine N. *How We Became Posthuman: Virtual Bodies in Cybernetics, Literature, and Informatics*. Chicago: U of Chicago P, 1999. Print.

Heidegger, Martin. *Being and Time*. Trans. John Macquarrie and Edward Robinson. New York: Harper, 2008. Print.

———. *Poetry, Language, Thought*. Trans. Albert Hofstadter. New York: HarperCollins, 1971. Print.

Hensley, Gordon R. "Position Statement." From "Environmental Groups Line Up to Oppose PG&E's Seismic Testing." *The Rock: Celebrating Ten Years of Guarding the Central Coast*. 20 Sept. 2012. Web. 7 July 2016. <http://www.rockofthecoast.com/2012/09/20/environmental-groups-line-up-to-oppose-pges-seismic-testing/>.

———. "San Luis Obispo Coastkeeper." Environment in the Public Interest, 2014. Web. 22 July 2016.

Hesford, Wendy S. "Reading Rape Stories: Material Rhetoric and the Trauma of Representation." *College English* 62.2 (1999): 192–221. Print.

Hirschfeld Davis, Julie. "Obama to Create World's Largest Marine Reserve Off Hawaii." *New York Times* 26 Aug. 2016. Web. 2 Apr. 2017. <https://www.nytimes.com/2016/08/26/us/politics/obamas-action-will-create-largest-marine-reserve-on-earth.html>.

Honolulu Museum of Art. *Plastic Fantastic?* Honolulu Museum of Art, 2016. Web. 31 Mar. 2017. <https://honolulumuseum.org/art/exhibitions/15453-plastic_fantastic/>.

"How Kernel Density Works." *ArcGIS Desktop 9.3 Help.* Environmental Systems Research Institute, n.d. Web. Nov. 2011.

Humane Society of the United States. "Feeding Your Backyard Birds." Humane Soc. of the U.S. 2017. Web. 8 July 2017. <http://www.humanesociety.org/animals/resources/tips/feeding_birds.html?credit=web_id86139783>.

Ingold, Tim. *Being Alive: Essays on Movement, Knowledge and Description.* New York: Routledge, 2011. Print.

Jack, Jordynn. "Leviathan and the Breast Pump: Toward an Embodied Rhetoric of Wearable Technology." *Rhetoric Society Quarterly* 46.3 (2016): 207–21. Print.

Jasny, Michael. "Blasting the Atlantic: Trump Admin Takes Big Step." Natural Resources Defense Council, 4 June 2017. Web. 9 July 2017. <https://www.nrdc.org/experts/blasting-atlantic-trump-admin-takes-next-step>.

Jessup, David A., et al. "Southern Sea Otter as a Sentinel of Marine Ecosystem Health." *EcoHealth* 1.3 (2004): 239–45. Print.

Jewell, Zoe. "Effect of Monitoring Technique on Quality of Conservation Science." *Conservation Biology* 27.3 (2013): 501–8. Print.

Jordan, Chris. "Midway: Message from the Gyre: About this Project." 2011. Web. 14 Nov. 2017. <http://www.chrisjordan.com/gallery/midway/#about>.

Jue, Melody. "The Anthropocene's Negative Media." *Humanities Circle: International Journal of Central University of Kerala, India* 3.2 (Winter 2015): 83–100. Print.

Kalof, Linda, Seven Bryant, and Amy Fitzgerald. "Animal Studies Bibliography." *Animal Studies at Michigan State University.* Michigan State University, 2011. Web. Nov. 2011. <http://animalstudies.msu.edu/bibliography.php>.

KCBX Newsroom. "PG&E Gets More Time for Seismic Risk Analysis of Diablo Canyon's Nuclear Reactors." *KCBXFM: Central Coast Public Radio* 27 Oct. 2015. Web. 24 June 2016.

Kitchin, Rob, Chris Perkins, and Martin Dodge. "Thinking about Maps." *Rethinking Maps: New Frontiers in Cartographic Theory.* Ed. Martin Dodge, Rob Kitchin, and Chris Perkins. New York: Routledge, 2009. 1–25. Print.

Koenen, Leon. "The Diablo Canyon Nuclear Power Plan, a 48-Year Odyssey." *KCET* 25 Mar. 2011. Web. 29 Oct. 2017. <https://www.kcet.org/socal-focus/the-diablo-canyon-nuclear-power-plant-a-48-year-odyssey>.

Kress, Gunther, and Theo van Leeuwen. *Reading Images: The Grammar of Visual Design.* New York: Routledge, 1996. Print.

Lambert, Cynthia. "County Supervisors Vote to Oppose Seismic Tests at Diablo Canyon." *San Luis Obispo Tribune* 30 Oct. 2012. Web. 30 May 2013.

Latour, Bruno. "Agency at the Time of the Anthropocene." *New Literary History* 45.1 (2014): 1–18. Print.

——. "Drawing Things Together." *Representation in Scientific Practice.* Ed. Michael Lynch and Steve Woolgar. Cambridge: MIT P, 1990. 19–68. Print.

———. *Pandora's Hope: Essays on the Reality of Science Studies.* Cambridge: Harvard UP, 1999. Print.

———. *We Have Never Been Modern.* Trans. Catherine Porter. Cambridge: Harvard UP, 1993. Print.

MacDonald, James. "The 'Keystone Species' Concept that Transformed Ecology." *JSTOR Daily* 30 June 2016. Web. 28 July 2016.

Mara, Andrew, and Byron Hawk. "Posthuman Rhetorics and Technical Communication." *Technical Communication Quarterly* 19.1 (2009): 1–10. Print.

Marks, Laura U. *The Skin of the Film: Intercultural Cinema, Embodiment, and the Senses.* Durham: Duke UP, 2000. Print.

Massey, Doreen. *Space, Place, and Gender.* Minneapolis: U of Minnesota P, 1994. Print.

Massumi, Brian. *Parables for the Virtual: Movement, Affect, Sensation.* Durham: Duke UP, 2002. Print.

McDowell, Linda, and Joanne P. Sharp. *A Feminist Glossary of Human Geography.* New York: Oxford UP, 1999. Print.

Michael, Mike. "Roadkill: Between Humans, Nonhuman Animals, and Technologies." *Society and Animals* 12.4 (2004): 277–98. Print.

Michel, Paul. "Proposed PG&E Seismic Survey Project." Monterey Bay National Marine Sanctuary. Memo. 18 Oct. 2012. Web. 29 Oct. 2017. Available as online attachment in Bert Etling, "More Critics Decry Seismic Testing Off the Central Coast," *San Luis Obispo Tribune* 18 Oct. 2012. <http://www.sanluisobispo.com/news/local/community/cambrian/article39426558.html>.

Miller, Carolyn R. "What Can Automation Tell Us About Agency?" *Rhetoric Society Quarterly* 37.2 (2007): 137–57. Print.

"Monkeying Around with New Materialism: An Interview with Laurie Gries." *Rhetoricity*, 18 May 2017. Web. <http://rhetoricity.libsyn.com/>.

Monterey Bay Aquarium. "Southern Sea Otters." Monterey Bay Aquarium Foundation, 2016. Web. 28 July 2016.

Moore, Captain Charles, and Cassandra Phillips. *Plastic Ocean: How a Sea Captain's Chance Discovery Launched a Determined Quest to Save the Oceans.* New York: Avery, 2011. Print.

Mothers for Peace. "Position Statement." From "Environmental Groups Line Up to Oppose PG&E's Seismic Testing." *The Rock: Celebrating Ten Years of Guarding the Central Coast.* 20 Sept. 2012. Web. 7 July 2016. <http://www.rockofthecoast.com/2012/09/20/environmental-groups-line-up-to-oppose-pges-seismic-testing/>.

Mothers for Peace. "2013 Mothers for Peace Response to Seismic Testing." *Mothers for Peace.* 2013. Web. 13 Feb. 2018. <https://mothersforpeace.org/data/2013-items/2013-mothers-for-peace-response-to-seismic-testing>.

———. "Welcome." Mothers for Peace, n.d. Web. 22 July 2016.

Mountford, Roxanne. "On Gender and Rhetorical Space." *Rhetoric Society Quarterly* 31.1 (2001): 41–71. Print.

National Geographic. "Albatross: Diomedeidae." National Geographic, n.d. Web. 5 Mar. 2016. <http://animals.nationalgeographic.com/animals/birds/albatross/>.

Natural Resources Defense Council. "Trump Administration Puts in Motion First Approvals for Atlantic Coast Drilling." Press release. Natural Resources Defense Council, 5 June 2017. Web. 9 July 2017. <https://www.nrdc.org/media/2017/170605>.

Navarra, Daniele. "Conceptualising Risk: A Theoretical and Practical Agenda." *Innovation, Risk and Governance.* Giannino Bassetti Foundation, 29 June 2004. Web. 4 Apr. 2014.

Nhat Hanh, Thich. "Please Call Me By My True Names." *Being Peace.* 1987. Berkeley: Parallax, 2005. Print.

Nicoletti, L. J. "Mediated Memory: The Language of Memorial Spaces." *Writing the Visual: A Practical Guide for Teachers of Composition and Communication.* Ed. Carol David and Anne R. Richards. West Lafayette: Parlor, 2008. 51–69. Print.

Nixon, Rob. *Slow Violence and the Environmentalism of the Poor.* Cambridge: Harvard UP, 2011. Print.

NOAA Fisheries. "About Us." NOAA Fisheries, 2016. Web. 9 July 2016.

Northern Chumash Tribal Council. "Barbareno Chumash Council (BCC) on PGE." *Northern Chumash Tribal Council.* 25 Sept. 2012. Web. 13 Feb. 2018. <https://northernchumash.wordpress.com/2012/09/25/bcc-on-pge/>.

O'Neill, Claire. "How Soda Caps Are Killing Birds." *National Public Radio.* Natl. Public Radio, 1 Nov. 2011. Web. 21 May 2015. <https://www.npr.org/sections/pictureshow/2011/10/31/141879837/how-soda-caps-are-killing-birds>.

"Palm Cockatoos aka Black Palm Cockatoos." *BeautyofBirds.com.* AvianWeb, 2011. Web. 5 July 2017. <https://www.beautyofbirds.com/palmcockatoos.html>.

"Parrots in the Land of Oz: Drumming Up Love." *You Tube.* NATURE, PBS, 23 Jan. 2008. Web. 20 Feb. 2018. <https://www.youtube.com/watch?v=udYdg270C-w>.

Paton Walsh, Nick. "Midway: A Plastic Island" *CNN* 30 Nov. 2016. Web. 18 Apr. 2017. <http://edition.cnn.com/videos/us/2016/11/30/midway-plastic-island-nick-paton-walsh-orig-jql.cnn>.

Penrose, Ann M., and Steven B. Katz. *Writing in the Sciences: Exploring Conventions of Scientific Discourse.* New York: Pearson, 2010. Print.

PG&E. "In Step With California's Evolving Energy Policy, PG&E, Labor and Environmental Groups Announce Proposal to Increase Energy Efficiency, Renewables and Storage While Phasing Out Nuclear Power Over the Next Decade." PG&E Corp., 21 June 2016. Web. 29 Oct. 2017. <https://www.pge.com/en/about/newsroom/newsdetails/index.page?title=20160621_in_step_with_californias_evolving_energy_policy_pge_labor_and_environmental_groups_announce_proposal_to_increase_energy_efficiency_renewables_and_storage_while_phasing_out_nuclear_power_over_the_next_decade>.

———. "Offshore Central Coastal California Seismic Imaging Project: Updated Expanded Project Description." California Coastal Commission, 28 Sept. 2012. Web. 29 Oct. 2017. <https://www.coastal.ca.gov/energy/seismic/PGE-Project-Description.pdf>.

———. "Seismic Safety and Advanced Seismic Testing." PG&E Corp., 2016. Web. 29 Oct. 2017. <http://pge.com/myhome/edusafety/systemworks/dcpp/seismic/3D.shtml>.

———. "Seismic Survey Safety." Downloadable flyer. PG&E Corp., 2016. Web. 29 Oct. 2017. <http://pge.com/myhome/edusafety/systemworks/dcpp/seismic/3D.shtml>; <https://pge.com/includes/docs/pdfs/shared/edusafety/systemworks/dcpp/seismic_survey8.pdf>.

———. "Seismic and Tsunami Safety at Diablo Canyon." PG&E Corp., 2016. Web. 29 Oct. 2017. <https://www.pge.com/en_US/safety/how-the-system-works/diablo-canyon-power-plant/seismic-safety-at-diablo-canyon/seismic-safety-at-diablo-canyon.page>.

———. "Survey Maps: 2012 Survey Area (Zone 4)." Downloadable map. PG&E Corp., 2016. Web. 29 Oct. 2017. <http://pge.com/myhome/edusafety/systemworks/dcpp/seismic/3D.shtml>; <http://pge.com/includes/docs/pdfs/shared/edusafety/systemworks/dcpp/Seismic_Tract_Map_Survey_Areas_4.pdf>.

———. "Survey Maps: 2013 Survey Area (Zones 1 & 2)." PG&E Corp., 2016. Web. 29 Oct. 2017. <http://pge.com/myhome/edusafety/systemworks/dcpp/seismic/3D.shtml>; <http://pge.com/includes/docs/pdfs/shared/edusafety/systemworks/dcpp/Seismic_Tract_Map_Survey_Areas_1_2.pdf>.

Polom, Cameron. "The Seismic Effect: Mysterious Dolphin Deaths in Peru." *KSBY News* 1 Nov. 2012. Web. 30 May 2013.

Propen, Amy D. "Cartographic Representation and the Construction of Lived Worlds: Understanding Cartographic Practice as Embodied Knowledge." *Rethinking Maps: New Frontiers in Cartographic Theory.* Ed. Martin Dodge, Rob Kitchin, and Chris Perkins. New York: Routledge, 2009. 113–30. Print.

———. "Critical GPS: Toward a New Politics of Location." *Critical Cartographies.* Spec. issue of *ACME: An International E-Journal of Critical Geographies* 4.1 (2005): 131–44. Print.

———. *Locating Visual-Material Rhetorics: The Map, the Mill, and the GPS.* Anderson: Parlor, 2012. Print.

Rice, Jenny Edbauer. "The New 'New': Making a Case for Critical Affect Studies." *Quarterly Journal of Speech* 94.2 (2008): 200–12. Print.

Rickert, Thomas. *Ambient Rhetoric: The Attunements of Rhetorical Being.* U of Pittsburgh P, 2013. Print.

Rivers, Nathaniel. "Deep Ambivalence and Wild Objects: Toward a Strange Environmental Rhetoric." *Rhetoric Society Quarterly* 45.5 (2015): 420–40. Print.

———. "Serial Exposition." Digital Writing and Research Lab, University of Texas, Austin, May 2017. Web. 10 May 2017.

The Rock: Celebrating Ten Years of Guarding the Central Coast. "Environmental Groups Line Up to Oppose PG&E's Seismic Testing." *The Rock* 20 Sept. 2012. Web. 7 July 2016. <http://www.rockofthecoast.com/2012/09/20/environmental-groups-line-up-to-oppose-pges-seismic-testing/>.

Roelvink, Gerda, and Magdalena Zolkos. "Posthumanist Perspectives on Affect." *Journal of the Theoretical Humanities* 20.3 (2015): 1–20. Print.

Rothfels, Nigel. Introduction. *Representing Animals.* Ed. Nigel Rothfels. Bloomington: Indiana UP, 2002. vii–xv. Print.

Rowland, Jesse. "Palm Cockatoo, *Probosciger aterrimus:* Targeted Species Survey Guidelines." Brisbane: Queensland Herbarium, Dept. of Science, Information Technology and Innovation, 2013. Web. 5 July 2017. <https://www.qld.gov.au/environment/assets/documents/plants-animals/biodiversity/palm-cockatoo.pdf>.

Sahagun, Louis. "PG&E Plan to Conduct Underwater Seismic Tests Is Shot Down." *Los Angeles Times* 15 Nov. 2012. Web. 21 June 2014.

———. "Yes, California's Drought Is All but Over, and the Dramatically Revived Cachuma Lake Proves It." *Los Angeles Times* 27 Feb. 2017. Web. 28 June 2017. <http://www.latimes.com/local/california/la-me-cachuma-rain-20170225-story.html>.

Schaffner, Spencer. "Field Guides to Birds: Images and Image/Text Positioned as Reference." *Ecosee: Image, Rhetoric, Nature.* Ed. Sidney I. Dobrin and Sean Morey. Albany: State U of New York P, 2009: 95–112. Print.

Schuster, Mary Lay. "A Different Place to Birth: A Material Rhetoric Analysis of Baby Haven, a Free-Standing Birth Center." *Women's Studies in Communication* 29 (2006): 1–38. Print.

Schuurman, Nadine. "Trouble in the Heartland: GIS and Its Critics in the 1990s." *Progress in Human Geography* 24 (2000): 569–90. Print.

Seigworth, Gregory J., and Melissa Gregg. "An Inventory of Shimmers." *The Affect Theory Reader.* Ed. Melissa Gregg and Gregory J. Seigworth. Durham: Duke UP, 2010. 1–25. Print.

Sheldon, Rebekah. "Form / Matter / Chora: Object-Oriented Ontology and Feminist New Materialism." *The Nonhuman Turn.* Ed. Richard Grusin. Minneapolis: U of Minnesota P, 2015: 193–222. Print.

Shukman, David. "Q&A: Your Midway Questions Answered." *BBC News* 2008 Mar. 28. Web. 2015 May 21.

Sidenstecker, Maris. "Urgent: Seismic Testing Could Begin by November 1. Thousands of Marine Mammals Could be Harmed and Killed." *Save the Whales* 2012. Web. 13 Feb. 2018. <https://savethewhales.org/wp-content/uploads/2017/07/9-12-E-News.html>.

Silk, John. "Caring at a Distance." *Ethics, Place and Environment* 1.2 (1998): 165–82. Print.

Smithsonian National Museum of Natural History. "Ocean Trash Plaguing Our Sea." *Ocean Portal* 31 May 2015. Web. 12 June 2017. <http://ocean.si.edu/ocean-news/ocean-trash-plaguing-our-sea>.

Sneed, David. "Diablo Canyon Can Withstand Earthquake, PG&E Study Concludes." *San Luis Obispo Tribune* 10 Sept. 2014. Web. 23 June 2016. <http://www.sanluisobispo.com/news/local/article39496224.html>.

———. "Nearly 3,000 Marine Mammals Will Be Harassed in Diablo Canyon Seismic Survey." *San Luis Obispo Tribune* 29 Sept. 2012. Web. 30 May 2013.

———. "Offshore Seismic Testing Will Impact Fishing near Diablo Canyon, but Long-Term Effects Unknown." *San Luis Obispo Tribune* 6 Oct. 2012. Web. 23 July 2016.

———. "PG&E Agrees to Close Diablo Canyon in 2025." *San Luis Obispo Tribune* 21 June 2016. Web. 21 June 2016.

———. "PG&E May Still Pursue Permits for Seismic Testing Off Diablo Canyon." *San Luis Obispo Tribune* 1 Dec. 2012. Web. 30 May 2013.

———. "Research to Track Otters' Response to Seismic Surveys." *San Luis Obispo Tribune* 20 Oct. 2012. Web. 30 May 2013.

Stormer, Nathan, and Bridie McGreavy. "Thinking Ecologically about Rhetoric's Ontology: Capacity, Vulnerability, and Resilience." *Philosophy and Rhetoric* 50.1 (2017): 1–25. Print.

Surfrider Foundation. "Opposition to Pacific Gas & Electric Seismic Survey." Letter. Surfrider Foundation, 24 Oct. 2012. Web. 9 July 2016. <http://public.surfrider.org/CCC%20seismic%20ltr.pdf>.

———. "Our Mission." *Surfrider Foundation* 2018. Web. 13 Feb. 2018. <http://www.surfrider.org/mission>.

Suter, Claudio. "Wandering Albatross (*Diomedea exulans*)." *Atlas of the Patagonian Sea. Species and Spaces.* Ed. Valeria Falabella, Claudio Campagna, and John Croxall. Buenos Aires: Wildlife Conservation Society and BirdLife International, 2009. Web. Nov. 2011. <http://atlas marpatagonico.org/species/8/wandering-albatross.htm>.

Teston, Christa. *Bodies in Flux: Scientific Methods for Negotiating Medical Uncertainty.* Chicago: U of Chicago P, 2017. Print.

———. "Rhetoric, Precarity, and mHealth Technologies." *Rhetoric Society Quarterly* 46.3 (2016): 251–68. Print.

Thompson, Nick. "Midway: Why Barack Obama Visited a Tiny Island in the Pacific." *CNN* 2 Sept. 2016. Web. 31. Mar. 2017. <http://www.cnn.com/2016/09/01/politics/midway-obama-preview/>.

Tobias, Michael Charles. "Compassionate Conservation: A Discussion from the Frontlines with Dr. Marc Bekoff." *Forbes* 9 May 2013. Web. 8 Mar. 2017. <https://www.forbes.com/sites/ michaeltobias/2013/05/09/compassionate-conservation-a-discussion-from-the-frontlines-with-dr-marc-bekoff/3/#2c75be34444a>.

Tribune Staff. "10 Milestones in the History of Diablo Canyon." *San Luis Obispo Tribune* 21 June 2016. Web. 29 Oct. 2017. <http://www.sanluisobispo.com/news/local/article85170162.html>.

Tsing, Anna Lowenhaupt. *The Mushroom at the End of the World: On the Possibility of Life in Capitalist Ruins.* Princeton: Princeton UP, 2015. Print.

Ulman, Lewis H. "Beyond Nature Photography: The Possibilities and Responsibilities of Seeing." *Ecomedia: Key Issues.* Ed. Stephen Rust, Salma Monani, and Sean Cubitt. New York: Routledge, 2015. 27–45. Print.

U.S. Department of the Navy. "Surtass LFA: Diver Studies." U.S. Dept. of the Navy, n.d. Web. 26 July 2016. <http://www.surtass-lfa-eis.com/DiverStudies/index.htm>.

U.S. Fish and Wildlife Service. "Wisdom, The Laysan Albatross: *Phoebastria immutabilis*." 12 Dec. 2016. Web. 21 Apr. 2017. <https://www.fws.gov/refuge/Midway_Atoll/wildlife_and_habitat/Wisdom_Profile.html>.

UTS. "About Us: What Is Compassionate Conservation?" Centre for Compassionate Conservation, U of Technology Sydney, 2015. Web. 20 Feb. 2018. <https://www.uts.edu.au/ research-and-teaching/our-research/centre-compassionate-conservation/about-us/ what-compassionate>.

UTS. "About Us: Who We Are." Centre for Compassionate Conservation, U of Technology Sydney, 2015. Web. 20 Feb. 2018. <https://www.uts.edu.au/research-and-teaching/our-research/ centre-compassionate-conservation/about-us/who-we-are>.

van Dooren, Thom. *Flight Ways: Life and Loss at the Edge of Extinction.* New York: Columbia UP, 2014. Print.

Weeks, Linton. "Hats Off to Women Who Saved the Birds." *National Public Radio.* Natl. Public Radio, 15 July 2015. Web. 12 June 2017. <http://www.npr.org/sections/ npr-history-dept/2015/07/15/422860307/hats-off-to-women-who-saved-the-birds>.

Weiss, Dennis M., Amy D. Propen, and Colbey Emmerson Reid. *Design, Mediation, and the Posthuman.* New York: Lexington, 2014. Print.

Willey, Angela. "A World of Materialisms: Postcolonial Feminist Science Studies and the New Natural." *Science, Technology, & Human Values* 41.6 (2016): 991–1014. Print.

Wolch, Jennifer, and Jody Emel. *Animal Geographies: Place, Politics and Identity in the Nature-Culture Borderlands.* London: Verso, 1998. Print.

Wolfe, Cary. "From *Dead Meat* to Glow-in-the-Dark Bunnies: Seeing 'the Animal Question' in Contemporary Art." *Ecosee: Image, Rhetoric, Nature.* Ed. Sidney I. Dobrin and Sean Morey. Albany: State U of New York P, 2009. 129–52. Print.

———. *What Is Posthumanism?* Minneapolis: U of Minnesota P, 2010. Print.

"Worlding." *How We Learn Media & Technology (Across the Lifespan).* Social Science and Humanities Research Council of Canada and University of British Columbia, 12 Sept. 2012. Web. 6 July 2017. <https://blogs.ubc.ca/hwlmt/2012/09/12/worlding/>.

Yin, Steph. "Drumming Cockatoos and the Rhythms of Love." *New York Times* 28 June 2017. Web. 28 June 2017. <https://www.nytimes.com/2017/06/28/science/drumming-palm-cocka-toos.html?hpw&rref=science&action=click&pgtype=Homepage&module=well-region&region=bottom-well&WT.nav=bottom-well>.

Zaragovia, Veronica. "Is Ocean Seismic Testing Endangering the Dolphins?" *Time Magazine* 29 Sept. 2009. Web. 3 Apr. 2014.

Zavattieri, Victoria. "Elephant Seal with Satellite Tracking Device." *Atlas of the Patagonian Sea. Species and Spaces.* Ed. Valeria Falabella, Claudio Campagna, and John Croxall. Buenos Aires: Wildlife Conservation Society and BirdLife International, 2009. Web. Nov. 2011. <http://atlas-marpatagonico.org/gis-database.html>.

Zertuche, Hayley. "Animal Representations in Visual Culture: An Overview and a Haunting." *Trace: Journal of Writing, Media, and Ecology* 1 (17 Apr. 2017): n. pag. Web. <http://tracejour-nal.net/trace-issues/issue1/06-zertuche.html>.

Zingsheim, Justine. "Probosciger aterrimus." *Animal Diversity Web.* University of Michigan Museum of Zoology, 2006. Web. 5 July 2017. <http://animaldiversity.org/accounts/Probosciger_aterrimus/>.

INDEX

Adams, John, 154

Adler-Kassner, Linda, 164n4

advocacy, 27–34, 50, 56, 80, 109, 112, 116, 129, 145, 150–51, 161n5, 164n4

affect, 31–32, 43, 61–65, 67, 69, 73–76

agency, 1–6; and compassionate conservation, 6, 11, 13–14, 16; distributive, 3, 8, 12, 81, 138; importance of how we think about, 6–16; and knowledge-making, 4, 12–15, 18–19, 33–34; and ocean wildlife tracking, 35, 118, 120–23, 131, 135–45; and plastic ocean debris, 32, 41, 43, 48, 51–53, 64–65, 67, 71; and seismic testing, 78–79, 81–84, 100–101, 103, 112–14, 166n2; Stormer and McGreavy on, 162n3; and technoscience, 1–35; and trans-corporeality, 11, 14, 16; and visual-material rhetorics, 11, 17–22, 161n5

agential assemblage, 6–8, 10, 162n1; and drumming cockatoos, 153; and ocean wildlife tracking, 136, 145; and plastic ocean debris, 52; and seismic testing, 34, 79, 82, 102–3, 115, 149, 167n8

agential cuts, 11, 13, 60, 64, 113, 140

agential realism, 3–4, 7, 10, 14–16, 32, 150, 163n8; and ocean wildlife tracking, 119, 137–40, 142–45; and plastic ocean debris, 33, 37, 41, 44, 52–53, 59, 76; and seismic testing, 81, 102

Ahmed, Sara, 63

Alaimo, Stacy: and agential intra-actions, 17, 19–20; and material ecocriticism, 15; and material intra-actions, 67, 140; and material memoirs, 166–67n8; and multispecies entanglements, 29; and ocean wildlife tracking, 118, 130–31, 140, 142; and plastic ocean debris, 43, 51, 54, 59–60, 67, 148; and seismic testing, 81, 84, 101, 103; and trans-corporeality, 3–4, 10, 22, 54, 59–60, 130–31

albatross: black-footed, 37; Laysan, 37, 44 fig. 1, 45, 72, 136; at Midway Atoll, 32–33, 36–76, 44 fig. 1, 148, 154, 164n3, 164n5; and ocean wildlife tracking, 122–30, 126 fig. 2, 128 fig. 3, 136; in the Patagonian Sea, 122–30, 126 fig. 2, 128 fig. 3, 136; and plastic ocean debris, 32–33, 36–76, 44 fig. 1, 148, 154, 164n3, 164n5; short-tailed, 37; spiritual significance of, Hawaiian, 45–46; vulnerable bodies of, 44–53; wandering, 122–30, 136; wandering, feeding areas of, 128 fig. 3; wandering, nesting sites of, 126 fig. 2

Albatross (film), 37

ambient rhetoric, 61, 137

NEW DIRECTIONS IN RHETORIC AND MATERIALITY

BARBARA A. BIESECKER, WENDY S. HESFORD, AND CHRISTA TESTON,
SERIES EDITORS

Current thinking about rhetoric signals a new attentiveness to and critical appraisal of material-discursive phenomena. New Directions in Rhetoric and Materiality provides a forum for established and emerging scholars to explore how rhetorical theories attuned to the everyday, material, lived conditions of human, nonhuman, and extra-human life are brought to bear upon a wide range of investigative foci, including bodies, biologies, economics, environments, borders, and social events of consequence. Of particular interest to the series' editors are monographs that push or push against the theoretical, analytical, and methodological orthodoxy on agency in various environs as well as those that pair rhetorical theory with an analysis of material conditions and the social-symbolic labor circulating therein.

CPSIA information can be obtained
at www.ICGtesting.com
Printed in the USA
FSHW011326201219
65187FS